Exploring
Social Life

Exploring Social Life

READINGS TO ACCOMPANY
ESSENTIALS OF SOCIOLOGY
A Down-to-Earth Approach
FIFTH EDITION

Edited by
James M. Henslin
Southern Illinois University, Edwardsville

Boston ■ New York ■ San Francisco
Mexico City ■ Montreal ■ Toronto ■ London ■ Madrid ■ Munich ■ Paris
Hong Kong ■ Singapore ■ Tokyo ■ Cape Town ■ Sydney

Senior Editor: Jeff Lasser
Editorial Assistant: Andrea Christie
Marketing Manager: Krista Groshong
Editorial-Production Service: Omegatype Typography, Inc.
Composition and Prepress Buyer: Linda Cox
Manufacturing Manager: Megan Cochran
Cover Administrator: Linda Knowles
Electronic Composition: Omegatype Typography, Inc.

For related titles and support materials, visit our online catalog at www.ablongman.com.

Between the time Website information is gathered and then published, it is not unusual for some sites to have closed. Also, the transcription of URLs can result in typographical errors. The publisher would appreciate notification where these errors occur so that they may be corrected in subsequent editions.

Library of Congress Cataloging-in-Publication Data

CIP data not available at time of publication.

0-205-40749-8

Printed in the United States of America

10   9   8   7   6   5   4   3   08   07   06   05   04

Contents

Social Change: Technology, Social Movements,
and the Environment

Preface

It is gratifying to see that students and instructors alike have responded so favorably to *Essentials of Sociology: A Down-to-Earth Approach*. Because so many instructors want to give their students the opportunity to read original sociological research, I have designed this brief anthology as a companion for *Essentials of Sociology*. Because these readings follow the text's outline chapter for chapter, it is easy to incorporate them into the course. In keeping with the *Essentials* theme, there is a single reading for each chapter. The one exception is the addition of a reading on human sexuality for those who incorporate this topic into their course.

As always, a selection may have several subthemes. This allows a reading to be incorporated into a different chapter than the one I have assigned it, or to be included in the course even though a particular chapter is not assigned.

Also in keeping with the *Essentials* theme, I will keep this preface brief. If you have any suggestions for the next edition of this reader, please let me know. As always, I look forward to hearing from you.

Jim Henslin
Henslin@aol.com

Exploring Social Life

I The Sociological Perspective

All of us, at least to some degree, want to understand social life. If nothing else, we want to understand why people react to us as they do. We may want to know why some people boast and tell lies, whereas others will undergo personal hardship to tell the truth. These are important questions, and they affect our everyday lives. So do issues on a much broader scale, such as why certain types of jobs are drying up around us, why we need more and more education to get a good job, why the divorce rate is so high, why people are prejudiced, why people are marrying later, or why cohabitation, which most people used to consider shameful behavior, is so common now. Then, too, there is the question of why nations go to war despite the common sentiment that war is evil and should be avoided.

The tool that sociology offers in our quest for understanding is called the *sociological perspective* (also known as the *sociological imagination*). Basically, the sociological perspective means that no behavior or event stands in isolation. Rather, it is connected to other events that surround it. To understand any particular behavior or event, we need to view it within the context in which it occurs. The sociological perspective sensitizes us to the need to uncover those connections.

C. Wright Mills, a sociologist who back in the 1950s and 1960s wrote on large-scale events such as war and politics, noted that world events were increasingly coming to play a significant role in our personal lives. More than ever, this is so today. What transpires in countries on the other side of the globe has profound effects on our own lives. An economic downturn in Japan and Europe, for example, pinches our economy—and may force us to put our lives on hold. When jobs are hard to get, we may decide that it is better to postpone getting married—no matter how much we are in love. Very reluctantly, we may even determine that it is prudent to move back in with our parents. If our country goes to war in some far-off region, it can have similar effects.

Economies surge, then tumble. Empires grow to a peak of power, then overreach and decline. Wars come and go, becoming a seemingly regular but strange part of our lives. New forms of communication change the way we do business, and even the way we write letters and do our homework. Morals change, and what was once considered wrong comes to be accepted as part of everyday life. What once were luxuries come to be considered as necessities.

Such far-reaching events affect both the ways we look at the world and how we see ourselves. Our aspirations—and our other innermost desires—do not originate within us. Instead, as we view them from the sociological perspective, we see that they are transplanted inside us. Most such influences on our personal desires, though, remain invisible to us. We tend to see only what we directly experience—our feelings, our interactions, our friendships, our problems—with causes and consequences beyond this intimate or personal level only dimly perceived.

In short, we cannot understand our lives by merely looking inside ourselves—at our own abilities, emotions, desires, or aspirations. Nor is it sufficient to look around only our own neighborhood, though it too is important. We have to also consider a world far beyond our immediate environment.

All these—our personal feelings, our everyday interactions, and events around the globe—come together in the *sociological perspective*. Learning to see ourselves and others from this perspective is a fascinating journey.

To begin this journey, we open the book with a selection that has become a classic in sociology. Peter Berger invites you to consider the excitement that comes with exploring social life. We follow this with a reading by Napoleon Chagnon, who recounts his fascinating adventure with a tribe in South America. In the third selection, Gwynne Dyer examines the techniques that the U.S. Marine Corps uses to turn boys into soldiers who will not hesitate to kill when the order is given. In the article that concludes this part, Stephen Miller takes us behind the scenes of an automobile agency. If you ever buy a car from a dealer, you may want to keep this report in mind.

Invitation to Sociology

Peter L. Berger

introduction ■ ■ ■ ■ ■

To grasp the *sociological perspective* is to see the social world in a new light. As your angle of vision changes, no longer do things look the same. As you peer beneath the surface of human relationships, other realities begin to emerge. The taken-for-granted may take on an unfamiliar hue. For example, if you place the sociological lens on something as familiar as friendship, you will find that rather than being a simple matter, friendship is based on complex rights and obligations. As you analyze friendship, the implicit understandings on which it is based will begin to emerge. You will make visible its reciprocal obligations (how social debts accumulate when your friend does something for you that you are expected to repay). Although seldom stated, these implicit understandings provide the background that rules the relationship. Violate them and you risk severing the friendship.

   Uncovering realities that lie beneath the surface and attaining a different understanding of social life are part of the fascination of sociology. Regardless of a sociologist's topic—whether as common and familiar as friendship or as uncommon and unfamiliar as how young women become prostitutes (Reading 6)—as Peter Berger points out in this selection, the sociologist's overriding motivation is curiosity, a desire to know and discover more about some aspect of social life.

Thinking Critically:

As you read this selection, ask yourself:

1. What is the difference between a sociologist and a pollster?

2. What does Berger mean by saying "Statistical data by themselves do not make sociology"?

3. What does Berger mean when he says that "an invitation to sociology is an invitation to a special kind of passion"?

It is gratifying from certain value positions (including some of this writer's) that sociological insights have served in a number of instances to improve the lot of groups of human beings by uncovering morally shocking conditions or by clearing away collective illusions or by showing that socially desired results could be obtained in more humane fashion. One might point, for example, to some applications of sociological knowledge in the penological practice of Western countries. Or one might cite the use made of sociological studies in the Supreme Court decision of 1954 on racial segregation in the public schools. Or one could look at the applications of other sociological studies to the humane planning of urban redevelopment. Certainly the sociologist who is morally and politically sensitive will derive gratification from such instances. But, once more, it will be well to keep in mind that what is at issue here is not sociological understanding as such but certain applications of this understanding. It is not difficult to see how the same understanding could be applied with opposite intentions. Thus the sociological understanding of the dynamics of racial prejudice can be applied effectively by those promoting intragroup hatred as well as by those wanting to spread tolerance. And the sociological understanding of the nature of human solidarity can be employed in the service of both totalitarian and democratic regimes....

One image [of the sociologist is that of] a gatherer of statistics about human behavior.... He* goes out with a questionnaire, interviews people selected at random, then goes home [and] enters his tabulations [into computers].... In all of this, of course, he is supported by a large staff and a very large budget. Included in this image is the implication that the results of all this effort are picayune, a pedantic restatement of what everybody knows anyway. As one observer remarked pithily, a sociologist is a fellow who spends $100,000 to find his way to a house of ill repute.

This image of the sociologist has been strengthened in the public mind by the activities of many agencies that might well be called parasociological, mainly agencies concerned with public opinion and market trends. The pollster has become a well-known figure in American life, inopportuning people about their views from foreign policy to toilet paper. Since the methods used in the pollster business bear close resemblance to sociological research, the growth of this image of the sociologist is understandable.... The fundamental sociological question, whether concerned with premarital petting or with Republican votes or with the incidence of gang knifings, is always presumed to be "how often?" or "how many?"...

Now it must be admitted, albeit regretfully, that this image of the sociologist and his trade is not altogether a product of fantasy.... [A good] part of the sociological enterprise in this country continues to consist of little studies of obscure fragments of social life, irrelevant to any broader theoretical concern. One glance at the table of contents of the major sociological journals or at the list of papers read at sociological conventions will confirm this statement....

From *An Invitation to Sociology* by Peter L. Berger. Copyright © 1963 by Peter L. Berger. Reprinted by permission of Doubleday, a division of Random House, Inc.

*Some classic articles in sociology that are reprinted in this anthology were written when "he" and "man" were generic, when they referred to both men and women. So it is with "his," "him," and so on. Although the writing style has changed, the sociological ideas have not.

Statistical data by themselves do not make sociology. They become sociology only when they are sociologically interpreted, put within a theoretical frame of reference that is sociological. Simple counting, or even correlating different items that one counts, is not sociology. There is almost no sociology in the Kinsey reports. This does not mean that the data in these studies are not true or that they cannot be relevant to sociological understanding. They are, taken by themselves, raw materials that can be used in sociological interpretation. The interpretation, however, must be broader than the data themselves. So the sociologist cannot arrest himself at the frequency tables of premarital petting or extramarital pederasty. These enumerations are meaningful to him only in terms of their much broader implications for an understanding of institutions and values in our society. To arrive at such understanding the sociologist will often have to apply statistical techniques, especially when he is dealing with the mass phenomena of modern social life. But sociology consists of statistics as little as philology consists of conjugating irregular verbs or chemistry of making nasty smells in test tubes.

Sociology has, from its beginnings, understood itself as a science.... [T]he allegiance of sociologists to the scientific ethos has meant everywhere a willingness to be bound by certain scientific canons of procedure. If the sociologist remains faithful to his calling, his statements must be arrived at through the observation of certain rules of evidence that allow others to check on or to repeat or to develop his findings further. It is this scientific discipline that often supplies the motive for reading a sociological work as against, say, a novel on the same topic that might describe matters in much more impressive and convincing language....

The charge that many sociologists write in a barbaric dialect must...be admitted.... Any scientific discipline must develop a terminology. This is self-evident for a discipline such as, say, nuclear physics that deals with matters unknown to most people and for which no words exist in common speech. However, terminology is possibly even more important for the social sciences, just because their subject matter *is* familiar and just because words *do* exist to denote it. Because we are well acquainted with the social institutions that surround us, our perception of them is imprecise and often erroneous. In very much the same way most of us will have considerable difficulty giving an accurate description of our parents, husbands or wives, children or close friends. Also, our language is often (and perhaps blessedly) vague and confusing in its references to social reality. Take for an example the concept of *class*, a very important one in sociology: There must be dozens of meanings that this term may have in common speech—income brackets, races, ethnic groups, power cliques, intelligence ratings, and many others. It is obvious that the sociologist must have a precise, unambiguous definition of the concept if his work is to proceed with any degree of scientific rigor. In view of these facts, one can understand that some sociologists have been tempted to invent altogether new words to avoid the semantic traps of the vernacular usage.

Finally, we would look at an image of the sociologist not so much in his professional role as in his being, supposedly, a certain kind of person. This is the image of the sociologist as a detached, sardonic observer, and a cold manipulator of men. Where this image prevails, it may represent an ironic triumph of the sociologist's own efforts to be accepted as a genuine scientist. The sociologist here becomes the self-appointed superior man, standing off from the warm vitality of common existence, finding his satisfactions not in living but in coolly appraising the lives of others, filing them away in little categories, and thus presumably missing the real significance of what he is observing. Further, there is the notion that, when he involves himself in social processes at all, the sociologist does so as an uncommitted technician, putting his manipulative skills at the disposal of the powers that be.

This last image is probably not very widely held.... The problem of the political role of the social scientist is, nevertheless, a very genuine one. For instance, the employment of sociologists by certain branches of industry and government raises moral questions that ought to be faced more widely than they have been so far. These are, however, moral questions that concern all men in positions of responsibility....

How then are we to conceive of the sociologist? In discussing the various images that abound in the popular mind we have already brought out certain elements that would have to go into our conception....

The sociologist, then, is someone concerned with understanding society in a disciplined way. The nature of this discipline is scientific. This means that what the sociologist finds and says about the social phenomena he studies occurs within a certain rather strictly defined frame of reference. One of the main characteristics of this scientific frame of reference is that operations are bound by certain rules of evidence. As a scientist, the sociologist tries to be objective, to control his personal preferences and prejudices, to perceive clearly rather than to judge normatively. This restraint, of course, does not embrace the totality of the sociologist's existence as a human being, but is limited to his operations *qua* sociologist. Nor does the sociologist claim that his frame of reference is the only one within which society can be looked at. For that matter, very few scientists in any field would claim today that one should look at the world only scientifically. The botanist looking at a daffodil has no reason to dispute the right of the poet to look at the same object in a very different manner. There are many ways of playing. The point is not that one denies other people's games but that one is clear about the rules of one's own. The game of the sociologist, then, uses scientific rules. As a result, the sociologist must be clear in his own mind as to the meaning of these rules. That is, he must concern himself with methodological questions. Methodology does not constitute his goal. The latter, let us recall once more, is the attempt to understand society. Methodology helps in reaching this goal. In order to understand society, or that segment of it that he is studying at the moment, the sociologist will use a variety of means. Among these are statistical techniques. Statistics can be very useful in answering certain sociological questions. But statistics does not constitute sociology. As a scientist, the sociologist will have to be concerned with the exact significance of the terms he is using. That is, he will have to be careful about terminology. This does not have to mean that he must invent a new language of his own, but it does mean that he cannot naively use the language of everyday discourse. Finally, the interest of the sociologist is primarily theoretical. That is, he is interested in understanding for its own sake. He may be aware of or even concerned with the practical applicability and consequences of his findings, but at that point he leaves the sociological frame of reference as such and moves into realms of values, beliefs and ideas that he shares with other men who are not sociologists....

[W]e would like to go a little bit further here and ask a somewhat more personal (and therefore, no doubt, more controversial) question. We would like to ask not only what it is that the sociologist is doing but also what it is that drives him to it. Or, to use the phrase Max Weber used in a similar connection, we want to inquire a little into the nature of the sociologist's demon. In doing so, we shall evoke an image that is not so much ideal-typical in the above sense but more confessional in the sense of personal commitment. Again, we are not interested in excommunicating anyone. The game of sociology goes on in a spacious playground. We are just describing a little more closely those we would like to tempt to join our game.

We would say then that the sociologist (that is, the one we would really like to invite to our game) is a person intensively, endlessly, shamelessly interested in the doings of men. His natural habitat is all the human gathering places of the world, wherever men come together. The sociologist may be interested in many other things. But his consuming interest remains in the world of men, their institutions, their history, their passions. And since he is interested in men, nothing that men do can be altogether tedious for him. He will naturally be interested in the events that engage men's ultimate beliefs, their moments of tragedy and grandeur and ecstasy. But he will also be fascinated by the common place, the everyday. He will know reverence, but this reverence will not prevent him from wanting to see and to understand. He may sometimes feel revulsion or contempt. But this also will not deter him from wanting to have his questions answered. The sociologist, in his quest for understanding, moves through the world of men without respect for the usual lines of demarcation. Nobility and degradation, power and obscurity, intelligence and folly—these are equally *interesting* to him, however unequal they may be in his personal values or tastes. Thus his questions may lead him to all possible levels of society, the best and the least known places, the most respected and the most despised. And, if he is a good sociologist, he will find himself in all these places because his own questions have so taken possession of him that he has little choice but to seek for answers.

It would be possible to say the same things in a lower key. We could say that the sociologist, but for the grace of his academic title, is the man who must listen to gossip despite himself, who is tempted to look through keyholes, to read other people's mail, to open closed cabinets. Before some otherwise unoccupied psychologist sets out now to construct an aptitude test for sociologists on the basis of sublimated voyeurism, let us quickly say that we are speaking merely by way of analogy. Perhaps some little boys consumed with curiosity to watch their maiden aunts in the bathroom later become inveterate sociologists. This is quite uninteresting. What interests us is the curiosity that grips any sociologist in front of a closed door behind which there are human voices. If he is a good sociologist, he will want to open that door, to understand these voices. Behind each closed door he will anticipate some new facet of human life not yet perceived and understood.

The sociologist will occupy himself with matters that others regard as too sacred or as too distasteful for dispassionate investigation. He will find rewarding the company of priests or of prostitutes, depending not on his personal preferences but on the questions he happens to be asking at the moment. He will also concern himself with matters that others may find much too boring. He will be interested in the human interaction that goes with warfare or with great intellectual discoveries, but also in the relations between people employed in a restaurant or between a group of little girls playing with their dolls. His main focus of attention is not the ultimate significance of what men do, but the action in itself, as another example of the infinite richness of human conduct. So much for the image of our playmate.

In these journeys through the world of men the sociologist will inevitably encounter other professional Peeping Toms. Sometimes these will resent his presence, feeling that he is poaching on their preserves. In some places the sociologist will meet up with the economist, in others with the political scientist, in yet others with the psychologist or the ethnologist. Yet chances are that the questions that have brought him to these same places are different from the ones that propelled his fellow-trespassers. The sociologist's questions always remain essentially the same: "What are people doing with each other here?" "What are their relationships to each other?" "How are these relationships organized in institutions?" "What are the collective ideas that move men and institutions?" In trying to answer these questions in specific instances, the sociologist will, of course, have to deal with economic or political matters, but he will do so in a way rather different from that of the economist or the political scientist. The scene that he contemplates is the same human scene that these other scientists concern themselves with. But the sociologist's angle of vision is different. When this is understood, it becomes clear that it makes little sense to try to stake out a special enclave within which the sociologist will carry on business in his own right. There is, however, one traveler whose path the sociologist will cross more often than anyone else's on his journeys. This is the historian. Indeed, as soon as the sociologist turns from the present to the past, his preoccupations are very hard indeed to distinguish from those of the historian. However, we shall leave this relationship to a later part of our considerations. Suffice it to say here that the sociological journey will be much impoverished unless it is punctuated frequently by conversation with that other particular traveler.

Any intellectual activity derives excitement from the moment it becomes a trail of discovery. In some fields of learning this is the discovery of worlds previously unthought and unthinkable. This is the excitement of the astronomer or of the nuclear physicist on the antipodal boundaries of the realities that man is capable of conceiving. But it can also be the excitement of bacteriology or geology. In a different way it can be the excitement of the linguist discovering new realms of human expression or of the anthropologist exploring human customs in faraway countries. In such discovery, when undertaken with passion, a widening of awareness, sometimes a veritable transformation of consciousness, occurs. The universe turns out to be much more wonder-full than one had ever dreamed. The excitement of sociology is usually of a different sort. Sometimes, it is true, the sociologist penetrates into worlds that had previously been quite unknown to him—for instance, the world of crime, or the world of some bizarre religious sect, or the world fashioned by the exclusive concerns of some group such as medical specialists or military leaders or advertising executives. However, much of the time the sociologist moves in sectors of experience that are familiar to him and to most people in his society. He investigates communities, institutions and activities that one can read about every day in the newspapers. Yet there is another excitement of discovery beckoning in his investigations. It is not the excitement of coming upon the totally unfamiliar, but rather the excitement of finding the familiar becoming transformed in its meaning. The fascination of sociology lies in the fact that its perspective makes us see in a new light the very world in which we have lived all our lives. This also constitutes a transformation of consciousness. Moreover, this transformation is more relevant existentially than that of many other intellectual disciplines, because it is more difficult to segregate in some special compartment of the mind. The astronomer does not live in the remote galaxies, and the nuclear physicist can, outside his laboratory, eat and laugh and marry and vote without thinking about the insides of the atom. The geologist looks at rocks only at appropriate times, and the linguist speaks English with his wife. The sociologist lives in society, on the job and off it. His own life, inevitably, is part of his subject matter. Men being what they are, sociologists too manage to segregate their professional insights from their everyday affairs. But it is a rather difficult feat to perform in good faith.

The sociologist moves in the common world of men, close to what most of them would call real. The categories he employs in his analyses are only refinements of the categories by which other men live—power, class, status, race, ethnicity. As a result, there is a deceptive simplicity and obviousness about some sociological investigations. One reads them, nods at the familiar scene, remarks that one has heard all this before and don't people have better things to do than to waste their time on truisms—until one is suddenly brought up against an insight that radically questions everything one had previously assumed about this familiar scene. This is the point at which one begins to sense the excitement of sociology.

Let us take a specific example. Imagine a sociology class in a Southern college where almost all the students are white Southerners. Imagine a lecture on the subject of the racial system of the South. The lecturer is talking here of matters that have been familiar to his students from the time of their infancy. Indeed, it may be that they are much more familiar with the minutiae of this system than he is. They are quite bored as a result. It seems to them that he is only using more pretentious words to describe what they already know. Thus he may use the term "caste," one commonly used now by American sociologists to describe the Southern racial system. But in explaining the term he shifts to traditional Hindu society, to make it clearer. He then goes on to analyze the magical beliefs inherent in caste tabus, the social dynamics of commensalism and connubium, the economic interests concealed within the system, the way in which religious beliefs relate to the tabus, the effects of the caste system upon the industrial development of the society and vice versa—all in India. But suddenly India is not very far away at all. The lecture then goes back to its Southern theme. The familiar now seems not quite so familiar any more. Questions are raised that are new, perhaps raised angrily, but raised all the same. And at least some of the students have begun to understand that there are functions involved in this business of race that they have not read about in the newspapers (at least not those in their hometowns) and that their parents have not told them—partly, at least, because neither the newspapers nor the parents knew about them.

It can be said that the first wisdom of sociology is this—things are not what they seem. This too is a deceptively simple statement. It ceases to be simple after a while. Social reality turns out to have many layers of meaning. The discovery of each new layer changes the perception of the whole.

Anthropologists use the term "culture shock" to describe the impact of a totally new culture upon a newcomer. In an extreme instance such shock will be experienced by the Western explorer who is told, halfway through dinner, that he is eating the nice old lady he had been chatting with the previous day—a shock with predictable physiological if not moral consequences. Most explorers no longer encounter cannibalism in their travels today. However, the first encounters with polygamy or with puberty rites or even with the way some nations drive their automobiles can be quite a shock to an American visitor. With the shock may go not only disapproval or disgust but a sense of excitement that things can *really* be that different from what they are at home. To some extent, at least, this is the excitement of any first travel abroad. The experience of sociological discovery could be described as "culture shock" minus geographical displacement. In other words, the sociologist travels at home—with shocking results. He is unlikely to find that he is eating a nice old lady for dinner. But the discovery, for instance, that his own church has considerable money invested in the missile industry or that a few blocks from his home there are people who engage in cultic orgies may not be drastically different in emotional impact. Yet we would not want to imply that sociological discoveries are always or even usually outrageous to moral sentiment. Not at all. What they have in common with exploration in distant lands, however, is the sudden illumination of new and unsuspected facets of human existence in society. This is the excitement and, as we shall try to show later, the humanistic justification of sociology.

People who like to avoid shocking discoveries, who prefer to believe that society is just what they were taught in Sunday School, who like the safety of the rules and the maxims of what Alfred Schuetz has called the "world-taken-for-granted," should stay away from sociology. People who feel no temptation before closed doors, who have no curiosity about human beings, who are content to admire scenery without wondering about the people who live in those houses on the other side of that river, should probably also stay away from sociology. They will find it unpleasant or, at any rate, unrewarding. People who are interested in human beings only if they can change, convert or reform them should also be warned, for they will find sociology much less useful than they hoped. And people whose interest is mainly in their own conceptual constructions will do just as well to turn to the study of little white mice. Sociology will be satisfying, in the long run, only to those who can think of nothing more entrancing than to watch men and to understand things human....

To be sure, sociology is an individual pastime in the sense that it interests some men and bores others. Some like to observe human beings, others to experiment with mice. The world is big enough to hold all kinds and there is no logical priority for one interest as against another. But the word "pastime" is weak in describing what we mean. Sociology is more like a passion. The sociological perspective is more like a demon that possesses one, that drives one compellingly, again and again, to the questions that are its own. An introduction to sociology is, therefore, an invitation to a very special kind of passion.

The Fierce People

Napoleon Chagnon

introduction ■ ■ ■ ■ ■

The many cultures of humans are fascinating. Each human group has its own culture, whether the group be an urban gang in the United States or a tribe in the jungles of South America. Like an envelope, our culture encloses us into a particular area. It sets boundaries and dictates what is significant and insignificant. It provides the rules for how we should interact with one another. And culture provides the framework from which we view life. Understand a people's culture, and you come a long way to understanding why they are the way they are.

Understanding and appreciation are two different things. To understand a group does not necessarily mean that you appreciate it. It might help, but not necessarily. In this selection, Napoleon Chagnon recounts his harrowing stay with the Yąnomamö, a tribe in South America. As you read this selection, you will see how uncomfortable he was during his lengthy fieldwork.

Thinking Critically:

As you read this selection, ask yourself:

1. Why didn't Chagnon develop an appreciation for the way of life of the Yąnomamö?

2. Why was Chagnon so stingy with his food—and so reluctant to accept food from others?

3. How does the culture of the Yąnomamö compare with your own culture? Be sure to compare gender relations (relationships among men and women).

The Yąnomamö Indians live in southern Venezuela and the adjacent portions of northern Brazil. Some 125 widely scattered villages have populations ranging from 40 to 250 inhabitants, with 75 to 80 people the most usual number. In total numbers their population probably approaches 10,000 people, but this is merely a guess. Many of the villages have not yet been contacted by outsiders, and nobody knows for sure exactly how many uncontacted villages there are, or how many people live in them. By comparison to African or Melanesian tribes, the Yąnomamö population is small. Still, they are one of the largest unacculturated tribes left in all of South America.

But they have a significance apart from tribal size and cultural purity: The Yąnomamö are still actively conducting warfare. It is in the nature of man to fight, according to one of their myths, because the blood of "Moon" spilled on this layer of the cosmos, causing men to become fierce. I describe the Yąnomamö as "the fierce people" because that is the most accurate single phrase that describes them. That is how they conceive themselves to be, and that is how they would like others to think of them.

I spent nineteen months with the Yąnomamö during which time I acquired some proficiency in their language and, up to a point, submerged myself in their culture and way of life. The thing that impressed me most was the importance of aggression in their culture. I had the opportunity to witness a good many incidents that expressed individual vindictiveness on the one hand and collective bellicosity on the other. These ranged in seriousness from the ordinary incidents of wife beating and chest pounding to dueling and organized raiding by parties that set out with the intention of ambushing and killing men from enemy villages. One of the villages was raided approximately twenty-five times while I conducted the fieldwork, six times by the group I lived among....

This is not to state that primitive man everywhere is unpleasant. By way of contrast, I have also done limited fieldwork among the Yąnomamö's northern neighbors, the Carib-speaking Makiritare Indians. This group was very pleasant and charming, all of them anxious to help me and honor bound to show any visitor the numerous courtesies of their system of etiquette. In short, they approached the image of primitive man that I had conjured up, and it was sheer pleasure to work with them....

My first day in the field illustrated to me what my teachers meant when they spoke of "culture shock." I had traveled in a small, aluminum rowboat propelled by a large outboard motor for two and a half days. This took me from the Territorial capital, a small town on the Orinoco River, deep into Yąnomamö country. On the morning of the third day we reached a small mission settlement, the field "head-quarters" of a group of Americans who were working in two Yąnomamö villages. The missionaries had come out of these villages to hold their annual conference on the progress of their mission work, and were conducting their meetings when I arrived. We picked up a passenger at the mission station, James P. Barker, the first non-Yąnomamö to make a sustained, permanent contact with the tribe (in 1950). He had just returned from a year's furlough in the United States, where I had earlier visited him before leaving for Venezuela. He agreed to accompany me to the village I had selected for my base of operations to introduce me to the Indians. This village was also his own home base, but he had not been there for over a year and did not plan to join me for another three months. Mr. Barker had been living with this particular group about five years.

We arrived at the village, Bisaasi-teri, about 2:00 P.M. and docked the boat along the muddy bank at the terminus of the path used by the Indians to fetch their drinking water. It was hot and muggy, and my clothing was soaked with perspiration.

It clung uncomfortably to my body, as it did thereafter for the remainder of the work. The small, biting gnats were out in astronomical numbers, for it was the beginning of the dry season. My face and hands were swollen from the venom of their numerous stings. In just a few moments I was to meet my first Yąnomamö, my first primitive man. What would it be like? I had visions of entering the village and seeing 125 social facts running about calling each other kinship terms and sharing food, each waiting and anxious to have me collect his genealogy. I would wear them out in turn. Would they like me? This was important to me; I wanted them to be so fond of me that they would adopt me into their kinship system and way of life, because I had heard that successful anthropologists always get adopted by their people. I had learned during my seven years of anthropological training at the University of Michigan that kinship was equivalent to society in primitive tribes and that it was a moral way of life, "moral" being something "good" and "desirable." I was determined to work my way into their moral system of kinship and become a member of their society.

My heart began to pound as we approached the village and heard the buzz of activity within the circular compound. Mr. Barker commented that he was anxious to see if any changes had taken place while he was away and wondered how many of them had died during his absence. I felt into my back pocket to make sure that my notebook was there and felt personally more secure when I touched it. Otherwise, I would not have known what to do with my hands.

I looked up and gasped when I saw a dozen burly, naked, filthy, hideous men staring at us down the shafts of their drawn arrows! Immense wads of green tobacco were stuck between their lower teeth and lips making them look even more hideous, and strands of dark-green slime dripped or hung from their noses. We arrived at the village while the men were blowing a hallucinogenic drug up their noses. One of the side effects of the drug is a runny nose. The mucus is always saturated with the green powder and the Indians usually let it run freely from their nostrils. My next discovery was that there were a dozen or so vicious, underfed dogs snapping at my legs, circling me as if I were going to be their next meal. I just stood there holding my notebook, helpless and pathetic. Then the stench of the decaying vegetation and filth struck me and I almost got sick. I was horrified. What sort of a welcome was this for the person who came here to live with you and learn your way of life, to become friends with you? They put their weapons down when they recognized Barker and returned to their chanting, keeping a nervous eye on the village entrances.

We had arrived just after a serious fight. Seven women had been abducted the day before by a neighboring group, and the local men and their guests had just that morning recovered five of them in a brutal club fight that nearly ended in a shooting war. The abductors, angry because they lost five of the seven captives, vowed to raid the Bisaasi-teri. When we arrived and entered the village unexpectedly, the Indians feared that we were the raiders. On several occasions during the next two hours the men in the village jumped to their feet, armed themselves, and waited nervously for the noise outside the village to be identified. My enthusiasm for collecting ethnographic curiosities diminished in proportion to the number of times such an alarm was raised. In fact, I was relieved when Mr. Barker suggested that we sleep across the river for the evening. It would be safer over there.

As we walked down the path to the boat, I pondered the wisdom of having decided to spend a year and a half with this tribe before I had even seen what they were like. I am not ashamed to admit, either, that had there been a diplomatic way out, I would have ended my fieldwork then and there. I did not look forward to the next day when I would be left alone with the Indians; I did not speak a word of their language, and they were decidedly different from what I had imagined them to be. The whole situation was depressing, and I wondered why I ever decided to switch from civil engineering to anthropology in the first place. I had not eaten all day, I was soaking wet from perspiration, the gnats were biting me, and I was covered with red pigment, the result of a dozen or so complete examinations I had been given by as many burly Indians. These examinations capped an otherwise grim day. The Indians would blow their noses into their hands, flick as much of the mucus off that would separate in a snap of the wrist, wipe the residue into their hair, and then carefully examine my face, arms, legs, hair, and the contents of my pockets. I asked Mr. Barker how to say "Your hands are dirty"; my comments were met by the Indians in the following way: They would "clean" their hands by spitting a quantity of slimy tobacco juice into them, rub them together, and then proceed with the examination.

Mr. Barker and I crossed the river and slung our hammocks. When he pulled his hammock out of a rubber bag, a heavy, disagreeable odor of mildewed cotton came with it. "Even the missionaries are filthy," I thought to myself. Within two weeks everything I owned smelled the same way, and I lived with the odor for the remainder of the fieldwork. My own habits of personal cleanliness reached such levels that I didn't even mind being examined by the Indians, as I was not much cleaner than they were after I had adjusted to the circumstances.

So much for my discovery that primitive man is not the picture of nobility and sanitation I had conceived him to be. I soon discovered that it was an enormously time-consuming task to maintain my own body in the manner to which it had grown accustomed in the relatively antiseptic environment of the northern United States. Either I could be relatively well fed and relatively comfortable in a fresh change of clothes and do very little fieldwork, or, I could do considerably more fieldwork and be less well fed and less comfortable.

It is appalling how complicated it can be to make oatmeal in the jungle. First, I had to make two trips to the river to haul the water. Next, I had to prime my kerosene stove with alcohol and get it burning, a tricky procedure when you are trying to mix powdered milk and fill a coffee pot at the same time: the alcohol prime always burned out before I could turn the kerosene on, and I would have to start all over. Or, I would turn the kerosene on, hoping that the element was still hot enough to vaporize the fuel, and not start a small fire in my palm-thatched hut as the liquid kerosene squirted all over the table and walls and ignited. It was safer to start over with the alcohol. Then I had to boil the oatmeal and pick the bugs out of it. All my supplies, of course, were carefully stored in Indian-proof, ratproof, moisture-proof, and insect-proof containers, not one of which ever served its purpose adequately. Just taking things out of the multiplicity of containers and repacking them afterward was a minor project in itself. By the time I had hauled the water to cook with, unpacked my food, prepared the oatmeal, milk, and coffee, heated water for dishes, washed and dried the dishes, repacked the food in the containers, stored the containers in locked trunks and cleaned up my mess, the ceremony of preparing breakfast had brought me almost up to lunch time.

Eating three meals a day was out of the question. I solved the problem by eating a single meal that could be prepared in a single container, or, at most, in two containers, washed my dishes only when there were no clean ones left, using cold river water, and wore each change of clothing at least a week to cut down on my laundry problem, a courageous undertaking in the tropics. I was also less concerned about sharing my provisions with the rats, insects, Indians, and the elements, thereby eliminating the need for my complicated storage process. I was able to last most of the day on *café con leche,* heavily sugared espresso coffee diluted about five to one with hot milk. I would prepare this in the evening and store it in a thermos. Frequently, my single meal was no more complicated than a can of sardines and a package of crackers. But at least two or three times a week I would do something sophisticated, like make oatmeal or boil rice and add a can of tuna fish or tomato paste to it. I even saved time by devising a water system that obviated the trips to the river. I had a few sheets of zinc roofing brought in and made a rain-water trap. I caught the water on the zinc surface, funneled it into an empty gasoline drum, and then ran a plastic hose from the drum to my hut. When the drum was exhausted in the dry season, I hired the Indians to fill it with water from the river.

I ate much less when I traveled with the Indians to visit other villages. Most of the time my travel diet consisted of roasted or boiled green plantains that I obtained from the Indians, but I always carried a few cans of sardines with me in case I got lost or stayed away longer than I had planned. I found peanut butter and crackers a very nourishing food, and a simple one to prepare on trips. It was nutritious and portable, and only one tool was required to prepare the meal, a hunting knife that could be cleaned by wiping the blade on a leaf. More importantly, it was one of the few foods the Indians would let me eat in relative peace. It looked too much like animal feces to them to excite their appetites.

I once referred to the peanut butter as the dung of cattle. They found this quite repugnant. They did not know what "cattle" were, but were generally aware that I ate several canned products of such an animal. I perpetrated this myth, if for no other reason than to have some peace of mind while I ate. Fieldworkers develop strange defense mechanisms, and this was one of my own forms of adaptation. On another occasion I was eating a can of frankfurters and growing very weary of the demands of one of my guests for a share in my meal. When he asked me what I was eating, I replied: "Beef." He then asked, "What part of the animal are you eating?" to which I replied, "Guess!" He stopped asking for a share.

Meals were a problem in another way. Food sharing is important to the Yạnomamö in the context of displaying friendship. "I am hungry," is almost a form of greeting with them. I could not possibly have brought enough food with me to feed the entire village, yet they seemed not to understand this. All they could see was that I did not share my food with them at each and every meal. Nor could I enter into their system of reciprocities with respect to food; every time one of them gave me something "freely," he would dog me for months to pay him back, not with food, but with steel tools. Thus, if I accepted a plantain from someone in a different village while I was on a visit, he would most likely visit me in the future and demand a machete as payment for the time that he "fed" me. I usually reacted to these kinds of demands by giving a banana, the customary reciprocity in their culture—food for food—but this would be a disappointment for the individual who had visions of that single plantain growing into a machete over time.

Despite the fact that most of them knew I would not share my food with them at their request, some of them always showed up at my hut during mealtime. I gradually became accustomed to this and learned to ignore their persistent demands while I ate. Some of them would get angry because I failed to give in, but most of them accepted it as just a peculiarity of the subhuman foreigner. When I did give in, my hut quickly filled with Indians, each demanding a sample of the food that I had given one of them. If I did not give all a share, I was that much more despicable in their eyes.

A few of them went out of their way to make my meals unpleasant, to spite me for not sharing; for example, one man arrived and watched me eat a cracker with honey on it. He immediately recognized the honey, a particularly esteemed Yąnomamö food. He knew that I would not share my tiny bottle and that it would be futile to ask. Instead, he glared at me and queried icily, "Shaki![1] What kind of animal semen are you eating on that cracker?" His question had the desired effect, and my meal ended.

Finally, there was the problem of being lonely and separated from your own kind, especially your family. I tried to overcome this by seeking personal friendships among the Indians. This only complicated the matter because all my friends simply used my confidence to gain privileged access to my cache of steel tools and trade goods, and looted me. I would be bitterly disappointed that my "friend" thought no more of me than to finesse our relationship exclusively with the intention of getting at any locked up possessions, and my depression would hit new lows every time I discovered this. The loss of the possession bothered me much less than the shock that I was, as far as most of them were concerned, nothing more than a source of desirable items; no holds were barred in relieving me of these, since I was considered something sub-human, a non-Yąnomamö.

The thing that bothered me most was the incessant, passioned, and aggressive demands the Indians made. It would become so unbearable that I would have to lock myself in my mud hut every once in a while just to escape from it: Privacy is one of Western culture's greatest achievements. But I did not want privacy for its own sake; rather, I simply had to get away from the begging. Day and night for the entire time I lived with the Yąnomamö I was plagued by such demands as: "Give me a knife, I am poor!"; "If you don't take me with you on your next trip to Widokaiya-teri, I'll chop a hole in your canoe!"; "Don't point your camera at me or I'll hit you!"; "Share your food with me!"; "Take me across the river in your canoe and be quick about it!"; "Give me a cooking pot!"; "Loan me your flashlight so I can go hunting tonight!"; "Give me medicine...I itch all over!"; "Take us on a week-long hunting trip with your shotgun!"; and "Give me an axe, or I'll break into your hut when you are away visiting and steal one!" And so I was bombarded by such demands day after day, months on end, until I could not bear to see an Indian.

It was not as difficult to become calloused to the incessant begging as it was to ignore the sense of urgency, the impassioned tone of voice, or the intimidation and aggression with which the demands were made. It was likewise difficult to adjust to the fact that the Yąnomamö refused to accept "no" for an answer until or unless it seethed with passion and intimidation—which it did after six months. Giving in to a demand always established a new threshold; the next demand would be for a bigger item or favor, and the anger of the Indians even greater if the demand was not met. I soon learned that I had to become very much like the Yąnomamö to be able to get along with them on their terms: sly, aggressive, and intimidating.

Had I failed to adjust in this fashion I would have lost six months of supplies to them in a single day or would have spent most of my time ferrying them around in my canoe or hunting for them. As it was, I did spend a considerable amount of time doing these things and did succumb to their outrageous demands for axes and machetes, at least at first. More importantly, had I failed to demonstrate that I could not be pushed around beyond a certain point, I would have been the subject of far more ridicule, theft, and practical jokes than was the actual case. In short, I had to acquire a certain proficiency in their kind of interpersonal politics and to learn how to imply subtly that certain potentially undesirable consequences might follow if they did such and such to me. They do this to each other in order to establish precisely the point at which they cannot goad an individual any further without precipitating retaliation. As soon as I caught on to this and realized that much of their aggression was stimulated by their desire to discover my flash point, I got along much better with them and regained some lost ground. It was sort of like a political game that everyone played, but one in which each individual sooner or later had to display some sign that his bluffs and implied threats could be backed up. I suspect that the frequency of wife beating is a component of this syndrome, since men can display their ferocity and show others that they are capable of violence. Beating a wife with a club is considered to be an acceptable way of displaying ferocity and one that does not expose the male to much danger. The important thing is that the man has displayed his potential for violence and the implication is that other men better treat him with respect and caution.

After six months, the level of demand was tolerable in the village I used for my headquarters. The Indians and I adjusted to each other and knew what to expect with regard to demands on their part for goods, favors, and services. Had I confined my fieldwork to just that village alone, the field experience would have been far more enjoyable. But, as I was interested in the demographic pattern and social organization of a much larger area, I made regular trips to some dozen different villages in order to collect genealogies or to recheck those I already had. Hence, the intensity of begging and intimidation was fairly constant for the duration of the fieldwork. I had to establish my position in some sort of pecking order of ferocity at each and every village.

For the most part, my own "fierceness" took the form of shouting back at the Yąnomamö as loudly and as passionately as they shouted at me, especially at first, when I did not know much of their language. As I became more proficient in their language and learned more about their political tactics, I became more sophisticated in the art of bluffing. For example, I paid one young man a machete to cut palm trees and make boards from the wood. I used these to fashion a platform in the bottom of my dugout canoe to keep my possessions dry when I traveled by river. That afternoon I was doing informant work in the village; the long-awaited mission supply boat arrived, and most of the Indians ran out of the village to beg goods from the crew. I continued to work in the village for another hour or so and went down to the river to say "hello" to the men on the supply boat. I was angry when I discovered that the Indians had chopped up all my palm boards and used them to paddle their own canoes across the river. I knew that if I overlooked this incident I would have invited them to take even greater liberties with my goods in the future. I crossed the river, docked amidst their dugouts, and shouted for the Indians to come out and see me. A few of the culprits appeared, mischievous grins on their faces. I gave a spirited lecture about how hard I had worked to put those boards in my canoe, how I had paid a machete for the wood, and how angry I was that they destroyed my work in their haste to cross the river. I then pulled out my hunting knife and, while their grins disappeared, cut each of their canoes loose, set them into the current, and let them float away. I left without further ado and without looking back.

They managed to borrow another canoe and, after some effort, recovered their dugouts. The headman of the village later told me with an approving chuckle that I had done the correct thing. Everyone in the village, except, of course, the culprits, supported and defended my action. This raised my status.

Whenever I took such action and defended my rights, I got along much better with the Yąnomamö. A good deal of their behavior toward me was directed with the forethought of establishing the point at which I would react defensively. Many of them later reminisced about the early days of my work when I was "timid" and a little afraid of them, and they could bully me into giving goods away.

Theft was the most persistent situation that required me to take some sort of defensive action. I simply could not keep everything I owned locked in trunks, and the Indians came into my hut and left at will. I developed a very effective means for recovering almost all the stolen items. I would simply ask a child who took the item and then take that person's hammock when he was not around, giving a spirited lecture to the others as I marched away in a faked rage with the thief's hammock. Nobody ever attempted to stop me from doing this, and almost all of them told me that my technique for recovering my possessions was admirable. By nightfall the thief would either appear with the stolen object or send it along with someone else to make an exchange. The others would heckle him for getting caught and being forced to return the item.

With respect to collecting the data I sought, there was a very frustrating problem. Primitive social organization is kinship organization, and to understand the Yąnomamö way of life I had to collect extensive genealogies. I could not have deliberately picked a more difficult group to work with in this regard: They have very stringent name taboos. They attempt to name people in such a way that when the person dies and they can no longer use his name, the loss of the word in the language is not inconvenient. Hence, they name people for specific and minute parts of things, such as "toenail of some rodent," thereby being able to retain the words "toenail" and "(specific) rodent," but not being able to refer directly to the toenail of that rodent. The taboo is maintained even for the living: One mark of prestige is the courtesy others show you by not using your name. The sanctions behind the taboo seem to be an unusual combination of fear and respect.

I tried to use kinship terms to collect genealogies at first, but the kinship terms were so ambiguous that I ultimately had to resort to names. They were quick to grasp that I was bound to learn everybody's name and reacted, without my knowing it, by inventing false names for everybody in the village. After having spent several months collecting names and learning them, this came as a disappointment to me: I could not cross-check the genealogies with other informants from distant villages.

They enjoyed watching me learn these names. I assumed, wrongly, that I would get the truth to each question and that I would get the best information by working in public. This set the stage for converting a serious project into a farce. Each informant tried to outdo his peers by inventing a name even more ridiculous than what I had been given earlier, or by asserting that the individual about whom I inquired was married to his mother or daughter, and the like. I would have the informant whisper the name of the individual in my ear, noting that he was the father of such and such a child. Everybody would then insist that I repeat the name aloud, roaring in hysterics as I clumsily pronounced the name. I assumed that the laughter was in response to the violation of the name taboo or to my pronunciation. This was a reasonable interpretation, since the individual whose name I said aloud invariably became angry. After I learned what some of the names meant, I began to understand what the laughter was all about. A few of the more colorful examples are: "hairy vagina," "long penis," "feces of the harpy eagle," and "dirty rectum." No wonder the victims were angry.

I was forced to do my genealogy work in private because of the horseplay and nonsense. Once I did so, my informants began to agree with each other and I managed to learn a few new names, real names. I could then test any new informant by collecting a genealogy from him that I knew to be accurate. I was able to weed out the more mischievous informants this way. Little by little I extended the genealogies and learned the real names. Still, I was unable to get the names of the dead and extend the genealogies back in time, and even my best informants continued to deceive me about their own close relatives. Most of them gave me the name of a living man as the father of some individual in order to avoid mentioning that the actual father was dead.

The quality of a genealogy depends in part on the number of generations it embraces, and the name taboo prevented me from getting any substantial information about deceased ancestors. Without this information, I could not detect marriage patterns through time. I had to rely on older informants for this information, but these were the most reluctant of all. As I became more proficient in the language and more skilled at detecting lies, my informants became better at lying. One of them in particular was so cunning and persuasive that I was shocked to discover that he had been inventing his information. He specialized in making a ceremony out of telling me false names. He would look around to make sure nobody was listening outside my hut, enjoin me to never mention the name again, act very nervous and spooky, and then grab me by the head to whisper the name very softly into my ear. I was always elated after an informant session with him, because I had several generations of dead ancestors for the living people. The others refused to give me this information. To show my gratitude, I paid him quadruple the rate I had given the others. When word got around that I had increased the pay, volunteers began pouring in to give me genealogies.

I discovered that the old man was lying quite by accident. A club fight broke out in the village one day, the result of a dispute over the possession of a woman. She had been promised to Rerebawa, a particularly aggressive young man who had married into the village. Rerebawa had already been given her older sister and was enraged when the younger girl began having an affair with another man in the village, making no attempt to conceal it from him. He challenged the young man to a club fight, but was so abusive in his challenge that the opponent's father took offense and entered the village circle with his son, wielding a long club. Rerebawa swaggered out to the duel and hurled insults at both of them, trying to goad them into striking him on the head with their clubs. This would have given him the opportunity to strike them on the head. His opponents refused to hit him, and the fight ended. Rerebawa had won a moral victory because his opponents were afraid to hit him. Thereafter, he swaggered around and insulted the two men behind their backs. He was genuinely angry with them, to the point of calling the older man by the name of his dead father. I quickly seized on this as an opportunity to collect an accurate genealogy and pumped him about his adversary's ancestors. Rerebawa had been particularly nasty to me up to this point, but we became staunch allies: We were both outsiders in the local village. I then asked about other dead ancestors and got immediate replies. He was angry with the whole group and not afraid to tell me the names of the dead. When I compared his version of the genealogies to that of the old man, it was obvious that one of them was lying. I challenged his information, and he explained that everybody knew that the old man was deceiving me and bragging about it in the village. The names the old man had given me were the dead ancestors of the members of a village so far away that he thought I would never have occasion to inquire about them. As it turned out, Rerebawa knew most of the people in that village and recognized the names.

I then went over the complete genealogical records with Rerebawa, genealogies I had presumed to be in final form. I had to revise them all because of the numerous lies and falsifications they contained. Thus, after five months of almost constant work on the genealogies of just one group, I had to begin almost from scratch!

Discouraging as it was to start over, it was still the first real turning point in my fieldwork. Thereafter, I began taking advantage of local arguments and animosities in selecting my informants, and used more extensively individuals who had married into the group. I began traveling to other villages to check the genealogies, picking villages that were on strained terms with the people about whom I wanted information. I would then return to my base camp and check with local informants the accuracy of the new information. If the informants became angry when I mentioned the new names I acquired from the unfriendly group, I was almost certain that the information was accurate. For this kind of checking I had to use informants whose genealogies I knew rather well: They had to be distantly enough related to the dead person that they would not go into a rage when I mentioned the name, but not so remotely related that they would be uncertain of the accuracy of the information. Thus, I had to make a list of names that I dared not use in the presence of each and every informant. Despite the precautions, I occasionally hit a name that put the informant into a rage, such as that of a dead brother or sister that other informants had not reported. This always terminated the day's work with that informant, for he would be too touchy to continue any further, and I would be reluctant to take a chance on accidentally discovering another dead kinsman so soon after the first.

These were always unpleasant experiences, and occasionally dangerous ones, depending on the temperament of the informant. On one occasion I was planning to visit a village that had been raided about a week earlier. A woman whose name I had on my list had been killed by the raiders. I planned to check each individual on the list one by one to estimate ages, and I wanted to remove her name so that I would not say it aloud in the village. I knew that I would be in considerable difficulty if I said this name aloud so soon after her death. I called on my original informant and asked him to tell me the name of the woman who had been killed. He refused, explaining that she was a close relative of his. I then asked him if he would become angry if I read off all the names on the list. This way he did not have to say her name and could merely nod when I mentioned the right one. He was a fairly good friend of mine, and I thought I could predict his reaction. He assured me that this would be a good way of doing it. We were alone in my hut so that nobody could overhear us. I read the names softly, continuing to the next when he gave a negative reply. When I finally spoke the name of the dead woman he flew out of his chair, raised his arm to strike me, and shouted: "You son-of-a-bitch![2] If you ever say that name again, I'll kill you!" He was shaking with rage, but left my hut quietly. I shudder to think what might have happened if I had said the name unknowingly in the woman's village. I had other, similar experiences in different villages, but luckily the dead person had been dead for some time and was not closely related to the individual into whose ear I whispered the name. I was merely cautioned to desist from saying any more names, lest I get people angry with me.

I had been working on the genealogies for nearly a year when another individual came to my aid. It was Kaobawa, the headman of Upper Bisaasi-teri, the group in which I spent most of my time. He visited me one day after the others had left the hut and volunteered to help me on the genealogies. He was poor, he explained, and needed a machete. He would work only on the condition that I did not ask him about his own parents and other very close kinsmen who were dead. He also added that he would not lie to me as the others had done in the past. This was perhaps the most important single event in my fieldwork, for out of this meeting evolved a very warm friendship and a very profitable informant-fieldworker relationship.

Kaobawa's familiarity with his group's history and his candidness were remarkable. His knowledge of details was almost encyclopedic. More than that, he was enthusiastic and encouraged me to learn details that I might otherwise have ignored. If there were things he did not know intimately, he would advise me to wait until he could check things out with someone in the village. This he would do clandestinely, giving me a report the next day. As I was constrained by my part of the bargain to avoid discussing his close dead kinsmen, I had to rely on Rerebawa for this information. I got Rerebawa's genealogy from Kaobawa.

Once again I went over the genealogies with Kaobawa to recheck them, a considerable task by this time: they included about two thousand names, representing several generations of individuals from four different villages. Rerebawa's information was very accurate, and Kaobawa's contribution enabled me to trace the genealogies further back in time. Thus, after nearly a year of constant work on genealogies, Yąnomamö demography and social organization began to fall into a pattern. Only then could I see how kin groups formed and exchanged women with each other over time, and only then did the fissioning of larger villages into smaller ones show a distinct pattern. At this point I was able to begin formulating more intelligent questions because there was now some sort of pattern to work with. Without the help of Rerebawa and Kaobawa, I could not have made very much sense of the plethora of details I had collected from dozens of other informants.

Kaobawa is about 40 years old. I say "about" because the Yąnomamö numeration system has only three numbers: one, two, and more-than-two. He is the headman of Upper Bisaasi-teri. He has had five or six wives so far and temporary affairs with as many more women, one of which resulted in a child. At the present time he has just two wives, Bahimi and Koamashima. He has had a daughter and a son by Bahimi, his eldest and favorite wife. Koamashima, about 20 years old, recently had her first child, a boy. Kaobawa may give Koamashima to his youngest brother. Even now the brother shares in her sexual services. Kaobawa recently gave his third wife to another of his brothers because she was beshi: "horny." In fact, this girl had been married to two other men, both of whom discarded her because of her infidelity. Kaobawa had one daughter by her; she is being raised by his brother.

Kaobawa's eldest wife, Bahimi, is about thirty-five years old. She is his first cross-cousin. Bahimi was pregnant when I began my fieldwork, but she killed the new baby, a boy, at birth, explaining tearfully that it would have competed with Ariwari, her nursing son, for milk. Rather than expose Ariwari to the dangers and uncertainty of an early weaning, she killed the new child instead. By Yąnomamö standards, she and Kaobawa have a very tranquil household. He only beats her once in a while, and never very hard. She never has affairs with other men.

Kaobawa is quiet, intense, wise, and unobtrusive. He leads more by example than by threats and coercion. He can afford to be this way as he established his reputation for being fierce long ago, and other men respect him. He also has five mature brothers who support him, and he has given a number of his sisters to other men in the village, thereby putting them under some obligation to him. In short, his "natural" following (kinsmen) is large, and he does not have to constantly display his ferocity. People already respect him and take his suggestions seriously.

Rerebawa is much younger, only about twenty-two years old. He has just one wife by whom he has had three children. He is from Karohi-teri, one of the villages to which Kaobawa is allied. Rerebawa left his village to seek a wife in Kaobawa's group because there were no eligible women there for him to marry.

Rerebawa is perhaps more typical than Kaobawa in the sense that he is concerned about his reputation for ferocity and goes out of his way to act tough. He is, however, much braver than the other men his age and backs up his threats with action. Moreover, he is concerned about politics and knows the details of intervillage relationships over a large area. In this respect he shows all the attributes of a headman, although he is still too young and has too many competent older brothers in his own village to expect to move easily into the position of leadership there.

He does not intend to stay in Kaobawa's group and has not made a garden. He feels that he has adequately discharged his obligations to his wife's parents by providing them with fresh game for three years. They should let him take the wife and return to his own village with her, but they refuse and try to entice him to remain permanently in Bisaasi-teri to provide them with game when they are old. They have even promised to give him their second daughter if he will stay permanently.

Although he has displayed his ferocity in many ways, one incident in particular shows what his character is like. Before he left his own village to seek a wife, he had an affair with the wife of an older brother. When he was discovered, his brother attacked him with a club. Rerebawa was infuriated so he grabbed an axe and drove his brother out of the village after soundly beating him with the flat of the blade. The brother was so afraid that he did not return to the village for several days. I recently visited his village with him. He made a point to introduce me to this brother. Rerebawa dragged him out of his hammock by the arm and told me, "This is the brother whose wife I had an affair with," a deadly insult. His brother did nothing and slunk back into his hammock, shamed, but relieved to have Rerebawa release the vise-grip on his arm.

Despite the fact that he admires Kaobawa, he has a low opinion of the others in Bisaasi-teri. He admitted confidentially that he thought Bisaasi-teri was an abominable group: "This is a terrible neighborhood! All the young men are lazy and cowards and everybody is committing incest! I'll be glad to get back home." He also admired Kaobawa's brother, the headman of Monou-teri. This man was killed by raiders while I was doing my fieldwork. Rerebawa was disgusted that the others did not chase the raiders when they discovered the shooting: "He was the only fierce one in the whole group; he was my close friend. The cowardly Monou-teri hid like women in the jungle and didn't even chase the raiders!"

Even though Rerebawa is fierce and capable of being quite nasty, he has a good side as well. He has a very biting sense of humor and can entertain the group for hours on end with jokes and witty comments. And, he is one of few Yąnomamö that I feel I can trust. When I returned to Bisaasi-teri after having been away for a year, Rerebawa was in his own village visiting his kinsmen. Word reached him that I had returned, and he immediately came to see me. He greeted me with an immense bear hug and exclaimed, "Shaki! Why did you stay away so long? Did you know that my will was so cold while you were gone that at times I could not eat for want of seeing you?" I had to admit that I missed him, too.

Of all the Yąnomamö I know, he is the most genuine and the most devoted to his culture's ways and values. I admire him for that, although I can't say that I subscribe to or endorse these same values. By contrast, Kaobawa is older and wiser. He sees his own culture in a different light and criticizes aspects of it he does not like. While many of his peers accept some of the superstitions and explanatory myths as truth and as the way things ought to be, Kaobawa questions them and privately pokes fun at some of them. Probably, more of the Yąnomamö are like Rerebawa, or at least try to be.

NOTES

1. "Shaki," or, rather, "Shakiwa," is the name they gave me because they could not pronounce "Chagnon." They like to name people for some distinctive feature when possible. *Shaki* is the name of a species of noisome bees; they accumulate in large numbers around ripening bananas and make pests of themselves by eating into the fruit, showering the people below with the debris. They probably adopted this name for me because I was also a nuisance, continuously prying into their business, taking pictures of them, and, in general, being where they did not want me.

2. This is the closest English translation of his actual statement, the literal translation of which would be nonsensical in our language.

READING **3** ∎ ▪ ∎ ▪ ▪ ∎ ▪ ∎ ▪ ∎ ▪ ∎ ▪ ∎ ▪ ∎ ▪ ∎ ▪ ∎ ▪ ∎ ▪ ∎ ▪ ∎ ∎

Anybody's Son Will Do

Gwynne Dyer

introduction ∎ ▪ ∎ ▪ ▪

To understand the term *socialization,* just substitute the word *learning.* Socialization does not refer only to children. All of us are being socialized all the time. Each time we are exposed to something new, we are being socialized. If we learn how to operate a new video control, play a new (or old) video game, watch a movie, read a book, or listen to a college lecture, we are being socialized. Even when we talk to a friend, socialization occurs. And socialization doesn't stop at a certain age. When we are old, we will still have experiences (even watching televised news) that influence our viewpoints. Socialization, then, is a lifelong process. You could say that in this process we are becoming more and more a part of our culture or of our subculture.

From the examples just given, you can see that socialization is usually gentle and gradual. But there are remarkable exceptions, and here we look at one of them. In this selection, Gwynne Dyer analyzes the process by which the U.S. Marine Corps turns young men into killers—and how this organization accomplishes such a drastic change in just a few weeks. As you will see, the Marines' techniques are brutal, swift, and effective.

Thinking Critically:

As you read this article, ask yourself:

1. How do the U.S. Marines socialize their recruits?

2. How do the socialization techniques of the Marines compare with the socialization techniques that have been used to bring you to your current place in life?

3. Why are the socialization techniques of the Marines so effective?

> *You think about it and you know you're going to have to kill but you don't understand the implications of that, because in the society in which you've lived murder is the most heinous of crimes...and you are in a situation in which it's turned the other way round....When you do actually kill someone the experience, my experience, was one of revulsion and disgust....*

From *War: Past, Present, and Future,* by Gwynne Dyer. Copyright © 1985 by Media Resources. Reprinted with the permission of Crown Publishers, a division of Random House, Inc.

I was utterly terrified—petrified—but I knew there had to be a Japanese sniper in a small fishing shack near the shore. He was firing in the other direction at Marines in another battalion, but I knew as soon as he picked off the people there—there was a window on our side—that he would start picking us off. And there was nobody else to go...and so I ran towards the shack and broke in and found myself in an empty room....

There was a door which meant there was another room and the sniper was in that—and I just broke that down. I was just absolutely gripped by the fear that this man would expect me and would shoot me. But as it turned out he was in a sniper harness and he couldn't turn around fast enough. He was entangled in the harness so I shot him with a .45, and I felt remorse and shame. I can remember whispering foolishly, "I'm sorry" and then just throwing up....I threw up all over myself. It was a betrayal of what I'd been taught since a child.

—William Manchester

Yet he did kill the Japanese soldier, just as he had been trained to—the revulsion only came afterward. And even after Manchester knew what it was like to kill another human being, a young man like himself, he went on trying to kill his "enemies" until the war was over. Like all the other tens of millions of soldiers who had been taught from infancy that killing was wrong, and had then been sent off to kill for their countries, he was almost helpless to disobey, for he had fallen into the hands of an institution so powerful and so subtle that it could quickly reverse the moral training of a lifetime.

The whole vast edifice of the military institution rests on its ability to obtain obedience from its members even unto death—and the killing of others. It has enormous powers of compulsion at its command, of course, but all authority must be based ultimately on consent. The task of extracting that consent from its members has probably grown harder in recent times, for the gulf between the military and the civilian worlds has undoubtedly widened: Civilians no longer perceive the threat of violent death as an everyday hazard of existence, and the categories of people whom it is not morally permissible to kill have broadened to include (in peacetime) the entire human race. Yet the armed forces of every country can still take almost any young male civilian and turn him into a soldier with all the right reflexes and attitudes in only a few weeks. Their recruits usually have no more than twenty years' experience of the world, most of it as children, while the armies have had all of history to practice and perfect their techniques.

Just think of how the soldier is treated. While still a child he is shut up in the barracks. During his training he is always being knocked about. If he makes the least mistake he is beaten, a burning blow on his body, another on his eye, perhaps his head is laid open with a wound. He is battered and bruised with flogging. On the march...they hang heavy loads round his neck like that of an ass.

—Egyptian, ca. 1500 B.C.

The moment I talk to the new conscripts about the homeland I strike a land mine. So I kept quiet. Instead, I try to make soldiers of them. I give them hell from morning to sunset. They begin to curse me, curse the army, curse the state.

Then they begin to curse together, and become a truly cohesive group, a unit, a fighting unit.

—Israeli, ca. A.D. 1970

All soldiers belong to the same profession, no matter what country they serve, and it makes them different from everybody else. They have to be different, for their job is ultimately about killing and dying, and those things are not a natural vocation for any human being. Yet all soldiers are born civilians. The method for turning young men into soldiers—people who kill other people and expose themselves to death—is basic training. It's essentially the same all over the world, and it always has been, because young men everywhere are pretty much alike.

Human beings are fairly malleable, especially when they are young, and in every young man there are attitudes for any army to work with: the inherited values and postures, more or less dimly recalled, of the tribal warriors who were once the model for every young boy to emulate. Civilization did not involve a sudden clean break in the way people behave, but merely the progressive distortion and redirection of all the ways in which people in the old tribal societies used to behave, and modern definitions of maleness still contain a great deal of the old warrior ethic. The anarchic machismo of the primitive warrior is not what modern armies really need in their soldiers, but it does provide them with promising raw material for the transformation they must work in their recruits.

Just how this transformation is wrought varies from time to time and from country to country. In totally militarized societies—ancient Sparta, the samurai class of medieval Japan, the areas controlled by organizations like the Eritrean People's Liberation Front today—it begins at puberty or before, when the young boy is immersed in a disciplined society in which only the military values are allowed to penetrate. In more sophisticated modern societies, the process is briefer and more concentrated, and the way it works is much more visible. It is, essentially, a conversion process in an almost religious sense—and as in all conversion phenomena, the emotions are far more important than the specific ideas....

Armies know this. It is their business to get men to fight, and they have had a long time to work out the best way of doing it. All of them pay lip service to the symbols and slogans of their political masters, though the amount of time they must devote to this activity varies from country to country.... Nor should it be thought that the armies are hypocritical—most of their members really do believe in their particular national symbols and slogans. But their secret is that they know these are not the things that sustain men in combat.

What really enables men to fight is their own self-respect, and a special kind of love that has nothing to do with sex or idealism. Very few men have died in battle, when the moment actually arrived, for the United States of America or for the sacred cause of Communism, or even for their homes and families; if they had any choice in the matter at all, they chose to die for each other and for their own vision of themselves....

The way armies produce this sense of brotherhood in a peacetime environment is basic training: a feat of psychological manipulation on the grand scale which has been so consistently successful and so universal that we fail to notice it as remarkable. In countries where the army must extract its recruits in their late teens, whether voluntarily or by conscription, from a civilian environment that does not share the military values, basic training involves a brief but intense period of indoctrination whose purpose is not really to teach the recruits basic military skills, but rather to change their values and their loyalties. "I guess you could say we brainwash them a little bit," admitted a U.S. Marine drill instructor, "but you know they're good people."

The duration and intensity of basic training, and even its major emphases, depend on what kind of society the recruits are coming from, and on what sort of military organization they are going to. It is obviously quicker to train men from a martial culture than from one in which the dominant values are civilian and commercial, and easier to deal with volunteers than with reluctant conscripts. Conscripts are not always unwilling, however; there are many instances in which the army is popular for economic reasons....

It's easier if you catch them young. You can train older men to be soldiers; it's done in every major war. But you can never get them to believe that they like it, which is the major reason armies try to get their recruits before they are 20. There are other reasons too, of course, like the physical fitness, lack of dependents, and economic dispensability of teenagers, that make armies prefer them, but the most important qualities teenagers bring to basic training are enthusiasm and naiveté. Many of them actively want the discipline and the closely structured environment that the armed forces will provide, so there is no need for the recruiters to deceive the kids about what will happen to them after they join.

> There is discipline. There is drill.... When you are relying on your mates and they are relying on you, there's no room for slackness or sloppiness. If you're not prepared to accept the rules, you're better off where you are.
> —British army recruiting advertisement, 1976

> People are not born soldiers, they become soldiers.... And it should not begin at the moment when a new recruit is enlisted into the ranks, but rather much earlier, at the time of the first signs of maturity, during the time of adolescent dreams.
> —Red Star (Soviet army newspaper), 1973

Young civilians who have volunteered and have been accepted by the Marine Corps arrive at Parris Island, the Corps's East Coast facility for basic training, in a state of considerable excitement and apprehension: Most are aware that they are about to undergo an extraordinary and very difficult experience. But they do not make their own way to the base; rather, they trickle in to Charleston airport on various flights throughout the day on which their training platoon is due to form, and are held there, in a state of suppressed but mounting nervous tension, until late in the evening. When the buses finally come to carry them the seventy-six miles to Parris Island, it is often after midnight—and this is not an administrative oversight. The shock treatment they are about to receive will work most efficiently if they are worn out and somewhat disoriented when they arrive.

The basic training organization is a machine, processing several thousand young men every month, and every facet and gear of it has been designed with the sole purpose of turning civilians into Marines as efficiently as possible. Provided it can have total control over their bodies and their environment for approximately three months, it can practically guarantee converts. Parris Island provides that controlled environment, and the recruits do not set foot outside it again until they graduate as Marine privates eleven weeks later.

> *They're allowed to call home, so long as it doesn't get out of hand—every three weeks or so they can call home and make sure everything's all right, if they haven't gotten a letter or there's a particular set of circumstances. If it's a case of an emergency call coming in, then they're allowed to accept that call; if not, one of my staff will take the message....*
>
> *In some cases I'll get calls from parents who haven't quite gotten adjusted to the idea that their son had cut the strings—and in a lot of cases that's what they're doing. The military provides them with an opportunity to leave home but they're still in a rather secure environment.*
>
> —Captain Brassington, USMC

For the young recruits, basic training is the closest thing their society can offer to a formal rite of passage, and the institution probably stands in an unbroken line of descent from the lengthy ordeals by which young males in precivilized groups were initiated into the adult community of warriors. But in civilized societies it is a highly functional institution whose product is not anarchic warriors, but trained soldiers.

Basic training is not really about teaching people skills; it's about changing them, so that they can do things they wouldn't have dreamt of otherwise. It works by applying enormous physical and mental pressure to men who have been isolated from their normal civilian environment and placed in one where the only right way to think and behave is the way the Marine Corps wants them to. The key word the men who run the machine use to describe this process is *motivation.*

> *I can motivate a recruit and in third phase, if I tell him to jump off the third deck, he'll jump off the third deck. Like I said before, it's a captive audience and I can train that guy; I can get him to do anything I want him to do.... They're good kids and they're out to do the right thing. We get some bad kids, but you know, we weed those out. But as far as motivation—here, we can motivate them to do anything you want, in recruit training.*
>
> —USMC drill instructor, Parris Island

The first three days the raw recruits spend at Parris Island are actually relatively easy, though they are hustled and shouted at continuously. It is during this time that they are documented and inoculated, receive uniforms, and learn the basic orders of drill that will enable young Americans (who are not very accustomed to this aspect of life) to do everything simultaneously in large groups. But the most important thing that happens in "forming" is the surrender of the recruits' own clothes, their hair—all the physical evidence of their individual civilian identities.

During a period of only 72 hours, in which they are allowed little sleep, the recruits lay aside their former lives in a series of hasty rituals (like being shaven to the scalp) whose symbolic significance is quite clear to them even though they are quite deliberately given absolutely no time for reflection, or any hint that they might have the option of turning back from their commitment. The men in charge of them know how delicate a tightrope they are walking, though, because at this stage the recruits are still newly caught civilians who have not yet made their ultimate inward submission to the discipline of the Corps.

> *Forming Day One makes me nervous. You've got a whole new mob of recruits, you know, 60 or 70 depending, and they don't know anything. You don't know what kind of a reaction you're going to get from the stress you're going to lay on them, and it just worries me the first day....*
>
> *Things could happen, I'm not going to lie to you. Something might happen. A recruit might decide he doesn't want any part of this stuff and maybe take a poke at you or something like that. In a situation like that it's going to be a spur-of-the-moment thing and that worries me.*
>
> —USMC drill instructor

But it rarely happens. The frantic bustle of forming is designed to give the recruit no time to think about resisting what is happening to him. And so the recruits emerge from their initiation into the system, stripped of their civilian clothes, shorn of their hair, and deprived of whatever confidence in their own identity they may previously have had as 18-year-olds, like so many blanks ready to have the Marine identity impressed upon them.

The first stage in any conversion process is the destruction of an individual's former beliefs and confidence, and his reduction to a position of helplessness and need. It isn't really as drastic as all that, of course, for three days cannot cancel out 18 years; the inner thoughts and the basic character are not erased. But the recruits have already learned that the only acceptable behavior is to repress any unorthodox thoughts and to mimic the character the Marine Corps wants. Nor are they, on the whole, reluctant to do so, for they *want* to be Marines. From the moment they arrive at Parris Island, the vague notion that has been passed down for a thousand generations that masculinity means being a warrior becomes an explicit article of faith, relentlessly preached: To be a man means to be a Marine.

There are very few 18-year-old boys who do not have highly romanticized ideas of what it means to be a man, so the Marine Corps has plenty of buttons to push. And it starts pushing them on the first day of real training: The officer in charge of the formation appears before them for the first time, in full dress uniform with medals, and tells them how to become men.

> *The United States Marine Corps has 205 years of illustrious history to speak for itself. You have made the most important decision in your life...by signing your name, your life, pledge to the Government of the United States, and even more importantly, to the United States Marine Corps—a brotherhood, an elite unit. In 10.3 weeks you are going to become a member of that history, those traditions, this organization—if you have what it takes....*

All of you want to do that by virtue of your signing your name as a man. The Marine Corps says that we build men. Well, I'll go a little bit further. We develop the tools that you have—and everybody has those tools to a certain extent right now. We're going to give you the blueprints, and we are going to show you how to build a Marine. You've got to build a Marine—you understand?
—Captain Pingree, USMC

The recruits, gazing at him with awe and adoration, shout in unison, "Yes, sir!" just as they have been taught. They do it willingly, because they are volunteers—but even conscripts tend to have the romantic fervor of volunteers if they are only 18 years old. Basic training, whatever its hardships, is a quick way to become a man among men, with an undeniable status, and beyond the initial consent to undergo it, it doesn't even require any decisions.

I had just dropped out of high school and I wasn't doing much on the street except hanging out, as most teenagers would be doing. So they gave me an opportunity—a recruiter picked me up, gave me a good line, and said that I could make it in the Marines, that I have a future ahead of me. And since I was living with my parents, I figured that I could start my own life here and grow up a little.
—USMC recruit

I like the hand-to-hand combat and…things like that. It's a little rough going on me, and since I have a small frame I would like to become deadly, as I would put it. I like to have them words, especially the way they've been teaching me here.
—USMC recruit (from Brooklyn), Parris Island

The training, when it starts, seems impossibly demanding physically for most of the recruits—and then it gets harder week by week. There is a constant barrage of abuse and insults aimed at the recruits, with the deliberate purpose of breaking down their pride and so destroying their ability to resist the transformation of values and attitudes that the Corps intends them to undergo. At the same time the demands for constant alertness and for instant obedience are continuously stepped up, and the standards by which the dress and behavior of the recruits are judged become steadily more unforgiving. But it is all carefully calculated by the men who run the machine, who think and talk in terms of the stress they are placing on the recruits: "We take so many c.c.'s of stress and we administer it to each man—they should be a little bit scared and they should be unsure, but they're adjusting." The aim is to keep the training arduous but just within most of the recruits' capability to withstand. One of the most striking achievements of the drill instructors is to create and maintain the illusion that basic training is an extraordinary challenge, one that will set those who graduate apart from others, when in fact almost everyone can succeed.

There has been some preliminary weeding out of potential recruits even before they begin training, to eliminate the obviously unsuitable minority, and some people do "fail" basic training and get sent home, at least in peacetime. The standards of acceptable performance in the U.S. armed forces, for example, tend to rise and fall in inverse proportion to the number and quality of recruits available to fill the forces to the authorized manpower levels. But there are very few young men who cannot be turned into passable soldiers if the forces are willing to invest enough effort in it.

Not even physical violence is necessary to effect the transformation, though it has been used by most armies at most times.

> It's not what it was 15 years ago down here. The Marine Corps still occupies the position of a tool which the society uses when it feels like that is a resort that they have to fall to. Our society changes as all societies do, and our society felt that through enlightened training methods we could still produce the same product— and when you examine it, they're right.... Our 100 c.c.'s of stress is really all we need, not two gallons of it, which is what used to be.... In some cases with some of the younger drill instructors it was more an initiation than it was an acute test, and so we introduced extra officers and we select our drill instructors to "fine-tune" it.
> —Captain Brassington, USMC

There is, indeed, a good deal of fine-tuning in the roles that the men in charge of training any specific group of recruits assume. At the simplest level, there is a sort of "good cop–bad cop" manipulation of the recruits' attitudes toward those applying the stress. The three younger drill instructors with a particular serial are quite close to them in age and unremittingly harsh in their demands for ever higher performance, but the senior drill instructor, a man almost old enough to be their father, plays a more benevolent and understanding part and is available for individual counseling. And generally offstage, but always looming in the background, is the company commander, an impossibly austere and almost godlike personage.

At least these are the images conveyed to the recruits, although of course all these men cooperate closely with an identical goal in view. It works: In the end they become not just role models and authority figures, but the focus of the recruits' developing loyalty to the organization.

> I imagine there's some fear, especially in the beginning, because they don't know what to expect.... I think they hate you at first, at least for a week or two, but it turns to respect.... They're seeking discipline, they're seeking someone to take charge, 'cause at home they never got it.... They're looking to be told what to do and then someone is standing there enforcing what they tell them to do, and it's kind of like the father-and-son game, all the way through. They form a fatherly image of the DI whether they want to or not.
> —Sergeant Carrington, USMC

Just the sheer physical exercise, administered in massive doses, soon has the recruits feeling stronger and more competent than ever before. Inspections, often several times daily, quickly build up their ability to wear the uniform and carry themselves like real Marines, which is a considerable source of pride. The inspections also help to set up the pattern in the recruits of unquestioning submission to military authority: Standing stock-still, staring straight ahead, while somebody else examines you closely for faults is about as extreme a ritual act of submission as you can make with your clothes on.

But they are not submitting themselves merely to the abusive sergeant making unpleasant remarks about the hair in their nostrils. All around them are deliberate reminders—the flags and insignia displayed on parade, the military music, the marching formations and drill instructors' cadenced calls—of the idealized organization, the "brotherhood" to which they will be admitted as full members if they submit and conform. Nowhere in the armed forces are the military courtesies so elaborately observed, the staffs' uniforms so immaculate (some DIs change several times a day), and the ritual aspects of military life so highly visible as on a basic training establishment.

Even the seeming inanity of close-order drill has a practical role in the conversion process. It has been over a century since mass formations of men were of any use on the battlefield, but every army in the world still drills its troops, especially during basic training, because marching in formation, with every man moving his body in the same way at the same moment, is a direct physical way of learning two things a soldier must believe: that orders have to be obeyed automatically and instantly, and that you are no longer an individual, but part of a group.

The recruits' total identification with the other members of their unit is the most important lesson of all, and everything possible is done to foster it. They spend almost every waking moment together—a recruit alone is an anomaly to be looked into at once—and during most of that time they are enduring shared hardships. They also undergo collective punishments, often for the misdeed or omission of a single individual (talking in the ranks, a bed not swept under during barracks inspection), which is a highly effective way of suppressing any tendencies toward individualism. And, of course, the DIs place relentless emphasis on competition with other "serials" in training: there may be something infinitely pathetic to outsiders about a marching group of anonymous recruits chanting, "Lift your heads and hold them high, 3313 is a-passin' by," but it doesn't seem like that to the men in the ranks.

Nothing is quite so effective in building up a group's morale and solidarity, though, as a steady diet of small triumphs. Quite early in basic training, the recruits begin to do things that seem, at first sight, quite dangerous: descend by ropes from fifty-foot towers, cross yawning gaps hand-over-hand on high wires (known as the Slide for Life, of course), and the like. The common denominator is that these activities are daunting but not really dangerous: the ropes will prevent anyone from falling to his death off the rappelling tower, and there is a pond of just the right depth—deep enough to cushion a falling man, but not deep enough that he is likely to drown—under the Slide for Life. The goal is not to kill recruits, but to build up their confidence as individuals and as a group by allowing them to overcome apparently frightening obstacles.

> You have an enemy here at Parris Island. The enemy that you're going to have at Parris Island is in every one of us. It's in the form of cowardice. The most rewarding experience you're going to have in recruit training is standing on line every evening, and you'll be able to look into each other's eyes, and you'll be able to say to each other with your eyes: "By God, we've made it one more day! We've defeated the coward."
>
> —Captain Pingree

> Number on deck, sir, 45...highly motivated, truly dedicated, rompin', stompin', bloodthirsty, kill-crazy United States Marine Corps recruits, SIR!
>
> —Marine chant, Parris Island

If somebody does fail a particular test, he tends to be alone, for the hurdles are deliberately set low enough that most recruits can clear them if they try. In any large group of people there is usually a goat: someone whose intelligence or manner or lack of physical stamina marks him for failure and contempt. The competent drill instructor, without deliberately setting up this unfortunate individual for disgrace, will use his failure to strengthen the solidarity and confidence of the rest. When one hapless young man fell off the Slide for Life into the pond, for example, his drill instructor shouted the usual invective—"Well, get out of the water. Don't contaminate it all day"—and then delivered the payoff line: "Go back and change your clothes. You're useless to your unit now."

"Useless to your unit" is the key phrase, and all the recruits know that what it means is "useless in *battle.*" The Marine drill instructors at Parris Island know exactly what they are doing to the recruits, and why. They are not rear-echelon people filling comfortable jobs, but the most dedicated and intelligent NCOs the Marine Corps can find; even now, many of them have combat experience. The Corps has a clear-eyed understanding of precisely what it is training its recruits for—combat—and it ensures that those who do the training keep that objective constantly in sight.

The DIs "stress" the recruits, feed them their daily ration of synthetic triumphs over apparent obstacles, and bear in mind all the time that the goal is to instill the foundations for the instinctive, selfless reactions and the fierce group loyalty that is what the recruits will need if they ever see combat. They are arch-manipulators, fully conscious of it, and utterly unashamed. These kids have signed up as Marines, and they could well see combat; this is the way they have to think if they want to live.

> *I've seen guys come to Vietnam from all over. They were all sorts of people that had been scared—some of them had been scared all their life and still scared. Some of them had been a country boy, city boys—you know, all different kinds of people—but when they got in combat they all reacted the same—99 percent of them reacted the same.... A lot of it is training here at Parris Island, but the other part of it is survival. They know if they don't conform—conform I call it, but if they don't react in the same way other people are reacting, they won't survive. That's just it. You know, if you don't react together, then nobody survives.*
>
> —USMC drill instructor, Parris Island

> *When I went to boot camp and did individual combat training they said if you walk into an ambush what you want to do is just do a right face—you just turn right or left, whichever way the fire is coming from, and assault. I said, "Man, that's crazy. I'd never do anything like that. It's stupid."...*
>
> *The first time we came under fire, on Hill 1044 in Operation Beauty Canyon in Laos, we did it automatically. Just like you look at your watch to see what time it is. We done a right face, assaulted the hill—a fortified position with concrete bunkers emplaced, machine guns, automatic weapons—and we took it. And we killed—I'd estimate probably 35 North Vietnamese soldiers in the assault, and we only lost three killed. I think it was about two or three, and about eight or ten wounded....*
>
> *But you know, what they teach you, it doesn't faze you until it comes down to the time to use it, but it's in the back of your head, like, What do you do when you come to a stop sign? It's in the back of your head, and you react automatically.*
>
> —USMC sergeant

Combat is the ultimate reality that Marines—or any other soldiers, under any flag—have to deal with. Physical fitness, weapons training, battle drills, are all indispensable elements of basic training, and it is absolutely essential that the recruits learn the attitudes of group loyalty and interdependency which will be their sole hope of survival and success in combat. The training inculcates or fosters all of those things, and even by the halfway point in the 11-week course, the recruits are generally responding with enthusiasm to their tasks....

In basic training establishments,...the malleability is all one way: in the direction of submission to military authority and the internalization of military values. What a place like Parris Island produces when it is successful, as it usually is, is a soldier who will kill because that is his job.

Secrets of Selling Cars

Stephen J. Miller

introduction ■ ■ ■ ■

Social life can be viewed as a game. As we interact with others, we try to maximize our position. We select the strategy that seems best to us at the time. Sometimes this means that we boast about something, but at other times we may feel that we will get more out of the situation if we show humility. One of the goals of the game is to give specific impressions of ourselves to others. The impression that we desire may be of the "good" self, the "capable" self, the "sexual" self, or even the "mean, bad" self. To this end, we constantly monitor the reactions of others. We want to know if what we are saying and doing is being received in the way we intend. If it isn't, we make changes in our performance.

Common language sometimes picks up this aspect of social life. People refer to the "selling game," for example. This is exactly the point of view that underlies this selection, as Stephen Miller analyzes the buying and selling of new cars. This reading alone may be worth more than the price of the book—if you ever purchase a new car, to know what occurs behind the scenes could one day save you a lot of money.

Thinking Critically:

As you read this selection, ask yourself:

1. In what ways is buying a new car like a game?

2. Explain the contact, the pitch, and the close.

3. How is this article related to the first article by Berger?

The automobile salesman, contrary to popular opinion, is no longer an economic entrepreneur operating without restraint and engaged solely in the pursuit of personal profit.[1] In the past, the automobile sales agency was somewhat of a provisional undertaking in which the salesman-customer relationship was a random, transitory and, in many cases, unrenewable encounter. Today, the increased complexity of the social organization of sales practices has resulted in the development of the manufacturer-authorized agency which depends upon mutually satisfactory relationships with its customers and encourages at least a modicum of continuity of clientele. Consequently, the salesman has evolved from the "wheeler and dealer" of the early postwar period to the agency employee who operates in a more restrained social situation. In addition, increased automobile production and a competitive market have modified the position of the customer, increasing his ability to direct or attempt to direct the conditions and outcome of the sales transaction. The salesman of today, in general, sells under conditions which are similar to those which influence the behavior of members of the service occupations—that is, he is subject to institutional prescription and comes into direct and personal contact with his customer.

The behavior of the salesman in the contemporary sales agency may be analyzed in a number of ways. The economic character of sales endeavors could be compared and contrasted to the service character of other occupations (for example, the physician) which enjoy a more reputable position in the hierarchy of work. However, such an analysis would exaggerate the obvious though not always legitimate distinction between service and business behavior—the altruistic motives of the former and the self-interest or profit motives of the latter.[2] A more comprehensive and meaningful approach, allowing for sociological as well as economic bases of sales behavior, would focus on the generality and constancy of sales behavior as affected by the normative patterns of the sales agency. In other words, the behavior of the salesman would be seen as influenced not only by the profit to be gained but also by his efforts to advance his self-interests by adherence to the prescribed patterns of behavior which have become institutionalized in the agency.[3] The analysis of sales behavior as the result of institutionalized patterns, though legitimate, would be somewhat limited in that it would not adequately take into account the influence of the direct and personal contact which occurs between salesman and customer.

The object of this paper is to analyze sales behavior by focusing on the interaction which occurs between the new car salesman and customer during the sales transaction: the "contact," marking the beginning; the "pitch," the middle; and the "close," signifying the end of the social encounter. The sales transaction, as interaction, will be treated as a series of events in which each phase arises logically out of and is influenced by the preceding phase. The underlying concern is with the effect of the course of the interaction on sales behavior rather than the influence of the inherent homeostatic tendencies of the agency. The discussion is based on information and materials gathered during a twelve-month period of observation and limited involvement in the social world of salesmen and operations of sales agencies. Most of the data were collected away from agencies, but frequent visits permitted observation of and actual involvement in more than a dozen completed sales transactions and numerous salesman-customer contacts.[4]

■ ■ ■ THE CONTACT

The initial social contact between the salesman and the customer occurs in one of two ways: (1) a random contact—the customer is interested in or has decided to buy a new automobile and presents himself to a salesman on the floor of the agency; (2) a solicited contact—the customer has been recruited by the salesman or referred to him. In the former case, the customer is either a "suspect" (a person who may need or want a new car but cannot afford or is not interested in making an actual purchase) or a "prospect" (a person who has decided to buy but has not decided on which automobile or where to make the purchase). The recruited customer is more often than not a "buyer" (a person who has decided which automobile to purchase and wishes to enter negotiations).

The unrecruited customer, the "drop in," constitutes a "cold call," a customer contact for which the salesman is not completely prepared and the determining of a proper sales approach is difficult. The majority of "drop ins" are nothing more than "suspects," offering the salesman little anticipation of a potential sale; this partially explains why salesmen prefer to invest as little time as possible in negotiations with unrecruited customers. The "drop in" may also have "shopped the car," gathering information which would "put him one-up on the salesman going into the deal," thereby putting the advantage on the side of the customer and reducing the salesman's control of the situation.[5] If personal profit and agency prescription were the primary motivations for sales behavior, the salesman could be expected to enter negotiations with customers regardless of the circumstances of the contact. A logical rationale would be that the more contacts with customers he has, the greater his opportunity for making a sale, gaining a profit, and meeting the expectations of the agency. However, salesmen are reluctant to enter negotiations if there is little anticipation of making a sale in a manner which affords them the greatest control of the negotiations and the outcome of the transaction.[6]

If a "drop in" proves promising, that is, accepts the role of "buyer," the salesman commits himself to the sales transaction. Though the agency expects a consistent degree of commitment, the salesman invests the majority of his time and effort in sales transactions which are the result of initiated contacts with recruited customers. The "good" salesman is one who not only can make his "pitch" and "close the deal" but can recruit customers as well. As one sales manager expressed it: "The good salesman does anything to get a customer onto the floor."[7] The recruitment of customers is vital to the occupational role of the salesman since it relates directly to his status as a salesman and increases his control of the transaction.

The means by which the salesman recruits his customers includes the usual direct mailings, telephone solicitations, and "would you takes" (throwaways which are placed on parked automobiles implying a favorable deal if the customer would take a certain amount, usually exaggerated, in trade for his present automobile). However, the most rewarding method of recruitment consists primarily in establishing a system of informants, "bird dogs," located at strategic places in the community (gas stations, repair garages, etc.) who introduce or refer "prospects" to the salesman. Such an informant is paid for his services, but the ideal "bird dog" is the satisfied customer who requires no remuneration.

The advantage of the "bird dog" system is that it assures that the majority of contacts will be with customers who are at least "prospects," thus increasing the chance of becoming involved in a transaction which will result in a sale. The "bird dog" referral system also facilitates the work of the salesman during the transaction by placing the seller-buyer relationship on a more personal basis and providing the salesman with information which will allow him to control negotiations. In addition, the "bird dog" has increased the chances of a sale by influencing the customer in favor of purchase. By doing some of the selling himself, the "bird dog" has increased the salesman's advantage.

▪ ▪ ▪ THE PITCH

If the customer accepts the role of "buyer," increasing the salesman's anticipation of a favorable outcome, the salesman commits himself to the role of "seller" by "making his pitch." The individual approach of each salesman to his customer has certain unique characteristics but sales behavior, once both parties accept their respective roles, is literally a performance, the dialogue and action of which reflects a generic character. The importance of the drama of the situation is well known to the salesman, as the following remarks indicate: "What sells a car? To sell a car it all boils down to this: if I can put a better show on than you had where you been, I stand a chance of selling you a car."

The customer is not simply a spectator but plays an important part in determining the nature of the dialogue and the direction of the action: "You can't sell unless you get the customer to tell you about himself...you got to listen and get to know the customer before you can make your pitch." The salesman attempts to develop an understanding of the attitudes and feelings of the particular customer—an understanding from which he can evolve hypotheses about customer reaction to the sales "pitch," and which allows him to modify his sales behavior to increase his control of the situation and the chances of a favorable outcome. The attitudes of the customer constitute a stimulus, the understanding of which and adjustment to necessitates roletaking. The anticipation and prediction of response to the role being played is a determinant of the course of sales behavior and the nature of the social activity.[8] Role taking is facilitated by the interpretation of symbols and cues presented to the salesman during two essential stages of the sales transaction: (1) the trade-in evaluation, which the salesman attempts to accomplish as early in the transaction as possible ("Let's see what you're driving"), even though the final appraisal of its value is usually done by someone other than the salesman; (2) the demonstration ride; "I ask him how he likes the way it handles, how about the power and a lot of other things...by the time we finish the ride, I have a good idea of what he wants in a car."

The automobile presently owned by the customer allows the salesman to "size-up the prospect," in terms of generalized customer categories, and set the stage for further action; for example, the car which is outfitted with dual exhaust pipes places the customer in the category of "kid" or "rod," while personal items in the car or trunk indicate the interests of the customer ("If he's got a fishing pole in his car, you know he's interested in fishing and you got something to talk about"). The salesman employs the demonstration ride to establish a situation in which the customer will communicate to the salesman what he values in an automobile and why, information which can be used to stress the merits of the automobile being considered and influence a decision.

The salesman, knowing that the customer is organizing his buying behavior to assure a favorable purchase, realizes that if he is to continue anticipating customer response correctly he must know with some degree of accuracy what the customer is thinking at all phases of the transaction. A number of methods are employed to facilitate accurate role ascription, including eavesdropping on the conversation between the customer and any person or persons who may have accompanied him to the agency, but the major means is inducing the customer to talk as much as possible: "By listening and getting you to talk, he [the salesman] is going to find out what you're thinking about...unless he does, he's not going to sell you...he's got to know what you'll take." A salesman who is a poor listener (for example, one who has a rapid-fire delivery of the merits of the automobile he is attempting to sell) is considered one who "talks himself out of a sale."

In addition to offering him information upon which to base his "pitch," "making the customer talk" allows the salesman to counter efforts by the customer to control the situation or set the terms of the deal: "You never let the customer tell you what you are going to do." The salesman desires to keep control, in fact, achieve mastery of his relationship with the customer. The operations of the salesman, similar to those of practitioners in all service relationships, are designed to control the interaction to his advantage.[9] The general sales opinion is that the customer is free to refuse the product and terms he is offered, but "when he tells you what he wants, all you have to do is find it." The customer is never given the opportunity to withdraw from involvement in the sales transaction since, by constantly being offered alternatives, he is not forced to make a decision to accept or reject the final terms; his anticipation of a favorable outcome is never diminished. On the other hand, the salesman is free to control his investment and involvement in the transaction in terms of his anticipation of future negotiations and their outcome.

■ ■ ■ ■ THE CLOSE

The salesman brings the customer to the point where he makes the decision to purchase by associating himself with the customer and with the customer's position by taking the customer role and anticipating the reactions to his own sales "pitch." The "close" of the sale, the acceptance of commitment to the terms of the deal by the customer, is accomplished by the salesman communicating to the customer that he has not only negotiated a mutually acceptable outcome to the transaction, but that he has gotten the best of the deal: "Before they buy they got to think they beat you and now you're on their side."

"Changing sides" is a characteristic of the "close." When a possible deal in mutually acceptable terms has been achieved, the salesman implies that the transaction, if completed, will be greatly in favor of the customer ("You're really beating me to death"). The salesman now suggests he will have to and well might act on the customer's behalf to convince the sales manager to accept the deal on the customer's terms ("I know the sales manager is going to jump all over me when I go in there but we've come to an agreement...let me go in there and work on him and see if I can get that car at your price"). Here is what actually happens, as described by one sales manager: "He [the salesman] comes to me and says, 'Here you are'...I OK the deal...he ain't going to come to me with a bad one...he waits, sits down, smokes a cigarette, then goes back to the customer." In fact, the salesman may well come to the sales manager "with a bad one," at least not the best possible deal for the agency.[10] The salesman considers his negotiations with the customer more or less sacrosanct and wishes the agency only to make clear the limits of his operation; for example, "We need at least _____" or "Don't sell for less than _____." He considers the manner in which he has written the contract and the terms of it his concern and resists any interference as long as he has not blatantly violated the economic limits set by the agency. The salesman, on his return to the customer, says he encountered difficulty in having the deal accepted ("You sure got me in a lot of trouble") but that he managed to convince the sales manager ("I got him to accept your deal"). By further implication, the salesman manages to communicate to the buyer that he is a unique and shrewd negotiator ("I'm glad I don't get many like you"). There are a number of variations in method, but "closing the sale" depends upon the customer feeling his negotiations have resulted in the outcome he anticipated.

■ ■ ■ ■ COOLING THE BUYER

The sales transaction has been, for the salesman, a process of "selling the prospect" on the automobile, by stressing not only its merits, but also the advantages of a continuing relationship, in terms of service, with the agency. It is only those transactions which are blatantly exploitative or in which the prospect has been obviously victimized that require he be cooled; that is, that the entire transaction be presented to him in such a way that he may accept its outcome without a feeling of personal failure or loss which would end the relationship. The majority of sales transactions that result in purchase require a less intense and continuing process of "cooling" through periodically communicating the wisdom of the purchase to the buyer as long as and in order that he maintain a relationship with the agency. The buyer may feel that there are no appreciable differences between the automobile he has purchased and the others he might have purchased, but he does wish to regard this particular transaction as evidence of his wisdom and judgment. In much the same way as the "mark" in the confidence game, by entering the sales transaction, he has committed himself to a concept of self as a shrewd buyer, a sharp bargainer, a wheeler and dealer, or at least not "an easy mark."[11]

The salesman, having exploited the self-concept of the buyer, realizes that it must be preserved and the buyer must be made to feel that the transaction is satisfactory; that is, the customer must continue to feel he has gotten the best of the deal and perceive himself as shrewd and sharp. Because the value of the buyer as a future prospect ("kept" or steady customer) and "bird dog" depends upon his satisfaction with the transaction, it is to the salesman's advantage to see that the customer's self-conception remain intact, that he continue to be cooled. The salesman states these reasons for the process of "cooling," though not in these terms, and rarely concerns himself with the image of the agency or its possible embarrassment. "What do I care what they [customers] think about them [agency]," said one salesman, "I sold the car and have to get the guy off my back but keep him happy."

Upon completion of the transaction, the salesman realizes that he cannot continue to "cool" the buyer; he must become disengaged from his involvement with the buyer for a number of reasons. Continued involvement requires that he expend his time in behavior which is not appropriate to his role as salesman and, therefore, costly to him in income and status. The more time he must spend "cooling" buyers, the less time he has for the selection and cultivation of "prospects," and involvement in other sales transactions. Involvement with the buyer after the sale may also involve the salesman in the blame for future disappointments which may be encountered with the agency later. By proper disengagement, the salesman is able to keep the good faith of the buyer and maintain his value as a future "prospect," "kept" customer, and/or "bird dog." In his role within the agency, by ending his involvement with the buyer, the salesman is free to act as "cooler" to the buyer-as-owner and make an effort to console him if he encounters any difficulty with the agency or finance company after the purchase. Though salesmen resist such a role, they will comply if they feel it will not subvert their relationship with the customer or if any future relationship has become impossible.

The salesman knowing for his own reasons that the customer must be "cooled," but that he cannot continue the "cooling," arranges for a formal and complimentary transition from buyer to owner. The buyer is ushered to the service department where he is literally promoted from the role of buyer to that of owner and presented with the purchased automobile. The salesman foists the customer on the agency and the service manager now enters into a relationship with the owner. His role is to see that the owner remains reasonably satisfied with the sales transaction (his role as buyer) by handling any complaints which may arise and by reassuring the owner of the wisdom of the purchase. The "cooling" of the buyer becomes a continuing feature of the service manager's role.

The buyer may resist what amounts to a depersonalization of his relationship with the salesman and resent any attempt to shift responsibility for the outcome of the sales transaction from the salesman to the service manager. Realizing the value of a personalistic approach to the buyer, the salesman attempts to create an atmosphere of comradeship, facilitated by a shift in the nature of the relationship from what was basically antagonistic—the objectives of both parties involved in the transaction were originally opposed—to one which is by implication cooperative. Salesman and buyer, at the salesman's suggestion, now enter into what appears to be a conspiracy against the agency and service manager.

Where the automobile has been oversold or the deal misrepresented by the salesman, the buyer may seek out the salesman and demand satisfaction. The salesman as a last resort then calls in the sales manager, who acts as the final "cooler." The principal technique he employs is to offer the buyer his money back, to rescind the sales transaction. Since the acceptance of the offer would suggest that the buyer himself had negotiated a bad deal, subverting his self-conceptions, it is not surprising that even the most outrageously dissatisfied buyer rarely accepts the offer.

■ ■ ■ WORK, SELF, AND CUSTOMER

A majority of automobile salesmen admit that their customers regard them as "con men," who attempt to "put one over" on the buyer. In informal conversations regarding what makes a "good salesman," salesmen describe their role in much the same way; for example, "Anybody can sell something they [the customers] want but the real bit is to make them think they need exactly what you got to sell, only more of it." The consensus appears to be that the "good" salesman is highly proficient at manipulating the situation and customer in such fashion as to produce a favorable deal for the salesman. The object of the sales transaction, as an experienced older salesman who was tutoring the writer in the techniques of "making out" expressed it, is to "make them think they are getting something instead of losing anything."

It would be an over-simplification to treat automobile salesmen as if they all operate with the same perspective, but their behavior appears organized around the premise that monetary and social success are the results of opportunistic dealing. Though such an attitude toward the work appears harsh and lacking in moral scruples, the salesman protects himself from feelings of guilt and resolves the problems presented by the exploitative aspects of his role by attributing to his customers the same characteristics which mark his own behavior. He sees them as opportunistic, "out to make or save a buck any way they can." The salesman's perception of the customer is clearly revealed in the following remarks directed to newly employed salesmen by a sales manager. "He [the customer] wants to get the most car for the least money and your job is to get the most money for your car.... If he gets what he wants, you lose." By selectively perceiving and, if necessary, by misinterpreting the behavior of the customer to fit his own pattern of expectations, the salesman is able to rationalize the exploitative and manipulative aspects of his role, making his work acceptable to himself and tolerable to others.

Salesmen insist that the approach to the customer is the most important factor in selling: "The pitch is the whole bit," but when the customer does not buy, thereby reflecting unfavorably on the way the salesman "made his pitch," the salesman blames the customer ("He only wanted to come in out of the rain") or the automobile ("You can't move [sell] that dog"), but rarely his own "pitch." The salesman has, by entering into negotiations with the customer, made a substantial investment in the sales transaction; an unsuccessful outcome is not only a loss of time but a threat to his self-conception and status as a salesman. In developing an appropriate "pitch," he is testing and revising, in terms of customer response, as measured by successful sales transactions, a behavior pattern. The salesman is usually always "on," that is, playing a role.[12] The "pitch" is the salesman's characteristic interpersonal style, his personal formula for adjusting and adapting to the demands of interacting with the customer.

The successful outcome of a sales transaction not only results in a monetary gain for the salesman but, by indicating to him that he found the formula which enables him to "win friends and influence people," adds to his personal feeling of worth and position as a salesman. He has demonstrated that he is highly proficient in manipulating situations and customers to produce an effect which is generally and occupationally desirable. His work satisfaction and occupational prestige are dependent upon successful interaction with the customer. Selling the automobile reflects favorably upon the way the salesman has performed his role and, in turn, adds to his status with his colleagues as a "good" salesman.

■ ■ ■ CONCLUSION

One type of economic behavior, sales behavior, has been explored by focusing on the relationship which occurs between the automobile salesman and his customer. The sales transaction, as well as sales tactics and the behavioral implications of the salesman's conception of himself, his work, and his customer, are influenced by the sociological circumstances of the sales encounter, as much by the dynamics of the salesman–customer relationship as by agency prescription and the immediate profit for the salesman.

The automobile sales agency expects the salesman to engage in negotiations with customers which will result in at least the minimum profit acceptable to the agency. The salesman, looking at the sales situation from the agency perspective, negotiates sales which are in keeping with the economic conditions and limits imposed by the agency. However, the perspective of the salesman, like the perspectives of members of other occupations who come into direct contact with a customer, client, or patient, includes strong opinions regarding the way the sales transaction should be conducted. If the customer, wishing to make the most advantageous purchase possible, attempts to direct the circumstances, conditions, and outcome of the sales transaction, a conflict results. The salesman either counters such attempts by employing the appropriate tactics or, in some manner, terminates his involvement with the customer. The conflict and the importance of control are substantiated by the attitudes and opinions of salesmen. The "good" salesman, as conceptualized by salesmen, is one who not only sells but is also adept at manipulating the circumstances of the negotiation so as to assure his control of the sales transaction.

The salesman engaged in the sales transaction is, of course, calculating the potential economic return to himself and the agency. However, in addition to economic gain, the salesman is vulnerable to loss in such non-economic areas as status, work satisfaction, and a personally acceptable and socially supportable concept of self. He protects himself from actual loss in noneconomic areas by at times refusing immediate or ultimate profit and by resisting agency prescription—for example, not entering into negotiations with a customer who may have information which would be to his advantage during negotiations. The salesman would prefer the loss of a profit, both for himself and the agency, to involvement in a situation which is controlled by the customer. The implications of the data are not that profit and agency prescription have no influence on the operations and actions of the salesman. Rather, the data suggest that, in addition to institutionalized patterns of economic behavior, there exist other socially based supports for sales behavior making that behavior more social and less economic than it is usually considered to be. The social circumstances and conflicts of the salesman–customer relationship, similar to those found in the practitioner–client relationships of service occupations, constitute such a social base for sales behavior.

NOTES

1. A revision of "The New Car Salesman and the Sales Transaction," a paper read at the annual meeting of the Midwest Sociological Society, 1963. The research on which the paper is based was supported, in part, by Community Studies, Inc., Kansas City, Mo. The writer is indebted to Robert W. Habenstein for his comments and criticism and to Howard S. Becker and Blanche Geer for their critical reading and suggested modification of the original paper.

2. For a discussion of such an analytical scheme and its shortcomings, see Talcott Parsons, "The Professions and Social Structure," in *Essays in Sociological Theory,* Glencoe, Ill.: The Free Press, 1954, pp. 34–49.

3. Talcott Parsons, "The Motivation of Economic Activities," *Canadian Journal of Economic and Political Science,* 6 (1940): 187–200. The analysis of sales behavior in terms of the thesis of Parsons' essay would be based primarily on the assumption that the salesman behaves the way he does because a pattern of sales behavior has become institutionalized in the sales agency.

4. Initial information regarding the salesman and agency operations came from contacts and interviews with the sales manager and a number of salesmen employed by one of the major, high-volume, manufacturer-authorized agencies located in Kansas City, Mo. It was difficult to arrange lengthy visits to other agencies or to engage salesmen in prolonged conversations while on the agency floor. Therefore, interviews were arranged with salesmen who were contacted informally in restaurants, bars and grills, etc., located on the metropolitan "automobile strip." Informal contact and conversation was the most practical method of gathering information and data. In addition, the writer acted as "bird dog" and "leg man" for a number of salesmen at various agencies. The writer, with few exceptions, was accepted as a person interested in automobiles and, though employed, considering a change in work, possibly employment as an automobile salesman.

5. Howard S. Becker, in "The Professional Dance Musician and His Audience," *American Journal of Sociology,* 57 (September, 1951): 136–44, has hypothesized that a desire on the part of the practitioner to control the interaction of the contact is chronic to service relationships. See, also, Eliot Freidson, *Patients' Views of Medical Practice,* New York: Russell Sage Foundation, 1961, in which the dilemma of the doctor–patient relationship is presented in terms of potential conflict for control between the doctor and patient.

6. These same factors explain what, at times, may appear to be a complete lack of interest on the part of the salesman in making a sale. The writer has observed salesmen who, with amazing accuracy, "size-up" a customer as one who is either attempting to verify the wisdom of a contemplated or completed purchase at another agency, or plans on "keeping the salesman honest" by employing information gathered at another agency. The salesman refuses to engage in conversation with such a customer unless it is to "foul him up" by supplying him with inaccurate or fabricated information. The accuracy of the salesmen's judgments were verified by subsequent conversations with customers so rebuked.

7. A reason, expressed by a salesman: "Play on your home court"—a basketball expression, implying that the home team has the advantage.

8. For its theoretical orientation, the analysis of sales behavior draws heavily on the work of George H. Mead; for example, *Mind, Self, and Society,* Chicago: The University of Chicago Press, 1934.

9. Becker, *op. cit.*

10. The agency attempts, in many cases, to control the salesman by paying him a percentage of the difference between the automobile being purchased and the one being traded in rather than a salary or straight commission. The obvious reason is that this increases the chances of the most favorable deal for the agency being written. However, salesmen admit that they have, at times, allowed more than they had to on a trade-in because they "liked the customer" or to "make the sale."

11. Erving Goffman, "On Cooling the Mark Out: Some Aspects of Adaptation to Failure," *Psychiatry*, 15 (November 1952): 451–63.

12. Sheldon L. Messinger, in his discussion of dramaturgical analysis, explains "to be on" as operating with a self and social perspective that requires a dramatic performance; the world is a theater in which the actor stages his show. Cf. "Life as a Theater: Some Notes on the Dramaturgic Approach to Social Reality," *Sociometry*, 25 (March 1962): 98–110.

II Social Groups and Social Control

It is easy to lose sight of the sociological significance of where we are born, that our birth ushers us into a world that already exists. For the most part, we yawn at such a statement. It seems to be an "of-course-we-all-know-that" type of thing, and we ordinarily fail to grasp its profound implications. That the world we enter is already constructed means that we join a human group with established ways of "doing social life." That is, we enter a group that has constructed an arbitrary system of norms and ideas that we are expected to follow. From birth, we are immersed in this sea of expectations. They may pinch, but we are only individuals. The group has already made the rules within which we are to live our lives. The game is in progress, and we have little choice but to play it.

Like a game, for social life to exist, rules are absolutely necessary. If you can't depend on people to do things, everything falls apart. For social groups to function, then—to do whatever they have set out to do—they must be able to depend on their members. This applies to all social groups, whether they be as small as our family or as large as a multinational corporation.

Deviance, however, is as inevitable as rules are necessary. Where there are rules, there will be rule breakers. *All* of us violate some of our group's many rules; that is, we all fail to meet some of the expectations that others have of us. When we do this, we become deviants. In sociology, *deviant* simply means someone who has deviated from the rules, someone who has wandered from the path that he or she was expected to follow. Deviant does *not* mean a horrible person—although horrible people are included in the term.

It has been said that the first rule of sociology is that nothing is as it appears, that behind the scenes lies a different reality. If so, then it is a goal of sociology to expose this hidden reality, the one that groups so carefully put forward for public consumption. We only have to peer deeply enough.

Sociologists have found that participant observation (reviewed in Chapter 1 of *Essentials*) is a good way of peering behind the scenes. It helps us explore this parallel reality that is usually open only to insiders. Just as the preceding article gave us a behind-the-scenes glimpse of car dealerships, so in the opening article of this part, Daniel Chambliss takes us behind the scenes of the hospital to reveal what really goes on there. This enables us to grasp an entirely different perspective than the one that is usually presented to us. To probe behind the scenes, sociologists also use in-depth interviews. In the second and concluding selection of this part, Nanette Davis turns the sociological lens on how young women become prostitutes. From her interviews, she found that theirs is not a conscious decision. Instead, they drift from promiscuity to prostitution. As you read this article, note how the self-identity of these women changes as they move from one status to another.

5∎▪∎∎▪∎∎▪∎∎▪∎∎▪∎∎▪∎∎▪∎∎▪∎∎▪∎∎▪∎

Just Another Routine Emergency

Daniel F. Chambliss

introduction ∎ ▪ ∎ ▪ ∎

Just as buildings have façades—attractive, carefully manicured front exteriors that are designed to give a good impression of what might be inside—so social groups and organizations have façades. Some organizations hire public relations firms to put out favorable messages. Others contribute to charitable causes to cultivate images of caring. Even oil companies that exploit the environment publish expensive, full-page glossy ads in national magazines to convince the public that they care more about the environment than does *Greenpeace* or *The Sea Shepards*.

Behind the social façade put out for public consumption lies a different reality. As in the case of some oil companies, the reality may conflict greatly with the cultivated public image. But in the typical case, the hidden reality has more to do with dissension among the group's members, or with less dedication to the group's goal, than the organization wants to reveal. At times, the façade may have more to do with maintaining an appearance of competence and order, whereas the reality is a looming incompetence and disorder. This selection by Daniel Chambliss takes a look behind the social façade of the hospital, revealing a reality that few of us are familiar with.

Thinking Critically

As you read this selection, ask yourself:

1. How do the personnel of hospitals keep outsiders from seeing past their social façade?

2. What did this participant observation study reveal about hospitals that we otherwise would not have known?

3. Use this reading to prove or disprove this statement: From their inappropriate humor, we can see that doctors and nurses don't really care about their patients.

*E*very unit in the hospital…has its own normality, its own typical patients, number of deaths, and crises to be faced. But just as predictably, every unit has its emergencies that threaten the routine and challenge the staff's ability to maintain workaday attitudes and practices. Emergencies threaten the staff's ability to carry on as usual, to maintain their own distance from the patient's suffering, and to hold at bay their awe at the enormity of events. Occasionally breakdowns occur in unit discipline or the ability to do the required work.

Staff follow several strategies when trying to manage the threat of breakdowns: they will keep outsiders outside, follow routinization rituals, or use humor to distance themselves. Finally, even when all efforts fail, they will keep going, no matter what. Consider in turn each of these implicit maxims:

■ ■ ■ 1. KEEP OUTSIDERS OUTSIDE

Every hospital has policies about visiting hours, designed not only to "let patients rest" but also to protect staff from outsiders' interference in their work. Visitors are limited to certain hours, perhaps two to a patient room for fifteen-minute visits; they may have to be announced before entering the unit or may be kept waiting in a room down the hall. No doubt many such policies are good for the patient. No doubt, too, they keep visitors out of the nurse's way, prevent too many obtrusive questions or requests for small services, and prevent curious laypersons from seeing the messier, less presentable sides of nursing care.

When visitors cannot be physically excluded, they can still be cognitively controlled, that is, prevented from knowing that something untoward is happening. Typically, the staff behave in such episodes as if everything were OK, even when it is not. This is similar to what Erving Goffman observed in conversations: when the shared flow of interaction is threatened by an accidental insult or a body failure such as a sneeze or flatulence, people simply try to ignore the break in reality and carry on as if nothing has happened. Such "reality maintenance" is often well-orchestrated, requiring cooperation on the part of several parties. For Goffman, normal people in normal interactions accept at face value each other's presentation of who they are:

> A state where everyone temporarily accepts everyone else's line is established. This kind of mutual acceptance seems to be a basic structural feature of interaction, especially the interaction of face-to-face talk. It is typically a "working" acceptance, not a "real" one.[1]

And when this routine breaks down, the immediate strategy is simple denial:

> When a person fails to prevent an incident, he can still attempt to maintain the fiction that no threat to face has occurred. The most blatant example of this is found where the person acts as if an event that contains a threatening expression has not occurred at all.[2]

In the hospital, the unexpected entrance of outsiders into a delicate situation can disrupt the staff's routine activities and create unmanageable chaos. To avoid this, the staff may pretend to outsiders that nothing special is happening; this pretense itself can be part of the routine. During a code (resuscitation) effort I witnessed, there were three such potential disruptions by outsiders: another patient calling for help, a new incoming patient being wheeled in, and the new patient's family members entering the unit. All three challenges were handled by the staff diverting the outsiders from the code with a show, as if nothing were happening:

> Code in CCU [Cardiac Care Unit]…woman patient, asystole [abnormal ventricle contractions]. Doc (res[ident]) pumping chest—*deep* pumps, I'm struck by how far down they push. Serious stuff. Matter of factness of process is striking. This was a surprise code, not expected. Patient was in Vtak [ventricular fibrillation], pulse started slowing, then asystole. N[urse]s pumping for a while, RT [Respiratory Therapist] ambu-bagging [pumping air into lungs]. Maybe 7–8 people in patient's room working. Calm, but busy. Occasionally a laugh.
>
> Pt in next room (no more than 10 feet away) called for nurse—a doc went in, real loose and casual, strolled in, pt said something; doc said, "There's something going on next door that's taking people's time; we'll get to you"—real easy, like nothing at all happening. Then strolls back to code room. Very calm…
>
> Two N[urse]s came into unit wheeling a new patient. One said, "Uh, oh, bad time," very quietly as she realized, going in the door, that a code was on. Somebody said, "Close the door"—the outside door to the unit, which the Ns with the new pt were holding open…
>
> When the new pt was brought in and rolled into his room, the family with him was stopped at unit door, told to stay in waiting room and "we'll call you" with a casual wave of hand, as if this is routine. [No one said a code was on. Patient lying on gurney was wheeled in, went right by the code room and never knew a thing.] [Field Notes]

This is a simple example of protecting the routine from the chaos of a panicking patient or a horrified family; the outsiders never knew that a resuscitation was occurring fifteen feet away. The staff's work was, in their own eyes, routine; their challenge was protecting that routine from outside disruption.

■ ■ ■ ■ 2. FOLLOW ROUTINIZATION RITUALS

The staff's sense of routine is maintained by the protective rituals of hospital life. Under stress, one may use them more and more compulsively, falling back on the old forms to reconvince oneself that order is still present. Frantic prayers in the foxhole are the prototype cases.

Most prominent of such rituals in hospitals are "rounds," the standard ritual for the routine handling of patient disasters in the hospital. "Rounds" is the generic term for almost any organized staff group discussion of patients' conditions. "Walking rounds" refers to a physician walking through the hospital, usually trailed by various residents and interns, going from patient to patient and reviewing their condition. "Grand rounds" are large meetings of the medical staff featuring the presentation of an interesting case, with elaborate discussion and questions, for the purpose of education and review of standard practices. Nursing rounds usually consist of a meeting between the staff for one (outgoing) shift reporting to the staff of the next (incoming) shift on the condition of all patients on the floor. Here the staff collectively explains what has happened and why, bringing every case into the staff's framework of thinking, and systematically enforcing the system's capability for handling medical problems without falling to pieces. In rounds, the staff confirm to each other that things are under control. Once a week, for instance, the Burn Unit at one hospital holds rounds in their conference room with a group of residents, one or two attending, several nurses, the social workers, dieticians, and physical therapists. The patients here are in terrible shape; one can sometimes hear moans in the hallway outside as patients are taken for walks by the nurses. But rounds continue:

> Macho style of the docs very evident.... Resident will present a case, then the attendings take rapid-fire shots at what he [the resident] had done: wrong dressing, wrong feeding schedule, failure to note some abnormality in the lab results. Much of the talk was a flurry of physiological jargon, many numbers and abbreviations. The intensity of the presentation, the mercilessness of the grilling, is surprising.... Focus is on no errors made in situation of extreme pressure—i.e., both in patient treatment and then here in rounds presenting the case. Goal here is to be predictable, *controlled,* nothing left out. [Field Notes]

■ ■ ■ 3. USE HUMOR TO DISTANCE YOURSELF

Keeping outsiders away and following the standard rituals for maintaining normality can help, but sometimes the pathos of hospital life becomes psychologically threatening to staff members. One response is to break down, cry, and run out, but this is what they are trying to avoid; the more common reaction is the sort of black humor that notoriously characterizes hospitals and armies everywhere. Humor provides an outlet; when physical space is not available, humor is a way to separate oneself psychologically from what is happening. It says both that I am not involved and that this really isn't so important. (In brain surgery, when parts of that organ are, essentially, vacuumed away, one may hear comments like "There goes 2d grade, there go the piano lessons," etc.) With laughter, things seem less consequential, less of a burden. What has been ghastly can perhaps be made funny:

> Today they got a 600-gram baby in the Newborn Unit. When Ns heard [the baby] was in Delivery, they were praying, "Please God let it be under 500 grams"—because that's the definite cutoff under which they won't try to save it—but the doc said admit it anyway. Ns unhappy.
> I came in the unit tonight; N came up to me and said brightly, with a big smile, "Have you seen our fetus?" Ns on the Newborn Unit have nicknames for some. There's "Fetus," the 600-gram one; "Munchkin"; and "Thrasher," in the corner, the one with constant seizures. Grim humor, but common. ["Fetus" was born at 24 weeks, "Munchkin" at 28.] [Field Notes]

The functions of such humor for medical workers have been described in a number of classic works of medical sociology. Renée Fox, writing in her book *Experiment Perilous* about physicians on a metabolic research unit, says, "The members of the group were especially inclined to make jokes about events that disturbed them a good deal," and she summarizes that

> by freeing them from some of the tension to which they were subject, enabling them to achieve greater detachment and equipoise, and strengthening their resolve to do something about the problems with which they were faced, the grim medical humor of the Metabolic Group helped them to come to terms with their situation in a useful and professionally acceptable way.[3]

Fox and other students of hospital culture (notably Rose Coser)[4] have emphasized that humor fills a functional purpose of "tension release," allowing medical workers to get on with the job in the face of trauma; their analyses usually focus on jokes explicitly told in medical settings. This analysis is correct as far as it goes, but in a sense I think it almost "explains away" hospital humor—as if to say that "these people are under a lot of strain, so it's understandable that they tell these gruesome jokes." It suggests, in a functionalist fallacy, that jokes are made because of the strain and that things somehow aren't "really" funny.

But they are. An appreciation of hospital life must recognize that funny things—genuinely funny, even if sometimes simultaneously horrible—do happen. Hospitals are scenes of irony, where good and bad are inseparably blended, where funny things happen, where to analytically excuse laughter as a defense mechanism is simultaneously to deny the human reality, the experience, that even to a non-stressed outsider *this is funny*.[5] The humor isn't found only in contrived jokes but in the scenes one witnesses; laughter can be spontaneous, and it's not always nervous. True, one must usually have a fairly normalized sense of the hospital to laugh here, but laugh one does.

Certainly, the staff make jokes:

> In the OR [operating room]:
>   "This is his [pt's] 6th time [for a hernia repair]."
>   "After two, I hear you're officially disabled."
>   "Oh good, does that mean he gets a special parking place?"
>   [Field Notes]
> In the ICU [Intensive Care Unit], two Ns—one male, one female—working on pt.
> Nurse 1 (male): "This guy has bowel sounds in his scrotum."
> Nurse 2 (female): "In his scrotum?"
> Nurse 1: "Yeah, didn't you pick that up?"
> Nurse 2: "I didn't put my stethoscope there!" (Big laughs.) [Field Notes]

Sometimes jokes are more elaborate and are obviously derived from the tragedy of the situation:

> In another ICU, staff member taped a stick to the door of the unit, symbolizing (for them) "The Stake," a sign of some form of euthanasia [perhaps the expression sometimes used, "to stake" a patient, derives from the myth that vampires can only be killed by driving a stake through the heart]. Periodically word went around that a resident had just won the "Green Stake Award," meaning that he or she had, for the first time, allowed or helped a patient to die. [Field Notes]
> Some colorful balloons with "Get Well Soon" were delivered to a patient's room. The patient died the following night. Someone on the staff moved the balloons to the

door of another patient's room; that patient died! Now the staff has put the balloons at the door of the patient they believe is "most likely to die next." [Field Notes]

But jokes have to be contrived; they are deliberate efforts at humor and so make a good example of efforts to distance oneself, or to make the tragic funny. But the inherent irony of the hospital is better seen in situations that spontaneously provoke laughter. These things are funny in themselves; even an outsider can laugh at them:

Nurse preparing to wheel a patient into the OR tells him, "Take out your false teeth, take off your glasses...," and continuing, trying to make a joke, "Take off your leg, take out your eyes." The patient said, "Oh, I almost forgot—" and pulled out his [false] eye! [Interview]

Or:

Lady patient [Geriatric floor] is upset because she called home, there's no answer; she's afraid her husband has died. Sylvia [a nurse] told her he probably just went somewhere for lunch, but patient said he would have called. She's afraid.
    [Later] Sylvia went back in lady's room—she's crying. Husband called! Sylvia happy, smiling, "You should be happy!" "But," says the old lady, "he called to say he was out burying the dog!"
    Sylvia had to leave the room because she was starting to laugh; she and Janie laughing at this at the N's station, saying it's really sad but funny at the same time. [Field Notes]

Or:

In looking at X-rays of a patient's colon, the resident explains to the team a shadow on the film: "Radiology says it could be a tumor, or it might just be stool." Jokes all around about how "helpful" Rays [Radiology] is. [Field Notes]

One needn't be under pressure to find such things funny. People do laugh to ease pressure or to distance oneself. But sometimes the distance comes first: laughter is made possible by the routinization that has gone before.

■ ■ ■ ■ 4. WHEN THINGS FALL APART, KEEP GOING

Sometimes routinization fails: outsiders come into the room and, seeing their dead mother, break down, screaming and wailing; or a longtime, cared-for patient begins irretrievably to "decompensate" and lose blood pressure, sliding quickly to death; or emergency surgery goes bad, the trauma shakes the staff, and there are other patients coming in from the ambulances. Any of these can destroy the staff's sense of "work as usual." In such cases, the typical practice seems to be, remarkably: just keep going. Trauma teams specialize in the psychological strength (or cold-bloodedness, perhaps) to continue working when the world seems to be falling apart. Finally, nurses and physicians are notable for continuing to work even, in the final case, after the patient is for almost all purposes dead, or will be soon.

> A resident said to the attending [physician] on one floor, discussing a terminal patient: "If we transfuse him, he might get hepatitis."
>   Another resident: "By the time he gets hepatitis he'll be dead."
>   Attending: "OK, so let's transfuse." [Field Notes]

Perseverance is a habit; it's also a moral imperative, a way of managing disaster as if it were routine.

In every unit there are nurses known for being good under pressure. These are people who, whatever their other skills (and, typically, their other skills are quite good), are able to maintain their presence of mind in any crisis. Whereas "being organized" is a key quality for nurses in routine situations, staying calm is crucial in emergency situations. Compare two nurses known for remaining calm (Mavis and Anna) to two others who are prone to alarm (Linda and Julie):

> Mavis [in Neonatal ICU] is cited as a good nurse (great starting IVs, e.g.) who doesn't get shook, even in a code, even if her pt is dying, she still keeps doing what you're supposed to do. Linda, by contrast, is real smart, very good technically, but can freak out, start yelling, etc., if things are going badly. [Field Notes]
>   Julie [in Medical ICU], hurrying around, looks just one step ahead of disaster, can't keep up, etc. Doc says something about the patient in room 1. Julie says, walking past, "He's not mine," keeps going. But Anna, calm, walks in pt's room—pt with oxygen mask, wants something. Anna goes out, calmly, comes back in a minute w/cup of crushed ice, gives pt a spoonful to ease thirst. She *always* seems to be doing that little thing that others "don't have time for"—never flustered and yet seems to get more done than anyone else. [Field Notes, Interview]

But to "keep going" depends not so much on the individual fortitude of nurses such Mavis and Anna, but on the professional and institutional habits of the nursing staff and the hospital. The continuance of care even in the face of obvious failure of efforts is itself a norm. Whatever one's personal disposition, one keeps working; the staff keep working, often when the patient is all but dead, or "dead" but not officially recognized as such:

> Dr. K., walking rounds with four residents, discussing a 30-year-old male patient, HIV-positive, gone totally septic [has bloodstream infection, a deadly problem], no hope at all of recovery—Dr. K. says this is a "100 percent mortality" case; so they decide how to proceed with minimal treatment, at the end of which Dr. K. says brightly, "And if he codes—code him!" [Field Notes]

Coding such a patient is an exercise in technique; there is no hope entailed, no optimism, no idea that he might be saved. There is only the institutional habit which substitutes for hope, which in many cases obviates the staff's pessimism or lack of interest. When standard procedure is followed, courage is unnecessary. It is one thing to be routinely busy, caring for vegetative patients; it happens every day. It is quite another to handle emergency surgery with no time and a life at stake. Sometimes such a case will challenge all the staff's resources—their personal fortitude, their habitualization of procedures, the self-protection offered by an indefatigable sense of humor. To maintain one's composure while under tremendous pressures of time and fatefulness requires all the courage a staff can muster.

One such case was that of emergency surgery on a thirty-five-year-old woman who came to Southwestern Regional hospital in severe abdominal pain; she was diagnosed with a ruptured ectopic [tubal] pregnancy estimated at sixteen weeks. The case provides us with a dramatic example of the pressure placed on the staff to retain their composure in the face of disaster.

The long description which follows is graphic. The scene was more than bloody; it was grotesque. More than one staff member—including one member of the surgical team itself—left the room during the operation, sickened. Other nurses, even very experienced ones, told me they have never witnessed such a scene and hope never to witness one. I include it here, in some detail, to exemplify both what health professionals face in their work and how, incredibly, some of them can carry on. The description is reconstructed from Field Notes (some written at the time on the inside of a surgical mask, some on sheets of paper carried in a pocket), and from interviews afterward with participants:

> Saturday night OR suite; hasn't been busy. Only one case so far, a guy who got beat up with a tire iron (drug deal), finished about 8:30 P.M. It's about 10:00. 2 Ns—the Saturday night staff—sitting around in the conference room, just chatting and waiting for anything that happens.
>
> Call comes over intercom: ruptured tubal (pregnancy) just came in OR, bringing to the crash room. 35-year-old black woman, very heavy—250 pounds maybe—apparently pregnant for 16 weeks, which means she's been in pain for 10 weeks or more without coming in. Friends brought her to ER screaming in pain. Blood pressure is at "60 over palpable," i.e., the diastolic doesn't even register on the manometer. She's obviously bleeding bad internally, will die fast if not opened up. Ns run to OR and set up fast. I've never seen people work so quickly here, no wasted motion at all. This is full speed *emergency.*
>
> When patient is rolled in, fully conscious, there are more than a dozen staff people in the room, including three gynecological surgery residents, who will operate; all three are women. The surgeons are scrubbed and gowned and stand in a line, back from the table, watching without moving, the one in charge periodically giving orders to the nurses who are setting up. At one point there are twelve separate people working on the patient—IVs going into both arms, anesthesiologist putting mask on pt to gas, nurse inserting a Foley [bladder] catheter, others tying pt's arms to the straightout arms of the table, others scrubbing the huge belly, an incredible scene. The patient is shaking terribly, in pain and fear. Her eyes are bugging out, looking around terribly fast. She's whimpering, groaning as needles go in, crying out softly. No one has time even to speak to her; one nurse briefly leans over and speaks into her ear something like "try not to worry, we're going to take care of you," but there is no time for this. I've never seen anyone so afraid, sweating and crying and the violent shaking.
>
> As soon as they have prepped her—the belly cleansed and covered with Opsite, in a matter of minutes, very, very fast, the anesthesiologist says, "All set?" And someone says "yes," and they gas her. I'm standing right by her head, looking to the head side of the drape which separates her head from her body; the instant that her eyes close, I look to the other side—and the surgeon has already slit her belly open. No hesitation at all, maybe before the patient was out.

What happened next, more extraordinary than the very fast prep, was the opening. Usually in surgery the scalpel makes the skin cut, then slowly scissors are used, snipping piece by piece at muscle, the Bovie cauterizing each blood vessel on the way, very methodical and painstaking. This was nothing like that. It was an entirely different style. They cut fast and deep, sliced her open deep, just chopped through everything, in a—not a panic, but something like a "blitzkrieg," maybe—to get down into the Fallopian tube that had burst and was shooting blood into the abdomen.

When they first got into the abdominal cavity, usually there would be some oozing blood; here as they opened blood splattered out all over the draping on the belly. It was a godawful mess, blood everywhere. They had one surgeon mopping up with gauze sponges, another using a suction pump, a little plastic hose, trying to clean the way. Unbelievable. They got down to the tubes, reaching down and digging around with their hands. And then they found it—suddenly out of this bloody mess down in the abdomen, with the surgeons groping around trying to feel where things were, out of this popped up, right out of the patient and, literally, onto the sheet covering her, the 16-week fetus itself. Immediately one surgeon said mock-cheerfully, "It's a boy!" "God, don't do that," said the scrub tech, turning her head away.

The scrub tech then began to lose it, tears running down her cheeks. Two other people on the team—there were maybe six around the table—said about the same time, nearly together, "Damien!" and "Alien!" recalling recent horror movies, "children of the devil" themes. The fetus lay on the sheet just below the open abdomen for a few moments. The head surgery resident, working, just kept working. The scrub tech should have put the fetus into a specimen tray, but she was falling to pieces fast, crying, and starting to have trouble handing the proper tools to the surgeon, who said something like, "What are you doing?" At this point the circulating nurse, a man, said, "If nobody else will do it," picked up the fetus and put it in a specimen tray, which he then covered with a towel and put aside. He then told another nurse to help him into a gown—he wasn't scrubbed. This violates sterile technique badly, for him to start handling tools, but the scrub tech was becoming a problem. The circulating nurse then quickly gowned and gloved, gently pulled the scrub tech aside and said, "I'll do it." The scrub tech ran out of the room in tears. And the circulating nurse began passing tools to the surgeons himself. It is the circulating nurse's responsibility to handle problems this way, and he did. Another nurse had gone out to scrub properly, and when she came back, maybe ten minutes later, she gowned and gloved and relieved him; so he (the circulating nurse) went back to his regular job of charting the procedure, answering the phone, etc.

By this time, things were under control; the bleeding was stopped, the tube tied off. The other tube was OK and left alone so the pt can get pregnant again. The blood in the abdomen was cleaned up—over 1500 cc's were lost, that's just under a half-gallon of blood. The pt would have died fast if they hadn't gotten in there.

Within two hours after the patient had first rolled in, the room was quiet, only three staff members left, two surgeons and the scrub nurse closing up and talking quietly. Most of the mess—the bloody sponges, the used tools, and all—was gone, cleared away, and all the other staff people, including the chief surgeon, had left. Very calm. The patient, who two hours ago was on the end of a fast terrible death, will be out of the hospital in two days with no permanent damage beyond the loss of one Fallopian tube. [Field Notes, Interviews]

In this situation, we can see two somewhat distinct problems in maintaining the routine order of things: first, the challenge simply in getting the work done; and second, the challenge of upholding the moral order of the hospital.[6] The first issue was resolved by replacing the scrub tech so the operation could continue. The second issue is trickier. The scrub tech's response appeared to be set off not by the horror of what she saw—the bloody fetus—but by the reaction of the assisting surgeon—"It's a boy!" I can only guess that the joke was too much for her. In continuing to work without her, and continuing without noticeable change of demeanor, the surgical team was asserting not only the imperative to protect the operational routine but also, I think, to protect the moral order of emergency surgery as well. That order includes:

1. The job comes first, before personal reactions of fear or disgust.
2. Cynicism is an acceptable form of expression if it helps to maintain composure and distance.
3. The medical team is rightfully in charge and above what may be happening in the OR [operating room].
4. Preserving life is the central value; others (such as niceties of language or etiquette) fall far behind.

There is clearly a morality here. Just as clearly, it is not the morality of everyday life.

NOTES

1. Erving Goffman, "On Face-Work," in *Interaction Ritual: Essays on Face-to-Face Behavior* (New York: Pantheon Books, 1967), p. 11.
2. Ibid., pp. 17–18.
3. Renée C. Fox, *Experiment Perilous* (New York: Free Press, 1959; reprint ed., Philadelphia: University of Pennsylvania Press, 1974), pp. 80–82.
4. Rose Laub Coser, "Some Social Functions of Laughter," in Lewis Coser, *The Pleasures of Sociology*, edited and with an introduction and notes by Lewis Coser (New York: New American Library, 1980), pp. 81–97.
5. The genius of Shem's *House of God* is that it accepts this fact and presents it honestly.
6. I am indebted to Robert Zussman, who suggested these in his review of the manuscript.

READING 6

Becoming a Prostitute

Nanette J. Davis

introduction

Society is set up to produce conforming individuals. As we learn the ways of our culture, we learn how we *ought* to act, think, and evaluate people, events, and ourselves. We learn what is expected of us if we are to be considered members of society in good standing. We learn this lesson as we are socialized within our family and later within other social institutions. The overall message we receive is to conform—in behavior and thought. And conformity is necessary, because if society is to survive, there must be rules, or norms, that allow its members to interact cooperatively with one another. This requires that people know what to expect of one another.

Most of us do conform most of the time, but not always. All of us break at least some of the rules, and some of us seem to break most of the rules. Most of us manage to skirt the rules when we want to, yet conform sufficiently to remain members of society in good standing. Some, however, flout the norms to such a degree that they are labeled outsiders. They know the label they receive, and this, in turn, affects how they think of themselves. Note how the women that Davis analyzes gradually move from one set of norms into another.

Thinking Critically

As you read this selection, ask yourself:

1. Why did these young women become prostitutes?

2. How does identity with hustler norms facilitate entry into prostitution?

3. If you were appointed by the Mayor of Minneapolis to develop a program to decrease the prostitution of young women, based on this article what program would you propose?

The source of data for this study is provided by a jail sample of thirty prostitutes from three correctional institutions (reformatory, workhouse, and training school) in Minnesota. Included are seventeen white women, twelve black women, and one Indian woman. The age range was fifteen to thirty-four, with an average age of twenty-one.

All of the thirty women were legally classified as "common prostitute," although only twenty-four of the thirty informants reported that they were professional prostitutes. The women operated at the "street-walker" level of prostitution, that is, lounging in bars or on streetcorners and openly soliciting clients. Data were elicited through structured interviews, with emphasis, however, on the informants' verbalized statements. The interviews averaged one and one-half to two hours in length. Official records also were used. Further, informal data were gained through participant observation....

THE PROCESS OF DRIFT FROM PROMISCUITY
TO THE FIRST ACT OF PROSTITUTION

Age at First Sexual Experience

The women in this sample were initiated into sexual experiences at an early age. The mean age at which they first had sexual intercourse was 13.6, with a range of seven to eighteen. Rape experiences, reported by two women, account for the lower age level (seven and nine years, respectively). Three other informants noted traumatic sexual experiences with brothers, step-father, or father, at age twelve or under. Nineteen of the thirty women report they had sexual intercourse by age thirteen, although almost one-half of the white girls had experienced intercourse by age twelve. The most characteristic pattern was coitus with a boyfriend, who was typically five or six years older than the girl was. Four informants were sexually initiated by another girl with heterosexual relations occurring within a year after such lesbian contacts.... First sexual contacts typically involved sexual intercourse, with only one girl reporting an initial petting experience.

Preconditions for those characterized by "early sexuality" are: (1) high levels of familial permissiveness led to association with older males at parties, neighboring houses, or street pickups, (2) familial social control was often lacking or inconsistent, (3) peer group norms encouraged early sexuality, and (4) sexuality was associated with freedom (a movement away from a disliked family) or, conversely, security (the certainty of male companionship). Three girls, on the other hand, did not experience their first sexual intercourse until age seventeen or eighteen. Those having this "late sexuality" experienced these typical conditions: (1) sexual matters were taboo areas in the family, (2) the mother was highly protective, exerting strong religious and familial controls with consequent little freedom of opportunity in early adolescence, and (3) a rebellion pattern eventually developed in opposition to the rigidity of the controls.

Almost all of the women (twenty-eight of thirty) report that their first sex experience was either meaningless or distasteful; for example, "It was nothing," "I did it just to please him," "I really didn't like it," "I disliked it," "It was awful," "I was scared," "It made me sick." A need for conformity seems to be the most salient motive for this first sexuality, as:

> I did it just to belong. Everybody was doing it.

> I was the only virgin in the crowd (age fifteen). Five of my girlfriends had kids at sixteen....

The promiscuous pattern which developed for most girls (three women had early pregnancies which were followed by marriage, with promiscuity and prostitution occurring *after* these events) seems to reflect associates' expectations, the desire to attract males ("The boys were always hot after me"), and an opportunity structure which facilitated the behavior.

Perception of Childhood and Adolescent Years

The promiscuous pattern may provide one condition which can lead to informal labeling ("bad" girl, "easy mark") and subsequent stigmatization by parents, teachers, and conventional associates. But other circumstances may arise, prior to or following this sexual behavior.... These women perceived their childhood and adolescent years as marked by negative or degrading interactions with society, as the following data indicate:

1. Familial instability was typical for almost all of the white girls (sixteen of seventeen) and two-thirds of the blacks (eight of twelve). Such instability included a drunken, violent or absentee parent (usually the father), extreme poverty, or families larger than the parents could cope with. Conditions within the family were eventually brought to the attention of neighbors, welfare board, or court. Such attention was defined as humiliating or demoralizing.

2. More than half of the informants (eighteen of thirty) have spent one year or more of their childhood (under twelve) in foster homes, living with relatives, or in other separations from the nuclear family.

3. Almost all of the informants (twenty-eight) report that parents, neighbors, and/or teachers considered them "trouble-makers," "slow learners," or generally inadequate in relation to expectations.

4. The black women (nine of twelve), especially, reported "unfair" treatment by white teachers or students, inability to gain and/or hold a job, and frustration in cases where self-improvement was attempted.

5. Twenty-three of the thirty informants reported that they had been sentenced to a juvenile home or training school as adolescents for truancy, incorrigibility, or sex delinquency....

In the interactional processes with significant others (parents, teachers, neighbors, and friends), the girl [is seen as] "different." She is a person who is expected to behave in unconventional ways. Absenteeism from school, chronic disobedience at home, and later, promiscuity, categorize the girl as difficult, if not impossible to control. Low family cohesion with consequent weak affectional ties between parents and daughter leads the girl to seek street associates....

[T]he rationale for promiscuity, and initially for prostitution, is a hedonistic concern for fun, new experiences, excitement, and a response to peer group expectations. Sex as a status tool is exploited to gain male attention. The adolescent urge for liberation from the confines of the family and controls of school and job leads to involvement in drinking parties or hustler groups, where differential identification with sophisticated delinquents occurs.

The Drift from Promiscuity to First Act of Prostitution

Regardless of the age at which the girl first experienced intercourse, there then followed a *"drift" or "slide" process from promiscuity to prostitution,* with the girl first prostituting herself in late adolescence (mean = 17.3 years). There was a range, however, of fourteen to twenty-five years. The early age of prostitution was facilitated by a definition of the deviant situation as similar to sexual promiscuity—excitement and desire for male attention:...

> It was either jump in bed, and go with every Tom, Dick, and Harry, and just give it away, so I decided to turn tricks instead.... The money was so easy to get....

My data strongly suggest that the movement from casual delinquency to the first phase of [prostitution] is facilitated by the policy of confining deviants to correctional institutions. The adolescent girl who is labeled a sex offender for promiscuity or "mixing" (white girls associating with black males) may initially experience a conflict about her identity. Intimate association with sophisticated deviants, however, may provide an incentive to learn the hustler role ("The girls told me about it—I was such an avid listener."), and thus resolve the status anxiety by gaining prestige through association with deviants, and later, experimentation in the deviant role. Frequent and predictable escapes from the open institution are common. Lines of communication between urban vice neighborhoods and training school inmates assures the escapee of finding accommodations during a "run."

As an outlaw, the girl cannot seek the security of parents or the home neighborhood. Thus, isolated from conventional associates or activities, and dependent on deviant contacts for financial and social support, the girl may come to define the situation as one that inevitably leads her into enacting the deviant role, as:

> I ran away from the institution. I went and visited my girlfriends. I was out of the institution about a month, just loafing around. I talked to some friends of mine who were hustlers. Someone suggested I try it. I had been sponging off everybody. I got sick of sponging. I'd sleep here one night, and there another....

> I had run away (from the training school). I had no money or anything. I went walking the street. The older girls (institutionalized associates) told me about it.

Roads to Recruitment

Adolescent institutionalization, then, often prior to the actual commitment of a deviant act, may act as a structural condition which facilitates the learning of a deviant role. Induction into the career, on the other hand, proceeds through alternative routes, chief of which are: (1) response to peer group expectations, (2) involvement in a pimp-manager relationship, and (3) adolescent rebellion.

Response to *peer group expectations* undoubtedly provides the major avenue to recruitment ("It's the environment. Everyone is doing it.") Associating with hustlers, "party girls," or pimps, while viewed as prestigious, can only be maintained by "trying out" the behavior. Clearly, for twenty-eight of the thirty informants, differential identification with deviant associates accounts, in part, for the movement into prostitution.

> I was on run...I didn't get up until 3 P.M. I was staying with my boyfriend. He was unemployed. He was planning to set me up [for prostitution]. We had been talking about it. I took long precautions.... A friend helped me out. Everything happened so fast. It was kind of like prearranged for me. Crazy! We were staying in a hotel with lots of pimps and prostitutes living there. The first time was at the World's Series. I was dressed like a normal teenager....

Involvement in a *pimp-manager relationship* provides a typical method of entrance for some under-age girls (eight informants.) In other instances, the pimp may not have initially arranged the first contact, but he typically appears relatively early on the scene to direct the girl's activities. The uninitiated girl views the pimp relationship as a means of security in an otherwise rejecting world.

> I always had a need to belong.... A pimp moves in, and he sees you're attractive, and he sees you want to belong. Pimps are the most understanding. They're the least educated persons, though. I thought my pimp was my knight in shining armor....

The pimp's ability to "set the girl up" by arranging clients is a measure of the girl's arrival on the deviant scene. One informant, whose first experience was such an arrangement, recalled how the system operated.

> I was living with a girlfriend.... She wasn't a hustler—and started going with this one boy. He introduced me to this pimp. He asked me if I would [hustle]. I was against it, but they all said how easy it was. I went to this pimp's house. I was a call girl. There were three of us [hustlers]. The pimps would come in. They got all the contacts, and they'd say to the tricks, "Lookee here, I got these girls, see," and he'd line up the tricks. Then he'd say to the girls that there was a trick in this hotel, and you'd go to a room number.

Another girl commented that the pimp used alternate techniques of violence ("He hit me on the head when I said no") and persuasion: "He told me, 'I can put you in big business. You won't have to hustle hard.' I saw the girls and how they did it. It was like a dream."

Adolescent rebellion operates for girls who have experienced oppressive familial controls (six women), forming another typical pattern.

> Well, I started hustling, I suppose, because the party group I ran around with were always talking about it. My mother had always picked my friends. She wouldn't allow any bad influences—the square friends only, the goody-goody club activities at church. My parents were very old-fashioned. They didn't drink or smoke, and were very church-going. But when I got in with this group, it was really different, man!...

Dominant Motives During the First Stage

Underlying these main roads to recruitment into prostitution are curiosity and a desire for new experience, defined idleness, identification with hustler norms, and a strong present-time orientation.

Curiosity and access to new experiences (or "kicks") act as a dominant motive to the naive girl who seeks esteem from the hustler group. "I was unemployed at the time, just hanging around with a group. I wanted some excitement—kicks, you know."

Remarks such as, "It was the glamor and game of it," "I did it just for the fun of it," "There's a lot of excitement to that—the cops on you and everything," indicate a perception of deviance as part of the excitement and risk of street life....

Idleness is typical for most of the women (twenty-three of thirty). Separations from family, school, job, or other conventional activities characterize this first deviant phase. For the runaway training school girl, prostitution may relieve the dullness of an otherwise undirected existence.

> I was sixteen and on the run, just loafing around my girlfriend's house. One of my girlfriends gave me the pointers, so I decided to try it.

> I had run away—like I was lost or something. I had been walking the streets all day, and at 6 P.M. I met this guy. I was really looking for love and attention, but not necessarily the men.

Identification with hustler norms undoubtedly accounts for the frequently expressed (twenty-seven of thirty) money rationale. However, economic deprivation is not the dominant element for most girls. Only two women, for instance, expressed intense financial need because of child support. Independence, isolation from conventional supports, and the lure of "easy" money, were major considerations.

> I was on run—no job or anything. I was by myself. It was about 8. I went out, went downtown. My boyfriend worked in the _____ Hotel. He called me up to say that he had a man who had fifty dollars to get a girl, and so there it was. I got forty-five dollars the first night—for four men. Everyone was doing it, anyway. Then I walked back downtown, and had three more, and then went back to my apartment.

A strong present-time orientation characterizes the younger girl particularly, who conceives of the act as satisfying immediate needs only, without considering long-range implications.

> The first time I did it was to buy a present for my boyfriend. The next time just to have some spending money. I've been asked to hustle lots of times. I know all the gimmicks, and how to do it…all that stuff.

> I was going to school and I wanted to go to this dance the night after. I needed new clothes. I went out at ten o'clock and home at twelve. I had three tricks the first time, and fifteen dollars for every trick.

Whatever the mode of recruitment, or the dominant motives involved, this study shows certain common elements present at this state of deviant involvement.

These generally include: informal labeling which early categorizes the girl as unconventional or "troublemaker"; isolation from conventional family, friends, or associates; response to deviant associates' expectations; and expressed need for economic self-sufficiency while "on run" or probation. Such motives indicate that: (1) episodic involvement, or *a drift into deviance,* is characteristic of prostitutes and is related to hedonistic and short-term concerns; and (2) stigmatized persons may respond to a morally degraded status by seeking associates who may reward the deviant behavior.

Transitional Deviance and Professionalization

Twenty-one of the thirty women interviewed experienced an "occasional" or "transitional" stage of deviance. Of the nine other labeled prostitutes, four repudiated the role after three or more deviant episodes, while five women moved directly into full-time deviance. The transitional stage lasted an average of six months (with a range from two weeks to four years). It could be viewed as an on-the-job learning period....

Motivational ambivalence during the transitional phase creates a zig-zag pattern of deviance for most prostitutes. They vacillate between conventionality and deviance. The conventional life, for instance, is not yet denied. Some girls make verbal commitments to stop, or even attempt to return to home, school, job or to set themselves up in an apartment with conventional associates. Conventional motives involve expressed reluctance to move into the act because of fear of discovery, interracial contacts, or belief that such conduct is immoral. ("It's not the right thing to do. I would get a bad reputation.")...

During this phase, they indicate indecision and confusion regarding their role. By hustling only occasionally, not more than two or three times a week, or engaging in prostitution "only when I wanted to," or "sometimes when I'm lonesome," or for "just something to do," the individual perceives that she is in control of the situation....

[T]he drift into deviance...occurs through *normalization of the act....* [This] may occur through rationalizations appropriate for promiscuity—the desire for male attention....

> I'm a person who likes to walk. There's nothing wrong with picking somebody up while you're walking. I always like walking around at night, and girls will be tempted. Girls like the offer. They like to see what the guy is going to say.

The "gaming" element, which revolves around the excitement of the "pickup" and independence on the street, is also linked to a promiscuous, rather than deviant, orientation. The promiscuous girl with conventional in-group supports may not define herself as a prostitute at this point.

In certain cases, role ambivalence may even lead to repudiation of the "trial" role after a few experiences (four informants). Negative experiences with a client, pimp, or policeman, for instance, may lead her to reject the role. Inadequate motivation is a typical condition leading to role failure in many areas of life. It was expressed by one seventeen-year old informant who had hustled on-and-off for about a month before her career had been interrupted by jail:

> Hustling—I don't get no kicks from it. I wouldn't go out and do it for a living. There
> are better ways to make money. I couldn't go through everything a prostitute goes
> through. I really don't have the guts for it. A prostitute picks up anyone off the street,
> and gets money for it. The tricks I had it with I did it just for sex, but not for me—not
> the whole self. I knew I couldn't make a career out of it. When you don't care about the
> guy, sex isn't for that.

Sex with affection, uncontaminated by money, still operates as a norm for the deviant dropout.

Their continuation in this sexually deviant behavior, on the other hand, is contingent on strong economic motivation (twenty-one women), loneliness (three), and/or expressed entrapment because of pimp control (six). For two girls, drug addiction acted as an inducement for continuation of the deviant role. Continuation in the deviant role is further contingent on an adequate learning period uninterrupted by police harassment or jail sentencing....

Delayed definitions of the act as immoral, degrading or repulsive (fifteen women report intense dissatisfaction or disgust with the situation) can no longer be postponed if situations occur that force unequivocal perception of a deviant self. Self-discovery, for instance, may be inevitable for some prostitutes when the pimp's behavior shifts from lover to exploiter, and, for example, nightly money quotas become the primary condition for the relationship ("I was just another one of his hustlers").... Another typical experience is contact with the police, court, or jail, where the label "common prostitute" is assigned. After the legal confrontation, public exposure proceeds in rapid order. Listing the girl's name in the paper, or passing the information to parents from "inside" sources, implies that, as a consequence, the girl soon renounces the pretense of conventional commitments. At this point, she may cut herself off from family and conventional others' support. Informants report such responses to the labeling procedure:

> They sent me up for something I didn't do, so I might as well do it. I wasn't afraid of
> anything.
>
> Society is really uninformed. They don't put themselves to the trouble to understand.
> There are lots worse things besides prostitution that happen. Society isn't helping at all.
> There's not a chance to be decent. Society has put the brand on us.

Personal integrity at earlier phases of the career had been maintained by secrecy regarding the deviant behavior. Role segmentation breaks down, however, if the woman has internalized the streetwalker's myth—"once a girl is on the streets, everyone knows what she is." For example,

> At first I was scared. The news gets out so fast. Everyone knows when a girl's on the
> streets a couple of nights. I thought about stopping, you know, but I just went on....

In-service training for this streetwalker group during the transitional period includes: (1) willingness to satisfy a broad range of client requests, requiring certain social and sexual skills; (2) elimination of fears regarding clients who are defined as

"odd" (sadomasochists); (3) adaptation to police surveillance and entrapment procedures; (4) avoidance of drunken clients, or those unable or unwilling to pay; and
(5) substitution of a "business" ethic for the earlier one of "gaming" or excitement....

[After a woman has gone through this process of learning and of making the
required adjustment in her identity, she has *become* a prostitute. Sex has become her
vocation.]

NOTE

This study is based on an unpublished Master's thesis, "Prostitution and Social Control:
An Empirical Inquiry into the Socialization Process of Deviant Behavior" (1967) University of Minnesota, under the direction of Professor David A. Ward.

The writer wishes to express appreciation to James M. Henslin, Peter K. Manning,
Bernard N. Meltzer, John Petras, and Ira Reiss for their helpful comments.

The selection is a condensed version of the author's more detailed analysis appearing
in *Studies in the Sociology of Sex,* James M. Henslin, ed. New York: Appleton-Century-
Crofts, 1971: 297–322, and the revised edition, *The Sociology of Sex: An Introductory
Reader,* James M. Henslin and Edward Sagarin, eds. New York: Schocken Books, 1978:
195–222.

PART
III Social Inequality

■■■

It is socially impossible to have a society of equals. Despite the strong desires of some to build an egalitarian society, every society will have inequality. Always there will be what sociologists call *social stratification*.

Each social group has a value system. That is, it values certain things above others. In a tribal group, this could be running, shooting arrows, throwing spears, or showing bravery. Some members of the tribe will have greater abilities to do the particular things that their group values—no matter what those things may be. Their abilities and accomplishments will mark them as different. These people will be looked up to, and they will likely be treated differently.

By considering abilities and accomplishments, as in a tribal group, we can see why social distinctions are inevitable. Social stratification, however, is based on much more than ability and accomplishment. In fact, ability and achievement are seldom the bases of social stratification. Much more common are inherited factors.

Every society stratifies its members according to whatever particular values and characteristics it cherishes. That is, every human group divides its people into layers, and treats each layer differently. Once a society is stratified, birth ushers children into different positions. By virtue of where their parents are located, children inherit some of the social distinctions of their parents. These can be their religion (Christian, Jew, Muslim), social class (upper, middle, lower), caste (Brahmin, Shudra), or any other distinction that their group makes.

Because their group has already set up the rules, children also inherit statuses (positions) based on their sex. With these come wide-ranging expectations of behaviors and attitudes. So it may be with their race or ethnicity. In addition, with today's geopolitical arrangements, their birth also ushers them onto a world stage, where they inherit their country's position in what is known as *global stratification*. Their nation may be rich and powerful or poor and weak. Wherever it is located on the world scene, this, too, has fundamental consequences for their lives.

In this third part of the book, we look at some of the major aspects of social inequality. We begin with the broad view of global stratification. William Greider's opening article makes it evident that where your nation is located in the global scheme of things makes a fundamental difference for what happens to you in life. Herbert Gans follows with a provocative analysis of poverty. Using a functionalist perspective, he suggests that poverty is inevitable because poor people perform valuable services for society. In his report on the social inequality of race, Lawrence Graham, a lawyer turned busboy, gives us a fascinating account of his experiences at an exclusive country club. With Robert Edgerton's controversial suggestion that some societies may be "sick," we close this part with a focus on the social inequality of gender.

One World, Ready or Not

William Greider

introduction ■ ■ ■ ■

Whether we welcome or fear it (or have no opinion), some form of a one-world government appears to be on our horizon. The trading blocs among nations have grown larger, encompassing more and more countries into the same organizations. Europe is in the midst of experimenting with an overarching government, one that has its own court, economic council, money, and military that supercede those of its individual members. The United Nations claims a peacekeeping function that includes its right to coordinate the military might of member nations against specified targets. These are just some of the indicators of a coming one-world government.

If such a government does become a reality, what it will consist of, or who will head it, is unknown at present. Apparently, though, its economic system will be capitalism. At least, this would be the logical conclusion we can draw from William Greider's analysis of how global economic changes are reshaping international politics.

Thinking Critically

As you read this selection, ask yourself:

1. Why does Greider say that capitalism is like a machine that reaps as it destroys?

2. What evidence does Greider give to support the idea that capitalism is changing international politics?

3. Greider says that multinational corporations are sharing "the tools of advanced civilization with other tribes" and that this has "explosive implications for the future of work and prosperity in the advanced economies." What does he mean by this?

Imagine a wondrous new machine, strong and supple, a machine that reaps as it destroys. It is huge and mobile, something like the machines of modern agriculture but vastly more complicated and powerful. Think of this awesome machine running over open terrain and ignoring familiar boundaries. It plows across fields and fencerows with a fierce momentum that is exhilarating to behold and also frightening. As it goes, the machine throws off enormous mows of wealth and bounty while it leaves behind great furrows of wreckage.

Now imagine that there are skillful hands on board, but no one is at the wheel. In fact, this machine has no wheel nor any internal governor to control the speed and direction. It is sustained by its own forward motion, guided mainly by its own appetites. And it is accelerating.

The machine is modern capitalism driven by the imperatives of global industrial revolution. The metaphor is imperfect, but it offers a simplified way to visualize what is dauntingly complex and abstract and impossibly diffuse—the drama of a free-running economic system that is reordering the world....

Before the machine can be understood, one must first be able to see it. The daunting shape and scope of the global system are usually described by opaque statistics from business and economics, but only the most sophisticated can grasp the explosive dynamics in those numbers. To visualize this great drama in its full dimensions, one must also see the people.

When I visited Bangkok, in Thailand, the newspapers were preoccupied with the melancholy saga of Honey, a work elephant who was severely injured when a truck sideswiped her on the highway. As doctors tried to mend the elephant's smashed hip, contributions poured in from heartsick citizens, including the king. Elephants have been the emblem of Thai culture for at least seven centuries, but are now gradually dying out. Honey's death prompted editorial reflections on the price of prosperity.

The new national symbol of Thailand, one could say, is the traffic jam. Bangkok's are the worst in Asia, citizens remark with an air of disgusted pride. Their daily commuting routines are the longest in developing Asia, and Thais manipulate schedules endlessly to try to avoid the hours of steaming in tropical congestions of cars. The problem is that Thais are buying cars much faster than the government is building a modern transportation system. Thailand may emerge as Toyota's biggest overseas market aside from the United States.

In Poland, the newly chartered Warsaw Stock Exchange was under way in a stately old pre-Communist building on Aleje Jeroszolimskie. Trading was quite thin since only two dozen companies had their shares listed and Poles were already experiencing the turbulence of Adam Smith's *niewidzialna ręka rynku,* "the invisible hand of the market." Stock prices rose fabulously in 1993, and many of the pioneer investors became instantly wealthy, zloty millionaires, at least on paper. The stock market crashed the following spring. As shares fell 40 to 70 percent in ten days, the Polish traders adopted the style of gallows humor familiar to mature financial markets around the world. Watching stocks plunge 27 percent in a single day, a broker observed: "The Warsaw Stock Exchange still awaits its first suicide."

The lobby of Warsaw's Victoria Intercontinental Hotel, a favorite of foreign business travelers, was filled with hopeful plungers. Each morning Polish entrepreneurs would spread their business prospectuses across the broad coffee tables and sit back, a bit fidgety, while visiting investors from Frankfurt or New York or Milan inspected the numbers.

On the city's industrial outskirts, meanwhile, workers at the Huta Luchini steelworks were on strike. They closed down the mill to demand a share of the ownership. These steelworkers had once been revolutionaries themselves, among the militant members of Solidarity, the free trade union that arose to confront the Polish Communist regime in the early 1980s and had campaigned for the autonomy of workers and enterprises organized on principles of self-management. The Warsaw steelworks is now owned by an Italian conglomerate.

In China, as the November days turned crisp and cold, the citizens of Beijing shopped at sidewalk markets for the traditional supplies of winter cabbage. High, squared-off mounds of cabbages attended by merchants in blue smocks with white kerchiefs on their heads were stacked at street corners along Chang An—Avenue of Eternal Peace—the mainstream boulevard. Farmers hauled cabbages into the city every day, stacked on trucks, bicycle-powered wagons and overloaded handcarts. The ritual reflects a national memory of poverty and famine. Every autumn a family acquires its store of winter cabbages as insurance against the ancient threat of scarcity. One can see the cabbages hanging atop communal walls or outside apartment windows, their outer leaves blackened by Beijing's sooty air.

Meanwhile, traffic on the boulevard was abruptly interrupted to make way for a caravan of important personages—a fleet of limousines and police escorts racing down the center lanes, with blue lights flashing. It was Jean Chrètien, the Canadian prime minister, and a trade delegation from Ottawa and the provinces. Kohl, Mitterand, Major, Balladur, Bentsen, Brown, Christopher—visiting political leaders from the most advanced economies, statesmen seeking contracts for home companies and access to China's explosive market, have become a commonplace.

As usual, McDonald's was already there, selling burgers to consumers. From Kuala Lumpur to Moscow, the company acts like an advanced scout for the global revolution, somehow able to detect the emergence of disposable incomes before other firms see it. Chinese buy their winter cabbages and also fast food. McDonald's measures its market potential with numbers like these: In the United States, there is a McDonald's restaurant for every 29,000 Americans. In China, despite rapid expansion, there is one McDonald's for every 40 million Chinese.

In Tokyo, the Sony Corporation, an authentic symbol of Japan's manufacturing excellence, is on the verge of becoming an un-Japanese company. The human resources manager, Yasunori Kirihara, lamented the prospect but explained it as an inevitable consequence of global economic integration. At present, he said, Sony's employees are split roughly fifty-fifty between Japanese and foreigners. As Sony continues to relocate its factories elsewhere, from Southeast Asia to Mexico, the substantial majority of its workforce, about 60 percent, will soon be outside Japan.

A new Japanese word, *kudoka*, has been popularized in business and political circles to describe this phenomenon. *Kudoka*, I was told, did not exist in the language before the 1980s. Its meaning should be familiar to American industrial workers who have seen their manufacturing jobs disappear. In English, it means "hollowing out."

In Everett, Washington, just north of Seattle, workers on the assembly line for Boeing's new 777, the company's latest addition to its line of large-body aircraft, gossiped that they might be shut down by the earthquake in Kobe, Japan. The main body section of the "Triple Seven," as Boeing people call their new plane, is manufactured by Mitsubishi Heavy Industries, though its plant, as it turned out, was not damaged by the quake. The 777 is a brilliant expression of America's productive prowess in advanced technologies, but their aircraft is manufactured, piece by piece, in twelve different countries.

As these scattered glimpses suggest, the symptoms of upheaval can be found most anywhere, since people in distant places are now connected by powerful strands of the same marketplace. The convergence has no fixed center, no reliable boundaries or settled outcomes. As enterprise opens up new territories, the maps keep changing—changing so rapidly that it has already become commonplace to speak of "one world" markets for everything from cars to capital. The earth's diverse societies are being rearranged and united in complicated ways by global capitalism. The idea evokes benumbed resignation among many. The complexity of it overwhelms. The enormity makes people feel small and helpless.

The essence of this industrial revolution, like others before it, is that commerce and finance have leapt inventively beyond the existing order and existing consciousness of peoples and societies. The global system of trade and production is fast constructing a new functional reality for most everyone's life, a new order based upon its own dynamics and not confined by the traditional social understandings. People may wish to turn away from that fact, but there is essentially no place to hide, not if one lives in any of the industrialized nations.

The only option people really have is to catch up with the reality. The only way to escape a sense of helplessness is to confront this new world on its own terms and try to understand its larger implications. The actual system, as we shall see, does not conform to the economic theory it presumes to follow. Nor are people and nations actually powerless to influence its behavior, as conventional wisdom asserts. But people and nations may restore a sense of control over their own destinies only if they are willing to face the complexity, only by grasping the operating imperatives that drive the global system and the full scope of human consequences that it yields.

Grasping the meaning of this new order requires one to set aside reflexive national loyalties in order to see the system whole. I have tried at least to do that. Above all, I avoid the standard nationalist complaints (most often aimed at Japan) that preoccupy so many books about the global economy, especially books written by Americans. (While I have tried to stand outside national identity and see things in a spirit of universality, I do not imagine for a moment that I have succeeded fully. Like most people, I am bound by culture and personal experience, by limitations of language and native biases, to one nation.)

The usual question—is America winning or losing?—can be disposed of quickly. The answer is yes. America is winning, and yes, it is losing. Some sectors of Americans are triumphant and other sectors are devastated, but not in equal measures. The same rough answer applies in differing degrees throughout most of the world, especially among the wealthiest nations—Germany, France or Britain, even Japan.

Books that nominate one country or another as "the winner" of global competition have a very short shelf life since these things change so rapidly. In 1992, a best-selling author heralded Europe, led by Germany, as the likely champion for its superior economic system; eighteen months later Europe and Germany were mired in gloomy forecasts from their own business leaders, complaining about their failure to keep up with American flexibility. Likewise, the United States has been written off and revived a number of times. Even Japan, so wealthy that many thought it had already won the race, is now experiencing its own tangible crisis of self-doubt.

The obsession with nations in competition misses the point of what is happening: The global economy divides every society into new camps of conflicting economic interests. It undermines every nation's ability to maintain social cohesion. It mocks the assumption of shared political values that supposedly unite people in the nation-state.

That is the fundamental reason politics has become so muddled in the leading capitalist democracies. In recent years, voters have turned on established parties and leaders, sometimes quite brutally, in the United States, Canada, Italy, France, Sweden and Japan, to name the most spectacular cases. Nor is there any ideological consistency to these voter rebellions. Socialists were tossed out in socialist Sweden, then restored to power a few years later. In a single election, the Conservative Party of Canada was reduced from governing majority to a remnant of two parliamentary seats. The business party that ruled Japan without interruption for four decades, the Liberal Democrats, was ousted by dissident reformers, then regained power in an unstable coalition of its own, this time led by a socialist.

Deeper political instability lies ahead for these societies because the global economy has put a different political question on the table: What exactly is the national interest in these new circumstances? No elected government in the richest countries, neither right nor left, has produced a definition that convinces its own electorate. Indeed, some important governments, clinging to the inherited postwar orthodoxy, are pursuing economic strategies that arguably do injury to majorities of their own citizens. This reflects not only the heavy hand of defunct theory, but also that insecure politicians do not know what else to do.

Political confusion in the dominant economies is set against a fundamental countervailing reality: For most people living in most parts of the world, the global economy began in 1492. In their history, the centuries of conquest and economic colonization were integral to the rise of industrial capitalism in Europe and North America, but the returns were never really shared with them. Books by Americans proclaiming "one world" may seem quite precious and self-centered to those people. For them, the global economy long ago consigned most regions of the world to lowly status as commodity producers—the hewers and haulers, the rubber tappers, tin miners and cane cutters. What William Faulkner said of the American South applies as well to those colonialized nations that used to be known as the Third World: the past is never dead, it is not even past. (The global economy has a language problem: The old labels for categories of nations are confused or obsolete. "Third World," a condescending term coined for the Cold War, is not meaningless. Even the "West" is useless if it is meant to designate the advanced economies, since Japan is among them and booming Asia lies west of the United States, not east. We are reduced to cruder terms like rich and poor nations, advanced and primitive economies.*)

---

*The more accurate terms coined for *Essentials of Sociology* are Most Industrialized Nations and Least Industrialized Nations.

From the perspective of most of these countries, the present industrial revolution is a rare opening in history, a chance to get out from under. Some of them are succeeding, climbing rapidly in wealth and establishing at least a fragile basis for national self-sufficiency. Dozens of others are trying to do the same. All of them approach the present with deep historical skepticism, the memory of how many times their aspirations were thwarted by the leading economic powers, how many previous openings turned out to be illusory.

When all the larger economic and political questions are exhausted, the heaviest legacy of this new "one world" may be the psychological blow to national arrogance. Americans reflexively think of themselves as without any real peers. Number One. In their own racialist ways so do the Japanese and the Germans. Tribal assumptions of inherited superiority are embedded in the cultures of the French and Chinese and Muslims, among many others. These folk illusions are now under vigorous assault, contradicted by the emerging economic reality.

During my travels I experienced certain small epiphanies: The amazement of watching a great modern industrial factory at work. The anguish of encountering exploited young people, peasant children turned into low-wage industrial workers, struggling to understand their own condition. The simple delight any tourist feels at glimpsing the weird variety of human life and also the underlying sameness.

The most powerful moments, however, were the recurring experience of witnessing poor people who dwell in marginal backwaters doing industrial work of the most advanced order. People of color, people who are black, yellow, red, brown, who exist in surroundings of primitive scarcity, are making complex things of world-class quality, mastering modern technologies that used to be confined to a select few. The tools of advanced civilization are being shared with other tribes. Multinational corporations, awesomely powerful and imperiously aloof, are the ironic vehicle for accomplishing this generous act of history.

The confident presumption that certain high-caliber work can be done only by certain people (mainly, it is assumed, by well-educated white people in a few chosen countries) is mistaken. Observing these scenes of industrial activity, I thought first of the explosive implications for the future of work and prosperity in the advanced economies, including America. The portents are stark and threatening. Yet the meaning also has to be understood in the broader sweep of human history. Watching former peasants making high-tech goods for the global market, I eventually reached a simpler, more nourishing understanding. Of course, I thought. People are capable, everywhere in the world.

Is it conceivable that commerce, pursuing narrow self-interested ends, might accomplish what idealistic politics has never been able to achieve—defeating stubborn ideas of racial superiority? I returned from my travels imagining it might someday be possible. Certainly, enormous conflicts lie ahead for the peoples of the world, political and economic collisions, possibly including the violence of wars between rival economies. Nevertheless, the process of globalization is visibly dismantling enduring stereotypes of race and culture, ancient assumptions of supremacy. This transformation will someday be understood as the most radical dimension of the revolution....

The raw energies of the global system, its power of excitement, can be glimpsed in the daily headlines about important business deals. Anheuser-Busch buys a stake in Kirin, Japan's biggest brewery, also a 5 percent share of China's

Tsingtao, then acquires 10 percent of Antarctica, the leading beer of Brazil. Siemens of Germany forms a partnership with Skoda Plzen to manufacture steam turbines in the Czech Republic. Volvo opens an assembly line near Xian, China, with Chinese machinists making Swedish tour buses. Switzerland's Roche bids $5.3 billion for the U.S. pharmaceutical Syntex, while Smith-Kline Beecham buys another American company for $2.3 billion. NEC, the Japanese electronics giant, agrees to collaborate with Samsung, the Korean multinational, to make DRAM memory chips, probably at a plant in Portugal, to supply the $5 billion European market.

The problem, of course, is that the stories are too diverse and plentiful to make the motivating principles very clear. As the announcements of new ventures accumulate in breathtaking number, the effect is like the blur of a major blizzard. IBM announces quarterly losses of $8 billion and plans to cut 35,000 jobs. Bausch & Lomb begins making contact lenses and Ray-Ban sunglasses in India. Colgate-Palmolive opens a toothbrush factory in Colombia. AT&T forms an alliance with the national telephone companies of Sweden, Switzerland and the Netherlands; its American rival MCI pairs off with British Telecommunications.

Coca-Cola returns to Vietnam, this time without the U.S. military forces. Toyota picks Kentucky to make automobiles, BMW picks South Carolina, Mercedes picks Alabama. Ford and General Motors hope the Chinese government will pick them to make cars in China....

After two decades of dramatic changes, the revolutionary pressures are not abating or leveling off into familiar patterns. The dynamics appear to be accelerating. What is the nature of the storm upon us? A new structure of power is gradually emerging in the world, forcing great changes everywhere it asserts itself. The broad dimensions are defined by a baseline of unsettling facts:

1. During the last generation the world's 500 largest multinational corporations have grown sevenfold in sales. Yet the worldwide employment of these global firms has remained virtually flat since the early 1970s, hovering around 26 million people.... [T]he human labor required for each unit of their output is diminished dramatically.

While this galaxy of major global firms grew in size, its center of gravity also shifted. America's flagship companies, from du Pont and IBM to GE and General Motors, were the modern progenitors of globalized manufacturing after World War II, but the United States has lost its dominance.... Europe's largest companies surpassed America's in number and sales volume.... A few important multinational corporations have even emerged in countries that were once very poor—Korea, Taiwan, even Thailand. The corporate girth of nations is gradually dispersing, leveling out.

2. The basic mechanism of globalization—companies investing capital in foreign countries, buying existing assets or building new factories—has accelerated explosively during the last fifteen years.... The United States became a debtor nation and sold off domestic assets to foreign investors; Japanese auto companies, among others, prudently located assembly plants in the States....

The growth of transnational corporate investments, the steady dispersal of production elements across many nations, has nearly obliterated the traditional understanding of trade. Though many of them know better, economists and politicians continue to portray the global trading system in terms that the public can understand—that is, as a collection of nations buying and selling things to each other. However, as the volume of world trade has grown, the traditional role of national markets is increasingly eclipsed by an alternative system: trade generated within the multinational companies themselves as they export and import among their own foreign-based subsidiaries.

According to one scholarly estimate, more than 40 percent of U.S. exports and nearly 50 percent of its imports are actually goods that travel not in the open marketplace, but through these intrafirm channels. A U.S. computer company ships design components to its assembly plant in Malaysia, then distributes the finished hardware back to the United States and to other buyers in Asia and Europe. A typical Japanese plant located in America "imports" most of its components from its parent corporation and allied suppliers, then "exports" products back to the parent in Japan or sister affiliates in other countries.

All of this intrafirm traffic is counted in the national trade statistics, but national identities are increasingly irrelevant to the buyers and sellers. Nation-to-nation trade flows are driven more and more by the proprietary strategies of the multinational corporations organizing their own diversified production, less and less by traditional concepts of comparative advantage among nations or the economic policies of home governments.

The shifting content of trade has led many leading governments, including the one in Washington, to embrace a strategy that might confound some citizens (if it were explained to them clearly) because it seems to offend nationalist intuition. The governments are actively promoting the dispersal of capital investment and production to foreign locations on the assumption that this will lead to increased exports for home-based production (and more jobs for domestic workers). As the flagship multinationals make more things overseas, they will presumably ship more homemade goods to their overseas affiliates. That, anyway, is the logic governments embrace.

3. Finance capital—the trading of stocks, bonds, currencies, and more exotic forms of financial paper—has accelerated its movements around the world at an astonishing pace.... The global exchange markets in national currencies—swapping dollars for yen or deutschemarks for francs or scores of other such trades—are moving faster still.... Since financial traders usually move in and out of different currencies in order to buy or sell a nation's stocks or bonds, this furious pace of currency exchange reflects the magnifying presence of borderless finance.

The entire global volume of publicly traded financial assets (about $24 trillion) turns over every twenty-four days. The International Monetary Fund, which attempts to monitor such matters, claims that this quickening pace is unexceptional since, it points out, the trading in U.S. government bonds is even faster. The entire traded volume of U.S. treasury debt ($2.6 trillion) turns over every eight days.

Despite the staggering volume the financial trading across borders is mostly transacted by a very small community: the world's largest thirty to fifty banks and a handful of major brokerages that do the actual trades in behalf of investor clients—wealthy individuals and the various pools of private capital, smaller banks and brokerages, pension funds, mutual funds and so on—as well as the banks' own portfolios.

As the volume has swelled, the global financial markets have become much more powerful—and much more erratic. Sentiment and prices can shift suddenly and sharply, cascading losses across innocent bystanders like the multinational corporations that depend on predictable currency values for their cross-border trade or national governments that watch helplessly as global finance raises their domestic interest rates or devalues their currencies. "Crisis" has become an overworked word. Market economists speak more politely of "disturbances." These are the decisive breaks in prices that occur when global investors suddenly lose confidence in one investment sector or an entire country and abruptly shift huge amounts of capital elsewhere quick as the electronic impulses of modern banking.

To make sense out of these bewildering facts, it helps to think of the global system in cruder terms, as a galaxy of four broad, competing power blocs—each losing or gaining influence over events. The biggest, most obvious loser in these terms is labor, both the organized union workers and wage earners in general. Wages are both rising and falling around the world, but workers at both ends of the global economy have lost substantial control over their labor markets and the terms of employment. "Now capital has wings," as New York financier Robert A. Johnson explained succinctly. "Capital can deal with twenty labor markets at once and pick and choose among them. Labor is fixed in one place. So power has shifted."

National governments, likewise, have lost ground on the whole, partly because many have retreated from trying to exercise their power over commerce and finance, implicitly ceding to the revolutionary spirit. In the advanced economies, most governments have become mere salesmen, promoting the fortunes of their own multinationals in the hope that this will provide a core prosperity that keeps everyone afloat. The clearest evidence that this strategy is not working is the condition of labor markets in the wealthiest nations: either mass unemployment or declining real wages (nominal pay adjusted for inflation), and, in some cases, both of these deleterious effects.

The more subtle evidence of the dilemma of leading governments is their deteriorating fiscal condition: most are threatened by rising, seemingly permanent budget deficits and accumulating debt. The swollen fiscal deficits of the United States are the largest in size, but far from the worst in relative terms. The general fiscal crisis of rich nations is driven by the same fundamental—disappointing economic growth that, year after year, fails to generate the tax revenues needed to keep up with the public obligations established in more prosperous times. The modern welfare state, the social protections that rich nations enacted to ameliorate the harsh inequalities of industrial capitalism, is now in peril. Some would say it is already obsolete.

Ironically, the governments of developing countries, at least the most successful ones, are less enthralled by the global system's theory and rhetoric and more willing to impose their own terms on capital and trade. Given their own historical memory, poor countries attempt, if they can, to bargain with the system—making nationalistic trade-offs with global firms and investors. Some succeed; many are overwhelmed.

The multinational corporations are, collectively, the muscle and brains of this new system, the engineers who are designing the brilliant networks of new relationships. It is their success at globalization that has inevitably weakened labor and degraded the control of governments. Some smart organizations are even reconfiguring themselves into what business futurists have dubbed "the virtual corporation," a quick-witted company so dispersed that it resembles the ganglia of a nervous system, a brain attached to many distant nodes but without much bodily substance at the center.

Despite their supple strengths the great multinationals are, one by one, insecure themselves. Even the most muscular industrial giants are quite vulnerable if they fail to adapt to the imperatives of reducing costs and improving rates of return. Critics who focus on the awesome size and sprawl of the global corporations find this point difficult to accept, but the executives of Volkswagen, GM, Volvo, IBM, Eastman Kodak and Pan American Airlines can attest to it. Those well-known firms, among many others, have experienced the harsh consequences of straying from the path of revolution. Their stocks were hammered, their managements ousted, tens of thousands of employees discarded. Behind corporate facades, the anxiety is genuine.

The Robespierre of this revolution is finance capital. Its principles are transparent and pure: maximizing the return on capital without regard to national identity or political and social consequences. Global finance collectively acts as the disinterested enforcer of these imperatives, like a Committee of Public Safety presiding over the Terror (though historians would note that Robespierre's revolutionaries pursued the opposite objective of reducing the great inequalities of wealth).

Financial investors monitor and punish corporations or whole industrial sectors if their returns weaken. Finance disciplines governments or even entire regions of the globe if those places appear to be creating impediments to profitable enterprise or unpleasant surprises for capital. If this sounds dictatorial, the global financiers also adhere to their own rough version of egalitarian values: they will turn on anyone, even their own home country's industry and government, if the defense of free capital seems to require it.

As the Jacobins learned during the French Revolution, it is the most zealous, principled advocates of new values who are ultimately most at risk in a revolutionary environment. Master financiers seem to appreciate this, too. George Soros, the Hungarian American billionaire who became fabulously wealthy by grasping the new principles of global investing before others, often emphasizes his own fallibility. In early 1994, when Soros got things wrong, he lost $600 million during two days of brisk disturbance in global bond markets. When Robespierre got things wrong, he was guillotined before a cheering mob in the Place de la Révolution.

Even the most powerful players—titans of finance or the multinationals regularly demonized in popular lore—are themselves dwarfed by the system and subject to its harsh, overwhelming consequences. To describe the power structure of the global system does not imply that anyone is in charge of the revolution. The revolution runs itself. This point is critical to understanding its anarchic energies and oblivious disregard for parochial victims or, for that matter, the seeming impotence of enterprises themselves to control things. This revolution is following historical patterns of behavior that industrial capitalism has reiterated across the centuries—an explosive cycle of renewal, migration and destruction that is typically ignited by human invention.

The Uses of Poverty: The Poor Pay All

Herbert J. Gans

introduction

Of the several social classes in the United States, sociologists have concentrated their studies on the poor. The super-rich and, for the most part, the ordinarily wealthy are beyond the reach of researchers. Sociologists are not members of the wealthy classes or of the power elite, and members of these groups have the means to insulate themselves from the prying eyes (and questionnaries and tape recorders) of sociologists. When it comes to the middle classes, sociologists are likely to take their members for granted. The middle classes are part of their everyday life, and, like others, sociologists often overlook the things closest to them. The characteristics and situations of the poor, however, are different enough to strike the interests of sociologists. And the poor are accessible. People in poverty are generally willing to be interviewed. They are even a bit flattered that sociologists, for the most part members of the upper middle class, will take the time to talk to them. Hardly anyone else takes them seriously.

A couple of thousand years ago, Jesus said, "The poor you'll always have with you." In this selection, as Herbert Gans places the sociological lens yet again on people in poverty, he uses a functionalist perspective to explain why we always will have people in poverty. Simply put, from a functionalist perspective, we *need* the poor.

Thinking Critically

As you read this selection, ask yourself:

1. What functions (or uses) of poverty does Gans identify?

2. Of the functions of poverty that Gans identifies, which two do you think are the most important? Which two the least important? Why?

3. Do you think that Gans has gone overboard with his analysis? That he has stretched the functionalist perspective beyond reason? Or do you agree with him? Why or why not?

*S*ome years ago Robert K. Merton applied the notion of functional analysis to explain the continuing though maligned existence of the urban political machine: If it continued to exist, perhaps it fulfilled latent—unintended or unrecognized—positive functions. Clearly it did. Merton pointed out how the political machine provided central authority to get things done when a decentralized local government could not act, humanized the services of the impersonal bureaucracy for fearful citizens, offered concrete help (rather than abstract law or justice) to the poor, and otherwise performed services needed or demanded by many people but considered unconventional or even illegal by formal public agencies.

Today, poverty is more maligned than the political machine ever was; yet it, too, is a persistent social phenomenon. Consequently, there may be some merit in applying functional analysis to poverty, in asking whether it also has positive functions that explain its persistence.

Merton defined functions as "those observed consequences [of a phenomenon] which make for the adaptation or adjustment of a given [social] system." I shall use a slightly different definition; instead of identifying functions for an entire social system, I shall identify them for the interest groups, socioeconomic classes, and other population aggregates with shared values that "inhabit" a social system. I suspect that in a modern heterogeneous society, few phenomena are functional or dysfunctional for the society as a whole, and that most result in benefits to some groups and costs to others. Nor are any phenomena indispensable; in most instances, one can suggest what Merton calls "functional alternatives" or equivalents for them, i.e., other social patterns or policies that achieve the same positive functions but avoid the dysfunction. (In the following discussion, positive functions will be abbreviated as functions and negative functions as dysfunctions. Functions and dysfunctions, in the planner's terminology, will be described as benefits and costs.)

Associating poverty with positive functions seems at first glance to be unimaginable. Of course, the slumlord and the loan shark are commonly known to profit from the existence of poverty, but they are viewed as evil men, so their activities are classified among the dysfunctions of poverty. However, what is less often recognized, at least by the conventional wisdom, is that poverty also makes possible the existence or expansion of respectable professions and occupations, for example, penology, criminology, social work, and public health. More recently, the poor have provided jobs for professional and para-professional "poverty warriors," and for journalists and social scientists, this author included, who have supplied the information demanded by the revival of public interest in poverty.

Clearly, then, poverty and the poor may well satisfy a number of positive functions for many nonpoor groups in American society. I shall describe 13 such functions—economic, social and political—that seem to me most significant.

■ ■ ■ ■ THE FUNCTIONS OF POVERTY

First, the existence of poverty ensures that society's "dirty work" will be done. Every society has such work: physically dirty or dangerous, temporary, dead-end and under-

From "The Uses of Poverty: The Poor Pay All," by Herbert J. Gans, *Social Policy,* July/August 1971. Copyright © 1971 by Social Policy. Reprinted by permission of the publisher.

paid, undignified, and menial jobs. Society can fill these jobs by paying higher wages than for "clean" work, or it can force people who have no other choice to do the dirty work—and at low wages. In America, poverty functions to provide a low-wage labor pool that is willing—or rather, unable to be *un*willing—to perform dirty work at low cost. Indeed, this function of the poor is so important that in some Southern states, welfare payments have been cut off during the summer months when the poor are needed to work in the fields. Moreover, much of the debate about the Negative Income Tax and the Family Assistance Plan [welfare programs] has concerned their impact on the work incentive, by which is actually meant the incentive of the poor to do the needed dirty work if the wages therefrom are no larger than the income grant. Many economic activities that involve dirty work depend on the poor for their existence: restaurants, hospitals, parts of the garment industry, and "truck farming," among others, could not persist in their present form without the poor.

Second, because the poor are required to work at low wages, they subsidize a variety of economic activities that benefit the affluent. For example, domestics subsidize the upper-middle and upper classes, making life easier for their employers and freeing affluent women for a variety of professional, cultural, civic, and partying activities. Similarly, because the poor pay a higher proportion of their income in property and sales taxes, among others, they subsidize many state and local governmental services that benefit more affluent groups. In addition, the poor support innovation in medical practice as patients in teaching and research hospitals and as guinea pigs in medical experiments.

Third, poverty creates jobs for a number of occupations and professions that serve or "service" the poor, or protect the rest of society from them. As already noted, penology would be minuscule without the poor, as would the police. Other activities and groups that flourish because of the existence of poverty are the numbers game, the sale of heroin and cheap wines and liquors, Pentecostal ministers, faith healers, prostitutes, pawn shops, and the peacetime army, which recruits its enlisted men mainly from among the poor.

Fourth, the poor buy goods others do not want and thus prolong the economic usefulness of such goods—day-old bread, fruit and vegetables that otherwise would have to be thrown out, secondhand clothes, and deteriorating automobiles and buildings. They also provide incomes for doctors, lawyers, teachers, and others who are too old, poorly trained or incompetent to attract more affluent clients.

In addition to economic functions, the poor perform a number of social functions.

Fifth, the poor can be identified and punished as alleged or real deviants in order to uphold the legitimacy of conventional norms. To justify the desirability of hard work, thrift, honesty, and monogamy, for example, the defenders of these norms must be able to find people who can be accused of being lazy, spendthrift, dishonest, and promiscuous. Although there is some evidence that the poor are about as moral and law-abiding as anyone else, they are more likely than middle-class transgressors to be caught and punished when they participate in deviant acts. Moreover, they lack the political and cultural power to correct the stereotypes that other people hold of them and thus continue to be thought of as lazy, spendthrift, etc., by those who need living proof that moral deviance does not pay.

Sixth, and conversely, the poor offer vicarious participation to the rest of the population in the uninhibited sexual, alcoholic, and narcotic behavior in which they are alleged to participate and which, being freed from the constraints of affluence, they are often thought to enjoy more than the middle classes. Thus many people, some social scientists included, believe that the poor not only are more given to uninhibited behavior (which may be true, although it is often motivated by despair more than by lack of inhibition) but derive more pleasure from it than affluent people (which research by Lee Rainwater, Walter Miller and others shows to be patently untrue). However, whether the poor actually have more sex and enjoy it more is irrelevant; so long as middle-class people believe this to be true, they can participate in it vicariously when instances are reported in factual or fictional form.

Seventh, the poor also serve a direct cultural function when culture created by or for them is adopted by the more affluent. The rich often collect artifacts from extinct folk cultures of poor people; and almost all Americans listen to the blues, Negro spirituals, and country music, which originated among the Southern poor. Recently they have enjoyed the rock styles that were born, like the Beatles, in the slums, and in the last year, poetry written by ghetto children has become popular in literary circles. The poor also serve as culture heroes, particularly, of course, to the left; but the hobo, the cowboy, the hipster, and the mythical prostitute with a heart of gold have performed this function for a variety of groups.

Eighth, poverty helps to guarantee the status of those who are not poor. In every hierarchical society, someone has to be at the bottom; but in American society, in which social mobility is an important goal for many and people need to know where they stand, the poor function as a reliable and relatively permanent measuring rod for status comparisons. This is particularly true for the working class, whose politics is influenced by the need to maintain status distinctions between themselves and the poor, much as the aristocracy must find ways of distinguishing itself from the *nouveaux riches.*

Ninth, the poor also aid the upward mobility of groups just above them in the class hierarchy. Thus a goodly number of Americans have entered the middle class through the profits earned from the provision of goods and services in the slums, including illegal or nonrespectable ones that upper-class and upper-middle-class businessmen shun because of their low prestige. As a result, members of almost every immigrant group have financed their upward mobility by providing slum housing, entertainment, gambling, narcotics, etc., to later arrivals—most recently to blacks and Puerto Ricans.

Tenth, the poor help to keep the aristocracy busy, thus justifying its continued existence. "Society" uses the poor as clients of settlement houses and beneficiaries of charity affairs; indeed, the aristocracy must have the poor to demonstrate its superiority over other elites who devote themselves to earning money.

Eleventh, the poor, being powerless, can be made to absorb the costs of change and growth in American society. During the nineteenth century, they did the backbreaking work that built the cities; today, they are pushed out of their neighborhoods to make room for "progress." Urban renewal projects to hold middle-class taxpayers in the city and expressways to enable suburbanites to commute downtown have typically been located in poor neighborhoods, since no other group will allow itself to be displaced. For the same reason, universities, hospitals, and civic centers also expand into land occupied by the poor. The major costs of the industrialization of agriculture have been borne by the poor, who are pushed off the land without recompense; and they have paid a large share of the human cost of the growth of American power overseas, for they have provided many of the foot soldiers for Vietnam and other wars.

Twelfth, the poor facilitate and stabilize the American political process. Because they vote and participate in politics less than other groups, the political system is often free to ignore them. Moreover, since they can rarely support Republicans, they often provide the Democrats with a captive constituency that has no other place to go. As a result, the Democrats can count on their votes, and be more responsive to voters—for example, the white working class—who might otherwise switch to the Republicans.

Thirteenth, the role of the poor in upholding conventional norms (see the *fifth* point, above) also has a significant political function. An economy based on the ideology of laissez-faire requires a deprived population that is allegedly unwilling to work or that can be considered inferior because it must accept charity or welfare in order to survive. Not only does the alleged moral deviancy of the poor reduce the moral pressure on the present political economy to eliminate poverty but socialist alternatives can be made to look quite unattractive if those who will benefit most from them can be described as lazy, spendthrift, dishonest and promiscuous.

■ ■ ■ THE ALTERNATIVES

I have described 13 of the more important functions poverty and the poor satisfy in American society, enough to support the functionalist thesis that poverty, like any other social phenomenon, survives in part because it is useful to society or some of its parts. This analysis is not intended to suggest that because it is often functional, poverty *should* exist, or that it *must* exist. For one thing, poverty has many more dysfunctions than functions; for another, it is possible to suggest functional alternatives.

For example, society's dirty work could be done without poverty, either by automation or by paying "dirty workers" decent wages. Nor is it necessary for the poor to subsidize the many activities they support through their low-wage jobs. This would, however, drive up the costs of these activities, which would result in higher prices to their customers and clients. Similarly, many of the professionals who flourish because of the poor could be given other roles. Social workers could provide counseling to the affluent, as they prefer to do anyway; and the police could devote themselves to traffic and organized crime. Other roles would have to be found for badly trained or incompetent professionals now relegated to serving the poor, and someone else would have to pay their salaries. Fewer penologists would be employable, however. And Pentecostal religion could probably not survive without the poor—nor would parts of the second- and third-hand-goods market. And in many cities, "used" housing that no one else wants would then have to be torn down at public expense.

Alternatives for the cultural functions of the poor could be found more easily and cheaply. Indeed, entertainers and adolescents are already serving as the deviants needed to uphold traditional morality and as devotees of orgies to "staff" the fantasies of vicarious participation.

The status functions of the poor are another matter. In a hierarchical society, some people must be defined as inferior to everyone else with respect to a variety of attributes, but they need not be poor in the absolute sense. One could conceive of a society in which the "lower class," though last in the pecking order, received 75 percent of the median income, rather than 15–40 percent, as is now the case. Needless to say, this would require considerable income redistribution.

The contribution the poor make to the upward mobility of the groups that provide them with goods and services could also be maintained without the poor's having such low incomes. However, it is true that if the poor were more affluent, they would have access to enough capital to take over the provider role, thus competing with, and perhaps rejecting, the "outsiders.".... Similarly, if the poor were more affluent, they would make less willing clients for upper-class philanthropy, although some would still use settlement houses to achieve upward mobility, as they do now. Thus "Society" could continue to run its philanthropic activities.

The political functions of the poor would be more difficult to replace. With increased affluence the poor would probably obtain more political power and be more active politically. With higher incomes and more political power, the poor would be likely to resist paying the costs of growth and change. Of course, it is possible to imagine urban renewal and highway projects that properly reimbursed the displaced people, but such projects would then become considerably more expensive, and many might never be built. This, in turn, would reduce the comfort and convenience of those who now benefit from urban renewal and expressways.

In sum, then, many of the functions served by the poor could be replaced if poverty were eliminated, but almost always at higher costs to others, particularly more affluent others. Consequently, a functional analysis must conclude that poverty persists not only because it fulfills a number of positive functions but also because many of the functional alternatives to poverty would be quite dysfunctional for the affluent members of society. A functional analysis thus ultimately arrives at much the same conclusion as radical sociology, except that radical thinkers treat as manifest what I describe as latent: that social phenomena that are functional for affluent or powerful groups and dysfunctional for poor or powerless ones persist; that when the elimination of such phenomena through functional alternatives would generate dysfunctions for the affluent or powerful, they will continue to persist; and that phenomena like poverty can be eliminated only when they become dysfunctional for the affluent or powerful, or when the powerless can obtain enough power to change society.

■ ■ ■ ■ POSTSCRIPT*

Over the years, this article has been interpreted as either a direct attack on functionalism or a tongue-in-cheek satirical comment on it. Neither interpretation is true. I

*A note from the author to the editor.

wrote the article for two reasons. First and foremost, I wanted to point out that there are, unfortunately, positive functions of poverty which have to be dealt with by antipoverty policy. Second, I was trying to show that functionalism is not the inherently conservative approach for which it has often been criticized, but that it can be employed in liberal and radical analyses.

Invisible Man

Lawrence Otis Graham

introduction ■ ■ ■ ■ ■

As you know, the circumstances we inherit at birth have serious consequences for what happens to us in life. Some of us are born poor, others rich, most of us in between. Each of us is born into an ethnic or racial group. Some of us are born to single mothers, others to married parents; some to parents who are college graduates, others to parents who have not finished high school. Even our geography (South, West, rural, urban) sets up background factors that play a significant role in our orientations to life. Sociologists use the term *life chances* to refer to how the background factors that surround our birth affect our fate in life.

A major issue in the sociology of race–ethnic relations is the relative significance of race-ethnicity and social class in determining people's life chances. Is the color of our skin more important than social class for setting us on a course in life? More specifically, does social class or race-ethnicity play a greater role in our everyday lives? Although not providing *the* answer to these provocative questions, this selection sheds light on some of the intricate interconnections between race-ethnicity and social class. As Lawrence Graham found, racism is far from dead, and race-ethnicity continues to play a pivotal role in what happens to us in everyday life.

Thinking Critically

As you read this selection, ask yourself:

1. Since Graham is an African American, he should know about racism. Why, then do you think he did this research?

2. What do you think Graham's most eye-opening experiences were?

3. What situation do you think embarrassed Graham the most? Why?

I drive up the winding lane past a long stone wall and beneath an archway of sixty-foot maples. At one bend of the drive, a freshly clipped lawn and a trail of yellow daffodils slope gently up to the four-pillared portico of a white Georgian colonial.

From *Member of the Club: Reflections on Life in a Racially Polarized World*, by Lawrence Otis Graham. Reprinted by permission of HarperCollins Publishers, Inc.

The building's six huge chimneys, the two wings with slate gray shutters, and the white-brick facade loom over a luxuriant golf course. Before me stands the one-hundred-year-old Greenwich Country Club—*the* country club—in the affluent, patrician, and very white town of Greenwich, Connecticut, where there are eight clubs for fifty nine thousand people.

I'm a thirty-year-old corporate lawyer at a Midtown Manhattan firm, and I make $105,000 a year. I'm a graduate of Princeton University (1983) and Harvard Law School (1988), and I've written ten nonfiction books. Although these may seem like impressive credentials, they're not the ones that brought me here. Quite frankly, I got into this country club the only way that a black man like me could—as a $7-an-hour busboy.

After seeing dozens of news stories about Dan Quayle, Billy Graham, Ross Perot, and others who either belonged to or frequented white country clubs, I decided to find out what things were really like at a club where I heard there were no black members.

I remember stepping up to the pool at the country club when I was ten and setting off a chain reaction: Several irate parents dragged their children out of the water and fled. When the other kids ran out of the pool, so did I—foolishly thinking that there was something in the water that was going to harm all of us. Back then, in 1972, I saw these clubs only as places where families socialized. I grew up in an affluent white neighborhood in Westchester, and all my playmates and neighbors belonged to one or more of these private institutions. Across the street, my best friend introduced me to the Westchester Country Club before he left for Groton and Yale. My teenage tennis partner from Scarsdale introduced me to the Beach Point Club on weekends before he left for Harvard. The family next door belonged to the Scarsdale Golf Club. In my crowd, the question wasn't "Do you belong?" It was "Where?"

My grandparents owned a Memphis trucking firm, and as far back as I can remember, our family was well off and we had little trouble fitting in even though I was the only black kid on the high school tennis team, the only one in the orchestra, the only one in my Roman Catholic confirmation class.

Today, I'm back where I started—on a street of five- and six-bedroom colonials with expensive cars and neighbors who all belong somewhere. Through my experience as a young lawyer, I have come to realize that these clubs are where business people network, where lawyers and investment bankers meet potential clients and arrange deals. How many clients and deals am I going to line up on the asphalt parking lot of my local public tennis courts?

I am not ashamed to admit that I one day want to be a partner and a part of this network. When I talk to my black lawyer or investment-banker friends or my wife, a brilliant black woman who has degrees from Harvard College, Harvard Law School, and Harvard Business School, I learn that our white counterparts are being accepted by dozens of these elite institutions. So why shouldn't we—especially when we have the same credentials, salaries, social graces, and ambitions?

My black Ivy League friends and I know of black company vice presidents who have to ask white subordinates to invite them out for golf or tennis. We talk about the club in Westchester that rejected black Scarsdale resident and millionaire magazine publisher Earl Graves, who sits on *Fortune* 500 boards, owns a Pepsi distribution franchise, raised three bright Ivy League children, and holds prestigious honorary degrees. We talk about all the clubs that face a scandal and then run out to sign up one quiet, deferential black man who will accept a special "limited-status" membership, remove the taint, and deflect further scrutiny.

I wanted some answers. I knew I could never be treated as an equal at this Greenwich oasis—a place so insular that the word *Negro* is still used in conversation. But I figured I could get close enough to understand what these people were thinking and why country clubs were so set on excluding people like me.

▪ ▪ ▪ MARCH 28 TO APRIL 7, 1992

I invented a completely new résumé for myself. I erased Harvard, Princeton, and my upper-middle-class suburban childhood from my life. So that I'd have to account for fewer years, I made myself seven years younger—an innocent twenty-three. I used my real name and made myself a graduate of the actual high school I attended. Since it would be difficult to pretend that I was from "the street," I decided to become a sophomore-year dropout from Tufts University, a midsize college in suburban Boston. My years at nearby Harvard and the fact that my brother had gone there had given me enough knowledge about the school to pull it off. I contacted some older friends who owned large companies and restaurants in the Boston and New York areas and asked them to serve as references. I was already on a short leave of absence from my law firm to work on a book.

I pieced together a wardrobe that consisted of a blue polyester blazer, white oxford shirt, ironed blue slacks, black loafers, and a horrendous pink, black, and silver tie, and I set up interviews at clubs. Over the telephone, five of the eight said that I sounded as if I would make a great waiter. During each of my phone conversations, I made sure that I spoke to the person who would make the hiring decision. I also confirmed exactly how many waiter positions were available, and I arranged a personal interview within forty minutes to an hour of the conversation, just to be sure that they could not tell me that no such job was available.

"We don't have any job openings—and if you don't leave the building, I will have to call security," the receptionist said at the first club I visited in Greenwich.

I was astounded by the speed with which she made this remark, particularly when I saw that she had just handed an application to a young-looking Hispanic man wearing jeans, sneakers, a T-shirt, and sunglasses. "I'm here to see Donna, your maître d'," I added defensively as I forced a smile at the pasty-looking woman who sat behind a window.

"There's no Donna here."

"But I just spoke to her thirty minutes ago and she said to come by to discuss the waiter job."

"Sorry, but there are no jobs and no one here named Donna."

After convincing the woman to give me an application, I completed it and then walked back into the dining room, which was visible from the foyer.

I came upon a white male waiter and asked him, "Is there a Donna here?"

"The maître d'?" he asked. "Yeah, she's in the kitchen."

When I found Donna and explained that I was the one she had talked to on the phone forty minutes earlier, she crossed her arms and shook her head. "You're the 'Larry' I talked to on the phone?"

"Yes," I answered.

"No way."

"I beg your pardon," I said.

"No. No way," she said while refusing to take the application I waved in front of her.

"We just talked on the phone less than an hour ago. You said I sounded perfect. And I've waited in three different restaurants—I've had two years of college—You said you have five waiter jobs open—I filled out the application—I can start right away—"

She still shook her head. And held her hands behind her back—unwilling to even touch my application. "No," she said. "Can't do it."

My talking did no good. It was 1992. This was the Northeast. If I hadn't been involved, I would never have believed it. I suddenly thought about all the times I quietly disbelieved certain poor blacks who said they had tried to get jobs but no one would hire them. I wanted to say then and there, "Not even as a waiter?"

Only an hour earlier, this woman had enthusiastically urged me to come right over for an interview. Now, as two white kitchen workers looked on, she would only hold her hands tightly behind her back and shake her head emphatically. So I left.

There were three other clubs to go to. When I met them, the club managers told me I "would probably make a much better busboy."

"Busboy? Over the phone, you said you needed a waiter," I argued.

"Yes, I know I said that, but you seem very alert, and I think you'd make an excellent busboy instead."

In his heavy Irish brogue, the club manager said he needed to give me a "perception test." He explained it this way: "This ten-question test will give us an idea of your perception, intellectual strength, and conscious ability to perform the duties assigned to you as a busboy."

I had no idea how much intellectual strength and conscious ability (whatever that meant) could be required of a busboy, but here are some of the questions he asked me:

1. If there are three apples and you take two away, how many do you have?
2. How many of each species of animal did Moses put on his new ark?
3. It's 1963 and you set your digital clock to ring at 9:00 A.M. when you go to bed at 8:00 P.M. How many hours will you sleep?
4. If a house gets southern exposure on all four sides, what color is the bear that walks by the house?

And the responses…

1. I answered "one apple" because I thought this was a simple math question, as in "three minus two equals one," but the correct answer was "two" because,

as the manager said, "You've got to think, Larry—if you take away two apples and put them in your pocket, you've got two apples, not one."

2. Fortunately, I answered this question as it was presumably designed to smoke out any applicants who hadn't been raised in a Judeo-Christian culture. It was Noah, not Moses, who built an ark.

3. I scored major credibility points here by lying and saying, "Wow, I wasn't even born yet in 1963...." The "right" answer was that there were no digital clocks in 1963. I took his word for it.

4. Although I believed that a house could get southern exposure on all four sides only at the South Pole—and thus the bear had to be a white polar bear—I was told that I was "trying to act too smart" and that all bears are, of course, brown.

■ ■ ■ APRIL 8 TO 11

After interviewing for advertised waiter jobs at five clubs, I had gotten only two offers—both for non-waiter jobs. One offer was to split my time as a towel boy in the locker room and a busboy in the dining room. The second offer—which followed a callback interview—was to work as a busboy. When I told the club manager that I had only wanted a waiter job, he responded, "Well, we've discussed it here and everyone would feel more comfortable if you took a busboy job instead."

"But I've never worked as a busboy," I reminded him.

He nodded sympathetically. "People here have decided that it's busboy or nothing."

Given these choices I made my final job selection in much the way I had decided on a college and a law school: I went for prestige. Not only was the Greenwich Country Club celebrating its hundredth anniversary but its roster boasted former president Gerald Ford, baseball star Tom Seaver, former Securities and Exchange Commission chairman and U.S. ambassador to the Netherlands John Shad, as well as former Timex spokesman John Cameron Swayze. Add to that a few dozen *Fortune* 500 executives, bankers, Wall Street lawyers, European entrepreneurs, a Presbyterian minister, and cartoonist Mort Walker, who does *Beetle Bailey*. (The Greenwich Country Club did not respond to any questions about the club and its members.)

For three days, I worked on my upper-arm muscles by walking around the house with a sterling-silver tray stacked high with heavy dictionaries. I allowed a mustache to grow in, then added a pair of arrestingly ugly Coke-bottle reading glasses.

■ ■ ■ APRIL 12 (SUNDAY)

Today was my first day at work. My shift didn't start until 10:30 A.M., so I laid out my clothes at home: a white button-down shirt, freshly ironed cotton khaki pants, white socks, and white leather sneakers. I'd get my official club uniform in two days. Looking in my wallet, I removed my American Express Gold Card, my Harvard club membership ID, and all of my business cards.

When I arrived at the club, I entered under the large portico, stepping through the heavy doors and onto the black-and-white checkerboard tiles of the entry hall.

A distracted receptionist pointed me toward Mr. Ryan's office. (*All names of club members and personnel have been changed.*) I walked past glistening silver trophies and a guest book on a pedestal to a windowless office with three desks. My new boss waved me in and abruptly hung up the phone.

"Good morning, Larry," he said with a sufficiently warm smile. The tight knot in his green tie made him look more fastidious than I had remembered from the interview.

"Hi, Mr. Ryan. How's it going?"

Glancing at his watch to check my punctuality, he shook my hand and handed me some papers. "Oh, and by the way, where'd you park?"

"In front, near the tennis courts."

Already shaking his head, he tossed his pencil onto the desk. "That's off-limits to you. You should always park in the back, enter in the back, and leave from the back. No exceptions."

"I'll do the forms right now," I said. "And then I'll be an official busboy."

Mr. Ryan threw me an ominous nod. "And Larry, let me stop you now. We don't like that term busboy. We find it demeaning. We prefer to call you busmen."

Leading me down the center stairwell to the basement, he added, "And in the future, you will always use the back stairway by the back entrance." He continued to talk as we trotted through a maze of hallways. "I think I'll have you trail with Carlos or Hector—no, Carlos. Unless you speak Spanish?"

"No." I ran to keep up with Mr. Ryan.

"That's the dishwasher room, where Juan works. And over here is where you'll be working." I looked at the brass sign. MEN'S GRILL.

It was a dark room with a mahogany finish, and it looked like a library in a large Victorian home. Dark walls, dark wood-beamed ceilings. Deep-green wool carpeting. Along one side of the room stood a long, highly polished mahogany bar with liquor bottles, wineglasses, and a two-and-a-half-foot-high silver trophy. Fifteen heavy round wooden tables, each encircled with four to six broad wooden armchairs padded with green leather on the backs and seats, broke up the room. A big-screen TV was set into the wall along with two shelves of books.

"This is the Men's Grill," Mr. Ryan said. "Ladies are not allowed except on Friday evenings."

Next was the brightly lit connecting kitchen. "Our kitchen serves hot and cold foods. You'll work six days a week here. The club is closed on Mondays. The kitchen serves the Men's Grill and an adjoining room called the Mixed Grill. That's where the ladies and kids can eat."

"And what about men? Can they eat in there, too?"

This elicited a laugh. "Of course they can. Time and place restrictions apply only to women and kids."

He showed me the Mixed Grill, a well-lit pastel-blue room with glass French doors and white wood trim.

"Guys, say hello to Larry. He's a new busman at the club."

I waved.

"And this is Rick, Stephen, Drew, Buddy, and Lee." Five white waiters dressed in white polo shirts with blue "1892" club insignias nodded while busily slicing lemons.

"And this is Hector, and Carlos, the other two busmen." Hector, Carlos, and I were the only nonwhites on the serving staff. They greeted me in a mix of English and Spanish.

"Nice to meet all of you," I responded.

"Thank God," one of the taller waiters cried out. "Finally—somebody who can speak English."

Mr. Ryan took me and Carlos through a hall lined with old black-and-white portraits of former presidents of the club. "This is our one hundredth year, so you're joining the club at an important time," Mr. Ryan added before walking off. "Carlos, I'm going to leave Larry to trail with you—and no funny stuff."

Standing outside the ice room, Carlos and I talked about our pasts. He was twenty-five, originally from Colombia, and hadn't finished school. I said I had dropped out, too.

As I stood there talking, Carlos suddenly gestured for me to move out of the hallway. I looked behind me and noticed something staring at us. "A video camera?"

"They're around," Carlos remarked quietly while scooping ice into large white tubs. "Now watch me scoop ice."

After we carried the heavy tubs back to the grill, I saw another video camera point down at us. I dropped my head.

"You gonna live in the Monkey House?" Carlos asked.

"What's that?"

We climbed the stairs to take our ten-minute lunch break before work began. "Monkey House is where workers live here," Carlos said.

I followed him through a rather filthy utility room and into a huge white kitchen. We got in line behind about twenty Hispanic men and women—all dressed in varying uniforms. At the head of the line were the white waiters I'd met earlier.

I was soon handed a hot plate with two red lumps of rice and some kind of sausage-shaped meat. There were two string beans, several pieces of zucchini, and a thin, broken slice of dried meat loaf that looked as if it had been cooked, burned, frozen, and then reheated. Lurking at the very edge of my dish was an ice-cream-scoop-sized helping of yellowish mashed potatoes.

I followed Carlos, plate in hand, out of the kitchen. To my surprise, we walked back into the dank and dingy utility room, which turned out to be the workers' dining area.

The white waiters huddled together at one end of the table, while the Hispanic workers ate quietly at the other end. Before I could decide which end to integrate, Carlos directed me to sit with him on the Hispanic end.

I was soon back downstairs working in the grill. At my first few tables, I tried to avoid making eye contact with members as I removed dirty plates and wiped down tables and chairs. Having known so many people who belonged to these clubs, I was sure I'd be recognized by someone from childhood, college, or work.

At around 1:15, four men who looked to be in their mid- to late fifties sat down at a six-chair table. They pulled off their cotton windbreakers and golf sweaters.

"It's these damned newspeople that cause all the problems," said golfer number one, shoving his hand deep into a popcorn bowl. "These Negroes wouldn't even be thinking about golf. They can't afford to join a club, anyway."

Golfer number two squirmed out of his navy blue sweater and nodded in agreement. "My big problem with this Clinton fellow is that he apologized." As I stood watching from the corner of the bar, I realized the men were talking about then-governor Bill Clinton's recent apology for playing at an all-white golf club in Little Rock, Arkansas.

"Holt, I couldn't agree with you more," added golfer number three, a hefty man who was biting off the end of a cigar.

"You got any iced tea?" golfer number one asked as I put the silverware and menus around the table. Popcorn flew out of his mouth as he attempted to speak and chew at the same time.

"Yes, we certainly do."

Golfer number three removed a beat-up Rolex from his wrist. "It just sets a bad precedent. Instead of apologizing, he should try to discredit them—undercut them somehow. What's to apologize for?" I cleared my throat and backed away from the table.

Suddenly, golfer number one waved me back to his side. "Should we get four iced teas or just a pitcher and four glasses?"

"I'd be happy to bring whatever you'd like, sir."

Throughout the day, I carried "bus buckets" filled with dirty dishes from the grill to the dishwasher room. And each time I returned to the grill, I scanned the room for recognizable faces. Fortunately, I saw none. After almost four hours of running back and forth, clearing dishes, wiping down tables, and thanking departing members who left spilled coffee, dirty napkins, and unwanted business cards in their wake, I helped out in the coed Mixed Grill.

"Oh, busboy," a voice called out as I made the rounds with two pots of coffee. "Here, busboy. Here, busboy," the woman called out. "Busboy, my coffee is cold. Give me a refill."

"Certainly, I would be happy to." I reached over for her cup.

The fiftyish woman pushed her hand through her straw blond hair and turned to look me in the face. "Decaf, thank you."

"You are quite welcome."

Before I turned toward the kitchen, the woman leaned over to her companion. "My goodness. Did you hear that? That busboy has diction like an educated white person."

A curly-haired waiter walked up to me in the kitchen. "Larry, are you living in the Monkey House?"

"No, but why do they call it that?"

"Well, no offense against you, but it got that name since it's the house where the workers have lived at the club. And since the workers used to be Negroes—blacks—it was nicknamed the Monkey House. And the name just stuck—even though Negroes have been replaced by Hispanics."

■ ■ ■ APRIL 13 (MONDAY)

I woke up and felt a pain shooting up my calves. As I turned to the clock, I realized I'd slept for eleven hours. I was thankful the club was closed on Mondays.

■ ■ ■ APRIL 14 (TUESDAY)

Rosa, the club seamstress, measured me for a uniform in the basement laundry room while her barking gray poodle jumped up on my feet and pants. "Down, Margarita, down," Rosa cried with pins in her mouth and marking chalk in her hand. But Margarita ignored her and continued to bark and do tiny pirouettes until I left with all of my new country-club polo shirts and pants.

Today, I worked exclusively with the "veterans," including sixty-five-year-old Sam, the Polish bartender in the Men's Grill. Hazel, an older waitress at the club, is quick, charming, and smart—the kind of waitress who makes any restaurant a success. She has worked for the club nearly twenty years and has become quite territorial with certain older male members. Whenever I was on my way to hand out menus or clear dishes at a table, Hazel would either outrun me or grab me by the arm when she saw that the table contained important male members. Inevitably, Hazel would say, "Oh, Larry, let me take care of Dr. Collingsworth. You go fill this salt shaker," or "Larry, I'll take Judge Wilson's dirty dish. You go slice some lemons in the kitchen," or "Larry, I'll clean up Reverend Gundersen's cracker crumbs. You go find some peanut oil."

During a lull, Sam, who I swear reminded me of a Norman Lear creation circa 1972, asked me to run out and get some supplies from a Mr. Chang.

"Who is Mr. Chang?" I asked.

"You know, the Chinaman. Mr. Chang."

I had recalled seeing an elderly Asian man with a gray uniform in the halls, but we had not been introduced.

"And where would I find him?"

"He's down at the other end of the hall beyond the stairs." Sam handed me a list of items on a printed form. "He's the Chinaman and it's easy to remember 'cause he's right next to the laundry room."

Hector came along and warned me not to lose the signed form because I could be accused of stealing food and supplies if the signed list wasn't given to Mr. Chang.

Down a dark, shadowy hall, we found Mr. Chang, who, in Spanish, shouted phrases at me while swinging his arms in the air.

"Do you understand him?" I asked Hector.

"He said to follow him and bring a cart."

We followed the methodical Mr. Chang from storage room to storage room, where he pulled out various items like a magician. Lemons were stored with paper goods, cans of ketchup were stored with pretzels and simultaneously served as shelves for large sacks of onions. Bottles of soda were stored with old boxes that had "Monkey House" written on them. Combustible popcorn oil and boxes of matches were stored with Styrofoam cups in the furnace room. It was all in a disorder that seemed to make complete sense to Mr. Chang.

Back in the Mixed Grill, members were talking about hotel queen and Greenwich resident Leona Helmsley, who was on the clubhouse TV because of her upcoming prison term for tax evasion.

"I'd like to see them haul her off to jail," one irate woman said to the rest of her table. "She's nothing but a garish you-know-what."

"In every sense of the word," nodded her companion as she adjusted a pink headband in her blondish white hair. "She makes the whole town look bad. The TV keeps showing those aerial shots of Greenwich and that dreadful house of hers."

A third woman shrugged her shoulders and looked into her bowl of salad. "Well, it is a beautiful piece of property."

"Yes, it is, except for those dreadful lampposts all over the lawn," said the first woman. "But why here? She should be in those other places like Beverly Hills or Scarsdale or Long Island, with the rest of them. What's she doing here?"

Woman number three looked up. "Well, you know, *he's* not Jewish."

"Really?"

"So that explains it," said the first woman with an understanding expression on her tanned forehead. "Because, you know, the name didn't sound Jewish."

The second woman agreed: "I can usually tell."

■ ■ ■ APRIL 15 (WEDNESDAY)

Today, we introduced a new, extended menu in the two grill rooms. We added shrimp quesadillas ($6) to the appetizer list—and neither the members nor Hazel could pronounce the name of the dish or fathom what it was. One man pounded on the table and demanded to know which country the dish had come from. He told Hazel how much he hated "changes like this. I like to know that some things are going to stay the same."

Another addition was the "New Dog in Town" ($3.50). It was billed as knockwurst, but one woman of German descent sent the dish back: "This is not knockwurst—this is just a big hot dog."

As I wiped down the length of the men's bar, I noticed a tall stack of postcards with color photos of nude busty women waving hello from sunny faraway beaches. I saw they had been sent from vacationing members with fond regards to Sam or Hazel. Several had come from married couples. One glossy photo boasted a detailed frontal shot of a red-haired beauty who was naked except for a shoestring around her waist. On the back, the message said, *Dear Sam, Pull string in an emergency. Love always, The Atkinson Family.*

■ ■ ■ APRIL 16 (THURSDAY)

This afternoon, I realized I was learning the routine. I was fairly comfortable with my few "serving" responsibilities and the rules that related to them:

- When a member is seated, bring out the silverware, cloth napkin, and a menu.
- Never take an order for food, but always bring water or iced tea if it is requested by a member or waiter.

- When a waiter takes a chili or salad order, bring out a basket of warm rolls and crackers along with a scoop of butter.
- When getting iced tea, fill a tall glass with ice and serve it with a long spoon, a napkin on the bottom, and a lemon on the rim.
- When a member wants his alcoholic drink refilled, politely respond, "Certainly, I will have your waiter come right over."
- Remember that the member is always right.
- Never make offensive eye contact with a member or his guest.
- When serving a member fresh popcorn, serve to the left.
- When a member is finished with a dish or a glass, clear it from the right.
- Never tell a member that the kitchen is out of something.

But there were also some "informal" rules that I discovered (but did not follow) while watching the more experienced waiters and kitchen staff in action:

- If you drop a hot roll on the floor in front of a member, apologize and throw it out. If you drop a hot roll on the floor in the kitchen, pick it up and put it back in the bread warmer.
- If you have cleared a table and are 75 percent sure that the member did not use the fork, put it back in the bin with the other clean forks.
- If, after pouring one glass of Coke and one of diet Coke, you get distracted and can't remember which is which, stick your finger in one of them to taste it.
- If a member asks for decaffeinated coffee and you have no time to make it, use regular coffee and add water to cut the flavor.
- When members complain that the chili is too hot and spicy, instead of making a new batch, take the sting out by adding some chocolate syrup.
- If you're making tuna on toasted wheat and you accidentally burn one side of the bread, don't throw it out. Instead, put the tuna on the burnt side and lather on some extra mayo.

■ ■ ■ APRIL 17 (FRIDAY)

Today, I heard the word "nigger" four times. And it came from someone on the staff.

In the grill, several members were discussing Arthur Ashe, who had recently announced that he had contracted AIDS through a blood transfusion.

"It's a shame that poor man has to be humiliated like this," one woman golfer remarked to a friend over pasta-and-vegetable salad. "He's been such a good example for his people."

"Well, quite frankly," added a woman in a white sunvisor, "I always knew he was gay. There was something about him that just seemed too perfect."

"No, Anne, he's not gay. It came from a blood transfusion."

"Ohh," said the woman. "I suppose that's a good reason to stay out of all those big-city hospitals. All that bad blood moving around."

Later that afternoon, one of the waiters, who had worked in the Mixed Grill for two years, told me that Tom Seaver and Gerald Ford were members. Of his brush with greatness, he added, "You know, Tom's real first name is George."

"That's something."

"And I've seen O. J. Simpson here, too."

"O. J. belongs here too?" I asked.

"Oh, no, there aren't any black members here. No way. I actually don't even think there are any Jews here either."

"Really? Why is that?" I asked.

"I don't know. I guess it's just that the members probably want to have a place where they can go and not have to think about Jews, blacks, and other minorities. It's not really hurting anyone. It's really a WASP club.... But now that I think of it, there's a guy here who some people think is Jewish, but I can't really tell. Upstairs, there's a Jewish secretary too."

"And what about O. J.?"

"Oh, yeah, it was so funny to see him out there playing golf on the eighteenth hole." The waiter paused and pointed outside the window. "It never occurred to me before, but it seemed so odd to see a black man with a golf club here on this course."

■ ■ ■ **APRIL 18 (SATURDAY)**

When I arrived, Stephen, one of the waiters, was hanging a poster and sign-up sheet for a soccer league whose main purpose was to "bridge the ethnic and language gap" between white and Hispanic workers at the country clubs in the Greenwich area. I congratulated Stephen on his idea. He said he was tired of seeing the whites and Hispanics split up during meals, breaks, and evening activities. "We even go to separate bars and diners," he explained. "I think a weekly soccer game might bring us all closer together."

Later, while I was wiping down a table, I heard a member snap his fingers in my direction. I turned to see a group of young men smoking cigars. They seemed to be my age or a couple of years younger. "Hey, do I know you?" the voice asked.

As I turned slowly toward the voice, I could hear my own heartbeat. I was sure it was someone I knew.

"No," I said, approaching the blond cigar smoker. He had on light green khaki pants and a light yellow V-neck cotton sweater adorned with a tiny green alligator. As I looked at the other men seated around the table, I noticed that all but one had alligators on their sweaters or shirts. Each one of them was a stranger to me.

"I didn't think so. You must be new—what's your name?"

"My name is Larry. I just started a few days ago."

The cigar-smoking host grabbed me by the wrist while looking at his guests. "Well, Larry, welcome to the club. I'm Mr. Billings. And this is Mr. Dennis, a friend and new member."

"Hello, Mr. Dennis," I heard myself saying to a freckle-faced young man who puffed uncomfortably on his fat roll of tobacco.

The first cigar smoker gestured for me to bend over as if he were about to share some important confidence. "Now, Larry, here's what I want you to do. Go get us some of those peanuts and then give my guests and me a fresh ashtray. Can you manage that?"

My workday ended at 4:20.

■ ■ ■ ■ EVENING OF APRIL 18 (SATURDAY)

After changing back into my street clothes at around 8:00 P.M., I drove back to the club to get together with Stephen and Lillie, two of the friendlier waiters (and the only ones willing to socialize with a busboy), in Stephen's room on the grounds. We sat, ate Hostess donuts, drank wine, watched the Saturday-night NBC-TV lineup, and talked about what it would be like to be a rich member of the club.

Squeezed into the tiny room and sitting on the bed, which was pushed against the wall, we each promised to look out for and warn the others if anyone else tried to backstab us in the grill. Stephen was talking about his plans for the intercultural soccer league and what it could do for all eight clubs in the area.

"After spending a couple semesters in Japan," Stephen explained, "I realized how afraid Americans are of other cultures." Stephen told me that he was working at the club to pay for the rest of his college education. He was taking a two-year break between his sophomore and junior years at a midwestern university, where he was majoring in Japanese.

Lillie talked about the formal dinner that she had just worked at that evening. It was then that I learned she was half South American. Her father, who was from Colombia, was an outdoor groundskeeper at the club. "I'm taking college courses now," she explained. "And maybe I'm crazy to say this, but I think I'd like to go into broadcasting." Given her nearly flawless English and her very white skin, I wondered if the members were aware of her Hispanic background. She felt very strong about her South American heritage, and she often acted as interpreter for some of the club workers who spoke only Spanish.

They were both such nice people, I felt terrible for intruding under such fraudulent circumstances.

■ ■ ■ ■ APRIL 19 (SUNDAY)

It was Easter Sunday and the Easter-egg hunt began with dozens of small children scampering around the tulips and daffodils while well-dressed parents watched from the rear patio of the club. A giant Easter bunny gave out little baskets filled with jelly beans to parents and then hopped over to the bushes, where he hugged the children. As we peered out from the closed blinds in the grill, we saw women in mink, husbands in gray suits, children in Ralph Lauren and Laura Ashley. Hazel let out a sigh. "Aren't they beautiful?" she said. For just a moment, I found myself agreeing.

"So, Larry." Sam laughed as I poured fresh oil into the popcorn machine's heated pan. It was my second day at the machine in the Men's Grill. "When you decide to move on from the club, you'll be able to get yourself a job at the popcorn counter in one of those big movie theaters."

I forced a smile.

"And you can tell them," he continued, "that you just about have a master's degree in popcorn popping. Tell 'em you learned everything you know from Sam at the country club."

I laughed. "Sure, Sam."

"Yeah, tell them I awarded you a master's degree."

I had already become an expert at yucking it up with Sam.

As I raced around taking out orders of coffee and baskets of hot rolls, I got a chance to see groups of families. The men seemed to be uniformly taller than six feet. Most of them were wearing blue blazers, white shirts, and incredibly out-of-style silk ties—the kind with little blue whales or little green ducks floating downward. They were bespectacled and conspicuously clean-shaven.

The "ladies," as the club prefers to call them, almost invariably had straight blond hair. Whether or not they had brown roots and whether they were twenty-five or forty-eight, they wore their hair blond, straight, and off the face. No dangling earrings, five-carat diamonds, or designer handbags. Black velvet or pastel headbands were de rigueur.

There were also groups of high school kids who wore torn jeans, sneakers, or unlaced L.L. Bean shoes, and sweatshirts that said things like "Hotchkiss Lacrosse" or "Andover Crew." At one table, two boys sat talking to two girls.

"No way, J.C.," one of the girls cried in disbelief while playing with the straw in her diet Coke.

The strawberry blond girl next to her flashed her unpainted nails in the air. "Way. She said that if she didn't get her grades up by this spring, they were going to take her out altogether."

"And where would they send her?" one of the guys asked.

The strawberry blond's grin disappeared as she leaned in close. "Public school."

The group, in hysterics, shook the table. The guys stomped their feet.

"Oh, my God, J.C., oh, J.C., J.C.," the diet-Coke girl cried.

Sitting in a tableless corner of the room beneath the TV set was a young, dark-skinned black woman dressed in a white uniform and a thick wool coat. On her lap was a baby with silky white blond hair. The woman sat patiently, shifting the baby in her lap while glancing over to where the baby's family ate, two tables away.

I ran to the kitchen, brought back a glass of tea, and offered it to her. The woman looked up at me, shook her head, and then turned back to the gurgling infant.

■ ■ ■ **APRIL 21 (TUESDAY)**

The TV in the Men's Grill was tuned to one of the all-day cable news channels and was reporting on the violent confrontations between pro-choice marchers and right-to-life protesters in Buffalo, New York.

"Look at all those women running around," a man in his late forties commented as he sat by himself at one of the larger tables in the Men's Grill.

At 11:10 A.M., the grill wasn't even officially opened yet.

As I walked around doing a final wipe of the tables, the man cried out into the empty room. "That's just a damned shame," he said while shaking his head and pulling at his yellow polo shirt in disbelief.

I nodded as he looked at me over his bowl of peanuts. "I agree with you."

He removed his sun visor and dropped it onto a table closer to the television. We both watched images of police dragging women who lay sprawled in the middle of a Buffalo city street.

"You know, it just scares me to see all these women running around like that," the middle-aged member continued as we both watched screaming crowds of placard-carrying activists and hand-cuffed protesters. "Someone's gotta keep these women reined in. A good, hard law that forces them to have those babies when they get pregnant will teach them to be responsible."

I looked at the man as he sat there hypnotized by the screen.

"All this equal rights bull," he finally added. "Running around getting pregnant and then running around doing what they want. Enough to make you sick."

Later, while Hector and I stood inside a deep walk-in freezer, we scooped balls of butter into separate butter dishes and talked about our life plans. "Will you go finish school sometime?" he asked as I dug deep into a vat of frozen butter.

"Maybe. In a couple of years, when I save more money, but I'm not sure." I felt lousy about having to lie.

"Maybe? If I had money, I'd go now—and I'm twenty-three years old." He shook his head in disapproval. "In my country, I had education. But here I don't because I don't know much English. It's tough because we have no work in South America. And here, there's work, but you need English to get it and make money."

We agreed that since 75 percent of the club employees were Spanish-speaking South Americans, the club really needed a bilingual manager or someone on staff who understood their concerns.

"Well," I offered. "I'll help you with English if you teach me some Spanish."

He joked that my Spanish was a lot worse than his English. After all, I only knew the words *gracias, buenos dias,* and *por favor.* So, during an illegal twelve-minute break, he ran through a quick vocabulary lesson while we walked to his minuscule room just across the sweaty congested halls of the noisy squash courts.

The room he took me into overlooked the driving range and was the size of a walk-in closet. The single bed touched three walls of the room. The quarter-sized refrigerator served as a stand for a stereo. There were a small dresser and a small desk plastered with many different pictures of a young Spanish-looking woman and a cute baby girl.

"My family" is all Hector would say in explanation while simultaneously pushing me out of the room and into the sweaty hall. "We go now—before we lose our job."

Just as we were leaving for the day, Mr. Ryan came down to hand out the new policies for those who were going to live in the Monkey House. Amazingly, without a trace of discomfort, he and everyone else referred to the building as "the Monkey

House." Many of the workers had been living temporarily in the squash building. Since it had recently been renovated, the club was requiring all new residents to sign the form. The policy included a rule that forbade the employees to have overnight guests. Rule 14 stated that the club management had the right to enter an employee's locked bedroom at any time, without permission and without giving notice.

As I was making rounds with my coffeepots, I overheard a raspy-voiced woman talking to a mother and daughter who were thumbing through a catalog of infants' clothing.

"The problem with au pairs is that they're usually only in the country for a year."

The mother and daughter nodded in agreement.

"But getting one that is a citizen has its own problems. For example, if you ever have to choose between a Negro and one of these Spanish people, always go for the Negro."

One of the women frowned, confused. "Really?"

"Yes," the raspy-voiced woman responded with cold logic, "Even though you can't trust either one, at least the Negroes can speak English and follow your directions."

Before I could refill the final cup, the raspy-voiced woman looked up at me and smiled. "Oh, thanks for the refill, Larry."

■ ■ ■   APRIL 22 (WEDNESDAY)

"This is our country, and don't forget it. They came here and have to live by our rules!" Hazel pounded her fist into the palm of her pale white hand.

I had made the mistake of telling her I had learned a few Spanish phrases to help me communicate better with some of my coworkers. She wasn't impressed.

"I'll be damned if I'm going to learn or speak one word of Spanish. And I'd suggest you do the same," she said. She took a long drag on her cigarette while I loaded the empty shelves with clean glasses.

Today, the TV was tuned to testimony and closing arguments from the Rodney King police-beating trial in California.

"I am so sick of seeing this awful videotape," one woman said to friends at her table. "It shouldn't be on TV."

At around two, Lois, the club's official secretary, asked me to help her send out a mailing to six hundred members after my shift. It seemed that none of the waiters wanted to stay late. And since the only other choice was the non-English-speaking bus staff and dishwashers, I was it.

She took me up to her office on the main floor and introduced me to the two women who sat with her.

"Larry, this is Marge, whom you'll talk with in three months, because she's in charge of employee benefits."

I smiled at the brunette.

"And Larry, this is Sandy, whom you'll talk with after you become a member at the club, because she's in charge of members' accounts."

Both Sandy and I looked up at Lois with shocked expressions.

Lois winked, and at the same moment, the three jovial women burst out laughing.

Lois sat me down at a table in the middle of the club's cavernous ballroom and had me stamp "Annual Member Guest" on the bottom of small postcards and stuff them into envelopes.

As I sat in the empty ballroom, I looked around at the mirrors and the silver-and-crystal chandeliers that dripped from the high ceiling. I thought about all the beautiful weddings and debutante balls that must have taken place in that room. I could imagine members asking themselves, "Why would anybody who is not like us want to join a club where they're not wanted?"

I stuffed my last envelope, forgot to clock out, and drove back to the Merritt Parkway and into New York.

■ ■ ■ APRIL 23 (THURSDAY)

"Wow, that's great," I said to Mr. Ryan as he posted a memo entitled "Employee Relations Policy Statement: Employee Golf Privileges."

After quickly reading the memo, I realized this "policy" was a crock. The memo opened optimistically. "The club provides golf privileges for staff.... Current employees will be allowed golf privileges as outlined below." Unfortunately, the only employees the memo listed "below" were department heads, golf-management personnel, teaching assistants, the general manager, and "key staff that appear on the club's organizational chart."

At the end of the day, Mr. Ryan handed me my first paycheck. Perhaps now the backbreaking work would seem worthwhile. When I opened the envelope and saw what I'd earned—$174.04 for five days—I laughed out loud.

Back in the security of a bathroom stall, where I had periodically been taking notes since my arrival, I studied the check and thought about how many hours—and how hard—I'd worked for so little money. It was less than one-tenth of what I'd make in the same time at my law firm. I went upstairs and asked Mr. Ryan about my paycheck.

"Well, we decided to give you $7 an hour," he said in a tone overflowing with generosity. I had never actually been told my hourly rate. "But if the check looks especially big, that's because you got some extra pay in there for all of your terrific work on Good Friday. And by the way, Larry, don't tell the others what you're getting, because we're giving you a special deal and it's really nobody else's business."

I nodded and thanked him for his largesse. I stuffed some more envelopes, emptied out my locker, and left.

The next morning, I was scheduled to work a double shift. Instead, I called and explained that I had a family emergency and would have to quit immediately. Mr. Ryan was very sympathetic and said I could return when things settled down. I told him, "No thanks," but asked that he send my last paycheck to my home. I put my uniform and the key to my locker in a brown padded envelope, and I mailed it all to Mr. Ryan.

Somehow it took two months of phone calls for me to get my final paycheck ($123.74 after taxes and a $30 deduction for my uniform).

I'm back at my law firm now, dressed in one of my dark gray Paul Stuart suits, sitting in a handsome office thirty floors above Midtown. While it's a long way from the Monkey House, we still have a long way to go.

Sick Societies

Robert B. Edgerton

All human groups develop a system to rank their members. In each group, people also attempt to display the status they have achieved. We are familiar with some of these: wearing clothing with labels deemed prestigious, driving a Rolls Royce, sporting a Rolex watch, getting admitted to a "name" school. In New York City, many reputable businesses have managed to get Park Avenue addresses, even though they are not located on Park Avenue. People who do business by mail with these firms aren't aware that the company's location is actually on an adjoining side street.

Although such matters are of interest, in their studies of social stratification sociologists probe much more deeply than this. Of special interest to sociologists is power, especially the means by which more powerful groups oppress groups with less power. Around the world, gender is a basis for sorting people into groups, with men the group in power. And around the world, men have developed practices to keep women submissive to them. In some instances, such as those documented by Robert Edgerton in this selection, the means men use to maintain dominance are severely oppressive. Both the practices described here and their acceptance by the oppressed group—which can be termed the *internalization of oppression*—may surprise you.

Thinking Critically

As you read this selection, ask yourself:

1. Why have men as a group dominated women as a group in every society of the world?

2. Why can practices that are painful and disfiguring persist for centuries?

3. What right do the people of one culture (such as one in the West) have to judge the customs of another culture (such as one in the East)?

How people feel about the established customs and institutions of their society can be a powerful indicator of how adequately that society and its culture serve their needs. But between blissful contentment and open rebellion lie many complexities and contradictions of human emotion and behavior. For example, women and men alike have gone to remarkable lengths to beautify themselves. They tattoo themselves over their entire bodies, cover themselves with scars, mutilate their genitals, and blacken their teeth, file them into points, and knock some of them out, among other things. These are only a few examples of painful practices that have been, and in some quarters still are, eagerly pursued in the quest for beauty. As painful as these practices are, few things done in the quest for beauty were more extreme than the Chinese practice of binding the feet of women. Young girls, some still in infancy, suffered excruciating pain because their feet were bandaged so tightly that normal growth could not occur. So tightly, in fact, were the toes folded under the foot that the bones were often broken. Accounts of the anguish these children suffered during the process of replacing blood- and pus-soaked bandages with new and still tighter ones are truly harrowing. The pain was so severe that the girls could not walk or even sleep, and they were too young to understand why they were being made to suffer. Eventually, the acute pain subsided, but for the rest of their lives these women were barely able to hobble, and some were carried everywhere in a sedan chair.

Chinese men have admired small feet in women since before Confucian times, but the practice of footbinding apparently did not begin until around 1100 A.D. It was at first confined to the Chinese elite, but it eventually spread throughout society, even including some peasants and the urban poor. The reasons for the origin and spread of footbinding were complex, but in addition to aesthetic considerations, Chinese men said that they saw the practice as an effective way to control the sexual liaisons of their increasingly bold wives. Once women's feet were bound, they could no longer "run around," so to speak, because they could not even leave their houses without assistance. What is more, a woman with bound feet could not work; so her husband achieved prestige by demonstrating that he could afford to have a wife who did not need to work. Men also saw the practice as a clear and necessary expression of their dominance over women. Before long, men also saw fit to praise the erotic advantages of footbinding, saying that the tottering style of walking it produced created more beautiful buttocks and tightened the vagina. The naked bound foot itself—"the golden lotus"—became as much a focus of erotic desire for Chinese men as women's breasts were for Westerners.

The Manchu conquerors outlawed footbinding, but to such little effect that some members of the Manchu court adopted a modified version of the practice themselves. Footbinding endured for over a thousand years without any widespread social protest by women. For one thing, Chinese women lacked political power, but at the same time they could appreciate the advantages of footbinding. It could give them beauty and sensuality, lead to a good marriage, and offer a life of leisure. Of at least equal importance, parents who imposed the practice on their young daughters were not thinking only of their daughters' futures. A daughter's marriage to a wealthy man was of obvious benefit to the entire family.

With these benefits in mind, it is perhaps less surprising that footbinding lasted so long than that it ended as suddenly as it did. Opposed by Christian missionaries, the expansionist Japanese, and Westerners of all sorts, the reform-minded revolutionary governments of early twentieth-century China were able to eradicate footbinding in a decade or so among their urban population although it lasted until the 1930s in some traditional rural areas. That a practice so painful and disfiguring to women can nonetheless persist should not be surprising. In Victorian times, the same Western women (some of whom were the wives of missionaries in China) who deplored footbinding as a "barbaric" custom willingly had themselves cinched into steel- and whalebone-reinforced canvas corsets so tightly that they had difficulty breathing and their internal organs were sometimes damaged. Girls as young as three were corseted, and over time their corsets became progressively tighter. By adolescence many girls' back muscles had atrophied to such an extent that they could neither sit nor walk for more than a few minutes without someone's support. The pursuit of beauty may be directed by men, even imposed by them, but women can find it to their advantage to acquiesce. With the controversy about silicone breast implants so freshly in mind, we need hardly be reminded that many American women (and some men) today endure painful and expensive cosmetic surgery in an effort to "beautify" their faces or bodies.

These cautionary examples alert us to the need to proceed judiciously in evaluating how dissatisfied people may be with their culture. For example, the practice of sending widows or household slaves to the grave with their deceased husbands or masters was known in many parts of the world, including China, Africa, ancient Greece, Scandinavia, and Russia. The reasons for putting a man's wives or slaves to death varied. Sometimes it was said that the deceased would need his wives or slaves to provide him with earthly comforts in the hereafter. Sometimes it was said (more cynically) that this practice would encourage wives or slaves to do everything in their power to keep their husbands or masters alive as long as possible. There were other reasons, too, ranging from jealousy about the sexual activities of surviving wives to elaborate religious justifications. Nowhere did the practice become as widespread or take on such profound metaphysical meaning as in Hindu India, where a widow could achieve virtual divinity by voluntarily immolating herself on her husband's funeral pyre.

Known as *sati* in Sanskrit and Anglicized as "suttee," this practice was observed as early as the fourth century B.C. when Alexander the Great recorded it, and despite heated controversy it has continued to occur now and then in contemporary India. Originally practiced by the wives of kings and great warriors, sati spread first to Brahmins, then to members of lower castes. Although Hindu scriptural justifications for the practice (or practices, since a widow could choose to be buried alive instead of being burned to death) were contradictory, many indicated that by choosing sati she could reduce the pollution that endangered her husband's surviving rela-

tives, absolve herself of sin (wives were thought to bear responsibility for their husbands' death), and rejoin her husband in a cycle of future rebirths. As Richard
Shweder has commented, sati can be a heroic act that represents and confirms the
"deepest properties of Hinduism's moral world."

Much like a wedding, the sati ceremony required elaborate ritual preparations.
Priests, mourners, and an excited crowd followed the ornately dressed widow and
her husband's corpse to the funeral pyre. After circling the fire, the widow distributed her jewels and money and looked into a mirror where she saw the past and the
future; then a priest quoted scriptural passages that likened the pyre to a marriage
bed. After the necessary ritual acts had been completed and the widow had joined
her husband's corpse on the pyre, it was set alight by her son (who sometimes col-
lapsed in grief after doing so). After the ceremony, the spot where the sati died became a shrine, and she was revered as a heroine and goddess.

As improbable as the spectacle of a woman willingly, even eagerly, burning
herself to death may seem, there are numerous eyewitness reports to the effect that
sometimes, at least, that is exactly what took place. William Carey witnessed a sati
in 1798 in which the widow actually danced on the pyre to show her contempt for
death before lying down next to the corpse of her husband and being consumed by
flames. In 1829 a British magistrate named Halliday attempted to convince a widow
not to become a sati. "At length she showed some impatience and asked to be allowed to proceed to the site." Horrified, Halliday tried once again to dissuade her
by asking if she understood how much pain she was about to suffer. The woman
looked scornfully at the Englishman, then demanded that a lamp be brought to her
and lighted. "Then steadfastly looking at me with an air of grave defiance she rested
her right elbow on the ground and put her finger in the flame of the lamp. The finger
scorched, blistered, and blackened and finally twisted up…this lasted for some time,
during which she never moved her hand, uttered a sound, or altered the expression
of her countenance." Halliday gave permission for the ceremony to proceed.

Over the centuries, many Hindu widows must have chosen sati deaths sublimely
and reverently. But there was another reality to sati, one that falls well short of sublim-
ity. First, it will not have escaped the reader's attention that sati was for women only;
widowers had no duty to join their deceased wives in the divine devotion of a fiery
death. Second, despite great pressure, very few widows actually chose sati. Even in
Bengal where sati was most common, only a small minority of widows—less than 10
percent—chose sati although the prospect of widowhood was a dismal one at best.
Widows were not only forbidden to remarry but were compelled to live in socially isolated asceticism—praying, fasting, reading holy books, and avoiding any hint of
worldly pleasure. Because widows were thought to endanger others and often were
accused of being witches, they were also scorned and feared. Despite the wretched
conditions of widowhood, the promised rewards of sati, and the often relentless pressure exerted by the deceased husband's relatives on the widow to choose this supreme
act of devotion, the great majority of widows preferred to live. Sometimes, however,
they were given no choice. Because many women were married as infants, they became widows and "chose" sati while still children. One wife burned with the corpse of
her adult husband was only four years old; others were scarcely older.

Sometimes the pressures imposed on a widow to choose sati were anything but subtle; indeed, they amounted to murder. In 1827 a British observer witnessed a sati ceremony in which the fire had no sooner been lighted than the widow leapt off the pyre and tried to flee; several men seized her and flung her back into the blaze. Once again the widow fled, and although badly burned she managed to outdistance her pursuers and throw herself into a nearby stream where she lay "weeping bitterly." She swore that she would not go through with the ceremony. Seeming to take pity on her, a man promised that if she would sit on a large cloth he had spread on the ground, he would carry her home. When she did so, she was once again seized, sewn into the cloth, and thrown back into the inferno. The cloth was immediately consumed by the flames, and the wretched victim once again tried to flee. This time she was beheaded with a sword, and her body was thrown back onto the pyre. Not exactly a serene act of wifely devotion.

It was not just tormented widows who frequently wanted no part of sati; some Hindu scriptures sharply criticized the custom. In *Mahamivantantra* (verses 79 and 80) it is said that a woman who accepts sati will go to hell. And there was a vigorous anti-sati movement in India even before the British attempted to abolish the practice (the movement was not led by women but by a Brahmin man). It was also observed that there were economic reasons for sati. It was most common in Bengal, and it was only in Bengal that a widow without a son had the same rights to the family property formerly possessed by her deceased husband. Surviving family members therefore attempted to protect family property by convincing the widow that it was her duty to join her husband in death (thereby conveniently leaving the property to her husband's family).

In recent years opposition to sati in India has grown, but the ceremony has not been abandoned. In 1987 Roop Kanwar, a beautiful eighteen-year-old, college-educated woman, immolated herself with her dead husband's head on her lap while a crowd estimated at 300,000 watched in admiration. But many Indians were outraged at the death of this young woman, partly because it was reported that she had been injected with morphine before the ceremony, which raised questions about undue influence on the part of her husband's relatives. Following Kanwar's death the government of Rajasthan, where the sati took place, made it a crime punishable by seven years in prison to "glorify" sati by collecting funds, building a temple, or performing a ceremony to preserve the memory of a person who committed sati; it also decreed that any attempt made to abet an act of sati was punishable by death. Many Indians were indignant about this criminalization of the ritual, arguing that a widow's immolation was a courageous, inspirational tradition that reaffirmed marital devotion and belief in rebirth.

The point of this example, perhaps overlong in the telling even though greatly oversimplified, is that people in a society can take quite different views of their customs and institutions. It is not only we outsiders who have differing views of sati; so have Indians themselves. A similar disagreement has existed, and indeed still does, in many parts of Africa with regard to the practice of female genital mutilation, generally known as female infibulation, circumcision, or clitoral excision. In parts of the Sudan, for example, the genitalia of young Nubian girls are still almost completely cut away, and the vaginal opening is sutured closed except for an opening the size of a matchstick for the passage of urine and menstrual blood. Done without anesthesia, the operation is excruciatingly painful, there can be dangerous complications, and some girls die. Nubian men are sometimes squeamish about the practice, but women have continued to support infibulation despite governmental efforts to abolish it. Farther south, in East Africa, the operation does not involve closing the vaginal opening, but it does require excision of the clitoris and both sets of labia—as in Nubia, the pain is terrible. There the operation does not take place until the girls are adolescents, and not every girl is able to stand the pain. Some have to be excised while they are held down by men. For many years, educated East Africans have deplored the practice, and it has been illegal in Kenya for some years. It nevertheless still takes place both in Kenya and elsewhere in Africa....

The extent to which women accept and value their culturally prescribed roles varies from society to society, but in a good many of them, women have been quite unhappy and have (not without justification, I might add) blamed men for their plight. Women have launched spirited verbal and even physical assaults against their husbands in various parts of the world, but with rare exceptions men physically dominate women, and they are often far from gentle about it. As a result, when women protest, they usually do so indirectly. Sometimes women consciously adopt a sick role, as in *susto* (or fright sickness, common in Latin America), to escape, if only temporarily, from the burdens of their lives. Writing about the Zapotec of Oaxaca, Douglas Uzzell concluded that women who claimed to suffer from *susto* were able to withdraw from ordinary relationships—including beatings from their husbands—because the illness was thought to be fatal unless the patient was indulged....

Another form of indirect protest was practiced by women among the Awald' Ali Bedouin in Egypt's western desert. Distressed by the cultural constraints of arranged marriage and enforced segregation, these women indulged in various kinds of irreverent discourse about men and masculinity, including oral lyric poetry that discreetly but pointedly ridiculed, chided, and sometimes excoriated men.

Women have also taken aggressive action against what they have perceived as intolerable behavior on the part of men. From Ulithi Atoll in Micronesia to the Inuit of the far north, aggrieved women sometimes gathered together to direct obscene and abusive taunts and songs against men. Women among the Andean people who were first incorporated into the Inca Empire and later subjugated to Spanish colonial rule protested against the misery of their lives in a number of ways. Sometimes they became so desperate that they preferred suicide to a tormented life. Other Andean women preferred killing their own children to allowing a new generation to suffer under the rule of colonial officials. Those who did so killed their sons rather than their daughters to protest the manifold ways in which men had betrayed them. Still other women fled with their children to inaccessible regions where they established an underground culture of resistance to colonial rule.

Among the Samburu [of Africa]...bands of twenty or so women would sing ribaldly abusive and threatening songs outside the house of an elder who, for instance, was unusually harsh with his wives. In other parts of Africa women's protests could become particularly overt and even painful. When women among the Igbo of Nigeria were offended by something a man did (such as mistreating his wife or infringing on women's economic rights), they would gather at his household where they danced and sang abusive songs that detailed his offenses (and not infrequently questioned his masculinity). They would also pound on the walls of his house, and if he came outside to object, they would even rough him up a bit. All this would continue until the man apologized and promised not to repeat his offenses. Among the Bakweri of West Cameroon, if a woman was offended by a man, she might call out all the women of the village, who then descended on the culprit and demanded an apology and recompense. A similar phenomenon occurred among the Kamba of Kenya, whose women were ordinarily quite subservient to their harshly domineering husbands. However, when Kamba women felt that something had taken place to endanger their crops or their general well-being and that the all-male council of elders had failed to remedy the problem, they would gather together and take direct action. Beating large drums and flailing thorny boughs about them, they would march on the offender to make their demands. Any man who was incautious enough to get in their way would become the target of verbal abuse, and some were even assaulted physically. In apparent recognition of the legitimacy of the women's indignation, the usually dominant Kamba men meekly acquiesced.

Like the Kamba, men among the Pokot of Kenya thoroughly dominated women during the course of everyday life; indeed, a husband rarely hesitated to beat his wife, sometimes severely, and it was considered his right to do so. Pokot women often expressed their anger to one another but typically seemed resigned to a life of subservience. It was common for them to remark, with as much fatalism as anger, that "we cannot rule men; we can only hate them." But sometimes when a man's abuse of his wife went beyond the very generous bounds of husbandly rights, the wife could and did organize other women to "shame" her husband, as the Pokot put it. If, for example, a man beat his wife excessively or failed to have sexual intercourse with her, she and the other women could tie him up while he slept; they then not only ridiculed and reviled him with every imaginable obscenity, but one woman after another showed their genitals to him—something that was ordinarily unthinkable among the Pokot—then urinated and even defecated on him before beating his testicles with small sticks. Finally, they would cut larger sticks and threaten to beat him even more severely. It was not until his wife intervened to halt the beating (no doubt with crocodile tears in her eyes) and the now thoroughly chastened man agreed to allow the women to slaughter and eat his favorite ox (something else that was ordinarily unthinkable) that the women would finally agree to release the man. Throughout this public event, men would make no attempt to intervene. Instead, they found that they were needed elsewhere....

■ ■ ■ CONCLUSION*

[Throughout history, the subjugation of women by men has taken many forms. In control of society, males have set the standards of beauty and loyalty that women

*Conclusion by the editor.

have had to meet in order to achieve social status. We reviewed footbinding as an example of how the male idea of beauty was forced upon women, female circumcision as a way of enforcing male standards of sexuality, and sati as a final act of male dominance. For some women, the consequence has been extreme pain; for others, death. We also reviewed examples of societies in which women banded together to rebel against their subjugation.]

PART
IV Social Institutions

▪ ▪

From the previous parts, you have seen many of the social forces that influence our lives, that twist and turn us in one direction or another. You have read about culture and socialization, social control and deviance, and various forms of social stratification. In this part, we turn our focus onto *social institutions*, the standard ways that society sets up to meet its basic needs.

To exist, every society must solve certain problems. Babies must be nourished and children given direction. The sex drive must also be held within bounds. To help accomplish these things, every society has set up some form of marriage and family, the first social institution we meet on the stage of life. Social order—keeping people from robbing and killing one another—also has to be established. To accomplish this, each social group sets up some form of what we call politics. Goods and services also have to be produced and distributed. This leads to what is called the economy. The new generation also has to be taught how to view the world in the correct way, as well as to have the skills to participate in the economy. For this, we have some form of education. Then there are views of the spiritual world, of God and morality, perhaps of an afterlife. For this, we have religion.

We are immersed in social institutions, and we never escape from them. We are born into one (the family), we attend school in another (education), and we make our living in still another (economy). Even if we don't vote, the political institution surrounds us with the demands of its laws. Even if we don't worship at a church, synagogue, or mosque, we can't avoid religion, for religious principles are the foundation of law. Even closing most offices, schools, and factories on Sunday is based on religion.

Social institutions, then, are another way that society nudges us to fit in. Like a curb or median is to an automobile, so social institutions are to us. They set boundaries around us, directing us to think and act along certain avenues, to turn one way instead of another.

Social institutions are so significant that some sociologists specialize in a single social institution. Some focus on marriage and family, others study politics or the economy, whereas still others do research on religion or education. After this introductory course, which is sort of a survey of sociology, students usually can take courses on specific social institutions. Often, for example, departments of sociology teach a course on marriage and family. In large departments, there may be a course on each social institution, one on the sociology of religion, another on the sociology of education, and so on. In very large departments, the social institutions may be broken down into smaller components, and there may be several courses on the sociology of politics, education, and so on.

To focus on social institutions, we open this part with an article that has become a classic in sociology. C. Wright Mills analyzes the ruling elite of the United States. What he calls the *power elite* is the group that makes the major decisions that affect our lives. Arlie Hochschild then analyzes a major change that is taking place in some work and family settings, where work becomes more enjoyable than family life. We conclude this part with a research report by Peter and Patricia Adler on the role of athletics in education—or perhaps we should say, the lack of education in athletes.

The Power Elite

C. Wright Mills

introduction ■ ■ ■ ■ ■

A theme that has run through many of the preceding selections is how groups influence us—how they direct and control our behavior. Our membership in some of these groups (as with gender in the immediately preceding selection) comes with birth and is involuntary. Other groups, we join because we desire the membership. All groups—whether our membership is voluntary or involuntary—try to control our behavior. The broad, overarching groups, which lay the general boundaries for our actions and even our thinking, are the *social institutions* of our society. We are born and we die within social institutions. And between birth and death, we live within them—from family and school to politics and religion.

A central question that sociologists ask concerns power. Who has it, and how is it exercised? In this selection, C. Wright Mills says that power in U.S. society has become concentrated in our political, military, and economic institutions. Not only have these three grown larger, but also they have become more centralized and interconnected. As a result, their power has outstripped that of our other social institutions. Together, these three form a "triangle of power." The interests of the top political, military, and business leaders have coalesced, says Mills, and in his term, they now form a *power elite*. It is this power elite that makes the major decisions that so vitally affect our welfare—and, increasingly, with the dominance of the United States in global affairs, the welfare of the world.

Thinking Critically

As you read this selection, ask yourself:

1. If the members of the power elite don't meet together as a group, how can they be considered the primary source of power in the United States today?

2. Not everyone agrees with Mills. Compare what Mills says in this selection with the *pluralist* view of power summarized in Chapter 11 of *Essentials*.

3. Mills identifies the top leaders of the top corporations as the pinnacle of power. Why doesn't he identify the top military or political leaders as this pinnacle?

The powers of ordinary men* are circumscribed by the everyday worlds in which they live, yet even in these rounds of job, family, and neighborhood they often seem driven by forces they can neither understand nor govern. "Great changes" are beyond their control, but affect their conduct and outlook nonetheless. The very framework of modern society confines them to projects not their own, but from every side, such changes now press upon the men and women of the mass society, who accordingly feel that they are without purpose in an epoch in which they are without power.

But not all men are in this sense ordinary. As the means of information and of power are centralized, some men come to occupy positions in American society from which they can look down upon, so to speak, and by their decisions mightily affect, the everyday worlds of ordinary men and women. They are not made by their jobs; they set up and break down jobs for thousands of others; they are not confined by simple family responsibilities; they can escape. They may live in many hotels and houses, but they are bound by no one community. They need not merely "meet the demands of the day and hour"; in some part, they create these demands, and cause others to meet them. Whether or not they profess their power, their technical and political experience of it far transcends that of the underlying population. What Jacob Burckhardt said of "great men," most Americans might well say of their elite: "They are all that we are not."

The power elite is composed of men whose positions enable them to transcend the ordinary environments of ordinary men and women; they are in positions to make decisions having major consequences. Whether they do or do not make such decisions is less important than the fact that they do occupy such pivotal positions: Their failure to act, their failure to make decisions, is itself an act that is often of greater consequence than the decisions they do make. For they are in command of the major hierarchies and organizations of modern society. They rule the big corporations. They run the machinery of the state and claim its prerogatives. They direct the military establishment. They occupy the strategic command posts of the social structure, in which are now centered the effective means of the power and the wealth and the celebrity which they enjoy.

The power elite are not solitary rulers. Advisers and consultants, spokesmen and opinion-makers are often the captains of their higher thought and decision. Immediately below the elite are the professional politicians of the middle levels of power, in the Congress and in the pressure groups, as well as among the new and old upper classes of town and city and region. Mingling with them, in curious ways which we shall explore, are those professional celebrities who live by being continually displayed but are never, so long as they remain celebrities, displayed enough. If such celebrities are not at the head of any dominating hierarchy, they do often have the power to distract the attention of the public or afford sensations to the masses,

---

*As with the first article in this anthology, when Mills wrote, "men" was used to refer to both men and women and "his" to both hers and his. Although the writing style has changed, the sociological ideas are as significant as ever.

or, more directly, to gain the ear of those who do occupy positions of direct power. More or less unattached, as critics of morality and technicians of power, as spokesmen of God and creators of mass sensibility, such celebrities and consultants are part of the immediate scene in which the drama of the elite is enacted. But that drama itself is centered in the command posts of the major institutional hierarchies.

The truth about the nature and the power of the elite is not some secret which men of affairs know but will not tell. Such men hold quite various theories about their own roles in the sequence of event and decision. Often they are uncertain about their roles, and even more often they allow their fears and their hopes to affect their assessment of their own power. No matter how great their actual power, they tend to be less acutely aware of it than of the resistances of others to its use. Moreover, most American men of affairs have learned well the rhetoric of public relations, in some cases even to the point of using it when they are alone, and thus coming to believe it. The personal awareness of the actors is only one of the several sources one must examine in order to understand the higher circles. Yet many who believe that there is no elite, or at any rate none of any consequence, rest their argument upon what men of affairs believe about themselves, or at least assert in public.

There is, however, another view: those who feel, even if vaguely, that a compact and powerful elite of great importance does now prevail in America often base that feeling upon the historical trend of our time. They have felt, for example, the domination of the military event, and from this they infer that generals and admirals, as well as other men of decision influenced by them, must be enormously powerful. They hear that the Congress has again abdicated to a handful of men decisions clearly related to the issue of war or peace. They know that the bomb was dropped over Japan in the name of the United States of America, although they were at no time consulted about the matter. They feel that they live in a time of big decisions; they know that they are not making any. Accordingly, as they consider the present as history, they infer that at its center, making decisions or failing to make them, there must be an elite of power.

On the one hand, those who share this feeling about big historical events assume that there is an elite and that its power is great. On the other hand, those who listen carefully to the reports of men apparently involved in the great decisions often do not believe that there is an elite whose powers are of decisive consequence.

Both views must be taken into account, but neither is adequate. The way to understand the power of the American elite lies neither solely in recognizing the historic scale of events nor in accepting the personal awareness reported by men of apparent decision. Behind such men and behind the events of history, linking the two, are the major institutions of modern society. *These hierarchies of state [politics] and corporation [business] and army [military] constitute the means of power* [italics added]; as such they are now of a consequence not before equaled in human history—and at their summits, there are now those command posts of modern society which offer us the sociological key to an understanding of the role of the higher circles in America.

Within American society, major national power now resides in the economic, the political, and the military domains. Other institutions seem off to the side of modern history, and, on occasion, duly subordinated to these. No family is as directly powerful in national affairs as any major corporation; no church is as directly powerful in the external biographies of young men in America today as the military establishment; no college is as powerful in the shaping of momentous events as the National Security Council. Religious, educational, and family institutions are not autonomous centers of national power; on the contrary, these decentralized areas are increasingly shaped by the big three, in which developments of decisive and immediate consequence now occur.

Families and churches and schools adapt to modern life; governments and armies and corporations shape it; and, as they do so, they turn these lesser institutions into means for their ends. Religious institutions provide chaplains to the armed forces where they are used as a means of increasing the effectiveness of its morale to kill. Schools select and train men for their jobs in corporations and their specialized tasks in the armed forces. The extended family has, of course, long been broken up by the industrial revolution, and now the son and the father are removed from the family, by compulsion if need be, whenever the army of the state sends out the call. And the symbols of all these lesser institutions are used to legitimate the power and the decisions of the big three.

The life-fate of the modern individual depends not only upon the family into which he was born or which he enters by marriage, but increasingly upon the corporation in which he spends the most alert hours of his best years; not only upon the school where he is educated as a child and adolescent, but also upon the state which touches him throughout his life; not only upon the church in which on occasion he hears the word of God, but also upon the army in which he is disciplined.

If the centralized state could not rely upon the inculcation of nationalist loyalties in public and private schools, its leaders would promptly seek to modify the decentralized educational system. If the bankruptcy rate among the top five hundred corporations were as high as the general divorce rate among the [57] million married couples, there would be economic catastrophe on an international scale. If members of armies gave to them no more of their lives than do believers to the churches to which they belong, there would be a military crisis.

Within each of the big three, the typical institutional unit has become enlarged, has become administrative, and, in the power of its decisions, has become centralized. Behind these developments there is a fabulous technology, for as institutions, they have incorporated this technology and guide it, even as it shapes and paces their developments.

The economy—once a great scatter of small productive units in autonomous balance—has become dominated by two or three hundred giant corporations, administratively and politically interrelated, which together hold the keys to economic decisions.

The political order, once a decentralized set of several dozen states with a weak spinal cord, has become a centralized, executive establishment which has taken up into itself many powers previously scattered, and now enters into each and every cranny of the social structure.

The military order, once a slim establishment in a context of distrust fed by state militia, has become the largest and most expensive feature of government, and, although well versed in smiling public relations, now has all the grim and clumsy efficiency of a sprawling bureaucratic domain.

In each of these institutional areas, the means of power at the disposal of decision makers have increased enormously; their central executive powers have been enhanced; within each of them modern administrative routines have been elaborated and tightened up.

As each of these domains becomes enlarged and centralized, the consequences of its activities become greater, and its traffic with the others increases. The decisions of a handful of corporations bear upon military and political as well as upon economic developments around the world. The decisions of the military establishment rest upon and grievously affect political life as well as the very level of economic activity. The decisions made within the political domain determine economic activities and military programs. There is no longer, on the one hand, an economy, and, on the other hand, a political order containing a military establishment unimportant to politics and to money-making. There is a political economy linked, in a thousand ways, with military institutions and decisions. On each side of the world-split running through central Europe and around the Asiatic rimlands, there is an ever-increasing inter-locking of economic, military, and political structures. If there is government intervention in the corporate economy, so is there corporate intervention in the governmental process. In the structural sense, this triangle of power is the source of the interlocking directorate that is most important for the historical structure of the present.

The fact of the interlocking is clearly revealed at each of the points of crisis of modern capitalist society—slump, war, and boom. In each, men of decision are led to an awareness of the interdependence of the major institutional orders. In the nineteenth century, when the scale of all institutions was smaller, their liberal integration was achieved in the automatic economy, by an autonomous play of market forces, and in the automatic political domain, by the bargain and the vote. It was then assumed that out of the imbalance and friction that followed the limited decisions then possible a new equilibrium would in due course emerge. That can no longer be assumed, and it is not assumed by the men at the top of each of the three dominant hierarchies.

For given the scope of their consequences, decisions—and indecisions—any one of these ramify into the others, and hence top decisions tend either to become coordinated or to lead to a commanding indecision. It has not always been like this. When numerous small entrepreneurs made up the economy, for example, many of them could fail and the consequences still remain local; political and military authorities did not intervene. But now, given political expectations and military commitments, can they afford to allow key units of the private corporate economy to break down in slump? Increasingly, they do intervene in economic affairs, and as they do so, the controlling decisions in each order are inspected by agents of the other two, and economic, military, and political structures are interlocked.

At the pinnacle of each of the three enlarged and centralized domains, there have arisen those higher circles which make up the economic, the political, and the military elites. At the top of the economy, among the corporate rich, there are the chief executives; at the top of the political order, the members of the political directorate; at the top of the military establishment, the elite of soldier-statesmen clustered in and around the Joint Chiefs of Staff and the upper echelon. As each of these domains has coincided with the others, as decisions tend to become total in their consequence, the leading men in each of the three domains of power—the warlords, the corporation chieftains, the political directorate—tend to come together, to form the power elite of America.

The higher circles in and around these command posts are often thought of in terms of what their members possess: They have a greater share than other people of the things and experiences that are most highly valued. From this point of view, the elite are simply those who have the most of what there is to have, which is generally held to include money, power, and prestige—as well as all the ways of life to which these lead. But the elite are not simply those who have the most, for they could not "have the most" were it not for their positions in the great institutions. For such institutions are the necessary bases of power, of wealth, and of prestige, and at the same time, the chief means of exercising power, of acquiring and retaining wealth, and of cashing in the higher claims for prestige.

By the powerful we mean, of course, those who are able to realize their will, even if others resist it. No one, accordingly, can be truly powerful unless he has access to the command of major institutions, for it is over these institutional means of power that the truly powerful are, in the first instance, powerful. Higher politicians and key officials of government command such institutional power; so do admirals and generals, and so do the major owners and executives of the larger corporations. Not all power, it is true, is anchored in and exercised by means of such institutions, but only within and through them can power be more or less continuous and important.

Wealth also is acquired and held in and through institutions. The pyramid of wealth cannot be understood merely in terms of the very rich; for the great inheriting families, as we shall see, are now supplemented by the corporate institutions of modern society: Every one of the very rich families has been and is closely connected—always legally and frequently managerially as well—with one of the multimillion-dollar corporations.

The modern corporation is the prime source of wealth, but, in latter-day capitalism, the political apparatus also opens and closes many avenues to wealth. The amount as well as the source of income, the power over consumers' goods as well as over productive capital, are determined by position within the political economy. If our interest in the very rich goes beyond their lavish or their miserly consumption, we must examine their relations to modern forms of corporate property as well as to the state; for such relations now determine the chances of men to secure big property and to receive high income.

Great prestige increasingly follows the major institutional units of the social structure. It is obvious that prestige depends, often quite decisively, upon access to the publicity machines that are now a central and normal feature of all the big institutions of modern America. Moreover, one feature of these hierarchies of corporation, state, and military establishment is that their top positions are increasingly interchangeable. One result of this is the accumulative nature of prestige. Claims for prestige, for example, may be initially based on military roles, then expressed in and augmented by an educational institution run by corporate executives; and cashed in, finally, in the political order, where, for [top military leaders who become president, such as] General Eisenhower and those [they represent], power and prestige finally meet at the very peak. Like wealth and power, prestige tends to be cumulative: The more of it you have, the more you can get. These values also tend to be translatable into one another: The wealthy find it easier than the poor to gain power; those with status find it easier than those without it to control opportunities for wealth.

If we took the one-hundred most powerful men in America, the one-hundred wealthiest, and the one-hundred most celebrated away from the institutional positions they now occupy, away from their resources of men and women and money, away from the media of mass communication that are now focused upon them— then they would be powerless and poor and uncelebrated. For power is not of a man. Wealth does not center in the person of the wealthy. Celebrity is not inherent in any personality. To be celebrated, to be wealthy, to have power requires access to major institutions, for the institutional positions men occupy determine in large part their chances to have and to hold these valued experiences.

The people of the higher circles may also be conceived as members of a top social stratum, as a set of groups whose members know one another, see one another socially and at business, and so, in making decisions, take one another into account. The elite, according to this conception, feel themselves to be, and are felt by others to be, the inner circle of "the upper social classes." They form a more or less compact social and psychological entity; they have become self-conscious members of a social class. People are either accepted into this class or they are not, and there is a qualitative split, rather than merely a numerical scale, separating them from those who are not elite. They are more or less aware of themselves as a social class and they behave toward one another differently from the way they do toward members of other classes. They accept one another, understand one another, marry one another, tend to work and to think if not together at least alike.

Now, we do not want by our definition to prejudge whether the elite of the command posts are conscious members of such a socially recognized class, or whether considerable proportions of the elite derive from such a clear and distinct class. These are matters to be investigated. Yet in order to be able to recognize what we intend to investigate, we must note something that all biographies and memoirs of the wealthy and the powerful and the eminent make clear: No matter what else they may be, the people of these higher circles are involved in a set of overlapping "crowds" and intricately connected "cliques." There is a kind of mutual attraction among those who "sit on the same terrace"—although this often becomes clear to them, as well as to others, only at the point at which they feel the need to draw the line; only when, in their common defense, they come to understand what they have in common, and so close their ranks against outsiders.

The idea of such ruling stratum implies that most of its members have similar social origins, that throughout their lives they maintain a network of internal connections, and that to some degree there is an interchangeability of position between the various hierarchies of money and power and celebrity. We must, of course, note at once that if such an elite stratum does exist, its social visibility and its form, for very solid historical reasons, are quite different from those of the noble cousin-hoods that once ruled various European nations.

That American society has never passed through a feudal epoch is of decisive importance to the nature of the American elite, as well as to American society as a historic whole. For it means that no nobility or aristocracy, established before the capitalist era, has stood in tense opposition to the higher bourgeoisie. It means that this bourgeoisie has monopolized not only wealth but prestige and power as well. It means that no set of noble families has commanded the top positions and monopolized the values that are generally held in high esteem; and certainly that no set has done so explicitly by inherited right. It means that no high church dignitaries or court nobilities, no entrenched landlords with honorific accouterments, no monopolists of high army posts have opposed the enriched bourgeoisie and in the name of birth and prerogative successfully resisted its self-making.

But this does *not* mean that there are no upper strata in the United States. That they emerged from a "middle class" that had no recognized aristocratic superiors does not mean they remained middle class when enormous increases in wealth made their own superiority possible. Their origins and their newness may have made the upper strata less visible in America than elsewhere. But in America today there are in fact tiers and ranges of wealth and power of which people in the middle and lower ranks know very little and may not even dream. There are families who, in their well-being, are quite insulated from the economic jolts and lurches felt by the merely prosperous and those farther down the scale. There are also men of power who in quite small groups make decisions of enormous consequence for the underlying population....

When Work Becomes Home and Home Becomes Work

Arlie Russell Hochschild

introduction ▪ ▪ ▪ ▪ ▪

The social institution that introduces us to society is the family. The family is our great socializer and is considered by most sociologists to be the basic building block of society. Within the family, we learn our basic orientations to social life. Here we learn our language, the norms of proper behavior, basic etiquette, even how much self-centeredness we are allowed to display in our interactions. Our family also introduces us to its acceptable ways of viewing gender, race–ethnicity, social class, religion, people with disabilities, the elderly—even our own body. With such far-reaching implications for what we become in life, it is difficult to overstate the influence of the family.

Like our other social institutions, U.S. families are changing. They have become smaller, they have more disposable income, parental authority has decreased, wives have more power, and divorce has made families fragile. (Some sociologists point out that because parents used to die at a much earlier age, today's children have about the same chance as children of two hundred years ago of living through childhood with both their parents.) Sociologists have uncovered another change, one that has just begun to appear. As we have moved away from factory work and vast numbers of women have joined the white-collar workforce, more emphasis is being placed on social relationships at work. This has made work more pleasant and satisfying. At the same time, the emotional demands of the family seem to have become greater. One result, as Arlie Hochschild found in her study of a company she calls Amerco, is a reversal of conditions: Some parents find work to be a refuge from home, rather than their family being a refuge from work.

Thinking Critically

As you read this selection, ask yourself:

1. Do you think you will prefer work to family life? Why or why not?

2. Hochschild says that because of a "time bind" there are two sides of the same family: the rushed family that they actually are and the relaxed family they imagine they might be if only they had time. How does this apply to your own family life?

3. What does Hochschild mean when she says that the corporate world is creating a sense of "neighborhood" and a "feminine culture"? How does this development pertain to family life?

It's 7:40 A.M. when Cassie Bell, 4, arrives at the Spotted Deer Child-Care Center, her hair half-combed, a blanket in one hand, a fudge bar in the other. "I'm late," her mother, Gwen, a sturdy young woman whose short-cropped hair frames a pleasant face, explains to the child-care worker in charge. "Cassie wanted the fudge bar so bad, I gave it to her," she adds apologetically.

"*Please,* can't you take me with you?" Cassie pleads.

"You know I can't take you to work," Gwen replies in a tone that suggests that she has been expecting this request. Cassie's shoulders droop. But she has struck a hard bargain—the morning fudge bar—aware of her mother's anxiety about the long day that lies ahead at the center. As Gwen explains later, she continually feels that she owes Cassie more time than she gives her—she has a "time debt."

Arriving at her office just before 8, Gwen finds on her desk a cup of coffee in her personal mug, milk no sugar (exactly as she likes it), prepared by a co-worker who managed to get in ahead of her. As the assistant to the head of public relations at a company I will call Amerco, Gwen has to handle responses to any reports that may appear about the company in the press—a challenging job, but one that gives her satisfaction. As she prepares for her first meeting of the day, she misses her daughter, but she also feels relief; there's a lot to get done at Amerco.

Gwen used to work a straight eight-hour day. But over the last three years, her workday has gradually stretched to eight and a half or nine hours, not counting the e-mail messages and faxes she answers from home. She complains about her hours to her co-workers and listens to their complaints—but she loves her job. Gwen picks up Cassie at 5:45 and gives her a long, affectionate hug.

At home, Gwen's husband, John, a computer programmer, plays with their daughter while Gwen prepares dinner. To protect the dinner "hour"—8:00–8:30—Gwen checks that the phone machine is on, hears the phone ring during dinner but resists the urge to answer. After Cassie's bath, Gwen and Cassie have "quality time," or "Q.T.," as John affectionately calls it. Half an hour later, at 9:30, Gwen tucks Cassie into bed.

There are, in a sense, two Bell households: the rushed family they actually are and the relaxed family they imagine they might be if only they had time. Gwen and John complain that they are in a time bind. What they say they want seems so modest—time to throw a ball, to read to Cassie, to witness the small dramas of her development, not to speak of having a little fun and romance themselves. Yet even these modest wishes seem strangely out of reach. Before going to bed, Gwen has to e-mail messages to her colleagues in preparation for the next day's meeting; John goes to bed early, exhausted—he's out the door by 7 every morning.

Nationwide, many working parents are in the same boat. More mothers of small children than ever now work outside the home. American men average 48.8 hours of work a week, and women 41.7 hours, including overtime and commuting. All in all, more women are on the economic train, and for many—men and women alike—that train is going faster.

But Amerco has "family-friendly" policies. If your division head and supervisor agree, you can work part time, share a job with another worker, work some hours at home, take parental leave or use "flex time." But hardly anyone uses these policies. In seven years, only two Amerco fathers have taken formal parental leave. Fewer than 1 percent have taken advantage of the opportunity to work part time. Of all such policies, only flex time—which rearranges but does not shorten work time—has had a significant number of takers (perhaps a third of working parents at Amerco).

Forgoing family-friendly policies is not exclusive to Amerco workers. A study of 188 companies conducted by the Families and Work Institute found that while a majority offered part-time shifts, fewer than 5 percent of employees made use of them. Thirty-five percent offered "flex place"—work from home—and fewer than 3 percent of their employees took advantage of it. And a Bureau of Labor Statistics survey asked workers whether they preferred a shorter workweek, a longer one or their present schedule. About 62 percent preferred their present schedule; 28 percent would have preferred longer hours. Fewer than 10 percent said they wanted a cut in hours.

Still, I found it hard to believe that people didn't protest their long hours at work. So I contacted Bright Horizons, a company that runs 136 company-based child-care centers associated with corporations, hospitals and Federal agencies in 25 states. Bright Horizons allowed me to add questions to a questionnaire they sent out to 3,000 parents whose children attended the centers. The respondents, mainly middle-class parents in their early 30s, largely confirmed the picture I'd found at Amerco. A third of fathers and a fifth of mothers described themselves as "workaholic," and 1 out of 3 said their partners were.

To be sure, some parents have tried to shorten their hours. Twenty-one percent of the nation's women voluntarily work part time, as do 7 percent of men. A number of others make under-the-table arrangements that don't show up on surveys. But while working parents say they need more time at home, the main story of their lives does not center on a struggle to get it. Why? Given the hours parents are working these days, why aren't they taking advantage of an opportunity to reduce their time at work?

The most widely held explanation is that working parents cannot afford to work shorter hours. Certainly this is true for many. But if money is the whole explanation, why would it be that at places like Amerco, the best-paid employees—upper-level managers and professionals—were the least interested in part-time work or job sharing, while clerical workers who earned less were more interested?

Similarly, if money were the answer, we would expect poorer new mothers to return to work more quickly after giving birth than rich mothers. But among working women nationwide, well-to-do new mothers are not much more likely to stay home after 13 weeks with a new baby than low-income new mothers. When asked what they look for in a job, only a third of respondents in a recent study said salary came first. Money is important, but by itself, money does not explain why many people don't want to cut back hours at work.

Were workers uninformed about the company's family-friendly policies? No. Some even mentioned that they were proud to work for a company that offered such enlightened policies. Were rigid middle managers standing in the way of workers using these policies? Sometimes. But when I compared Amerco employees who worked for flexible managers with those who worked for rigid managers, I found that the flexible managers reported only a few more applicants than the rigid ones. The evidence, however counterintuitive, pointed to a paradox: workers at the company I studied weren't protesting the time bind. They were accommodating to it.

Why? I did not anticipate the conclusion I found myself coming to: namely, that work has become a form of "home" and home has become "work." The worlds of home and work have not begun to blur, as the conventional wisdom goes, but to reverse places. We are used to thinking that home is where most people feel the most appreciated, the most truly "themselves," the most secure, the most relaxed. We are used to thinking that work is where most people feel like "just a number" or "a cog in a machine." It is where they have to be "on," have to "act," where they are least secure and most harried.

But new management techniques so pervasive in corporate life have helped transform the workplace into a more appreciative, personal sort of social world. Meanwhile, at home the divorce rate has risen, and the emotional demands have become more baffling and complex. In addition to teething, tantrums and the normal developments of growing children, the needs of elderly parents are creating more tasks for the modern family—as are the blending, unblending, reblending of new stepparents, stepchildren, exes and former in-laws.

This idea began to dawn on me during one of my first interviews with an Amerco worker. Linda Avery, a friendly, 38-year-old mother, is a shift supervisor at an Amerco plant. When I meet her in the factory's coffee-break room over a couple of Cokes, she is wearing blue jeans and a pink jersey, her hair pulled back in a long, blond ponytail. Linda's husband, Bill, is a technician in the same plant. By working different shifts, they manage to share the care of their 2-year-old son and Linda's 16-year-old daughter from a previous marriage. "Bill works the 7 A.M. to 3 P.M. shift while I watch the baby," she explains. "Then I work the 3 P.M. to 11 P.M. shift and he watches the baby. My daughter works at Walgreen's after school."

Linda is working overtime, and so I begin by asking whether Amerco required the overtime or whether she volunteered for it. "Oh, I put in for it," she replies. I ask her whether, if finances and company policy permitted, she'd be interested in cutting back on the overtime. She takes off her safety glasses, rubs her face and, without answering my question, explains: "I get home, and the minute I turn the key, my daughter is right there. Granted, she needs somebody to talk to about her day.... The baby is still up. He should have been in bed two hours ago, and that upsets me. The dishes are piled in the sink. My daughter comes right up to the door and complains about anything her stepfather said or did, and she wants to talk about her job. My husband is in the other room hollering to my daughter, 'Tracy, I don't ever get any time to talk to your mother, because you're always monopolizing her time before I even get a chance!' They all come at me at once."

Linda's description of the urgency of demands and the unarbitrated quarrels that await her homecoming contrast with her account of arriving at her job as a shift supervisor: "I usually come to work early, just to get away from the house. When I arrive, people are there waiting. We sit, we talk, we joke. I let them know what's going on, who has to be where, what changes I've made for the shift that day. We sit and chitchat for 5 or 10 minutes. There's laughing, joking, fun."

For Linda, home has come to feel like work and work has come to feel a bit like home. Indeed, she feels she can get relief from the "work" of being at home only by going to the "home" of work. Why has her life at home come to seem like this? Linda explains it this way: "My husband's a great help watching our baby. But as far as doing housework or even taking the baby when I'm at home, no. He figures he works five days a week; he's not going to come home and clean. But he doesn't stop to think that I work seven days a week. Why should I have to come home and do the housework without help from anybody else? My husband and I have been through this over and over again. Even if he would just pick up from the kitchen table and stack the dishes for me, that would make a big difference. He does nothing. On his weekends off, he goes fishing. If I want any time off, I have to get a sitter. He'll help out if I'm not here, but the minute I am, all the work at home is mine."

With a light laugh, she continues: "So I take a lot of overtime. The more I get out of the house, the better I am. It's a terrible thing to say, but that's the way I feel."

When Bill feels the need for time off, to relax, to have fun, to feel free, he climbs in his truck and takes his free time without his family. Largely in response, Linda grabs what she also calls "free time"—at work. Neither Linda nor Bill Avery wants more time together at home, not as things are arranged now.

How do Linda and Bill Avery fit into the broader picture of American family and work life? Current research suggests that however hectic their lives, women who do paid work feel less depressed, think better of themselves and are more satisfied than women who stay at home. One study reported that women who work outside the home feel more valued at home than housewives do. Meanwhile, work is where many women feel like "good mothers." As Linda reflects: "I'm a good mom at home, but I'm a better mom at work. At home, I get into fights with Tracy. I want her to apply to a junior college, but she's not interested. At work, I think I'm better at seeing the other person's point of view."

Many workers feel more confident they could "get the job done" at work than at home. One study found that only 59 percent of workers feel their "performance" in the family is "good or unusually good," while 86 percent rank their performance on the job this way.

Forces at work and at home are simultaneously reinforcing this "reversal." This lure of work has been enhanced in recent years by the rise of company cultural engineering—in particular, the shift from Frederick Taylor's principles of scientific management to the Total Quality principles originally set out by W. Edwards Deming. Under the influence of a Taylorist world view, the manager's job was to coerce the worker's mind and body, not to appeal to the worker's heart. The Taylorized worker was de-skilled, replaceable and cheap, and as a consequence felt bored, demeaned and unappreciated.

Using modern participative management techniques, many companies now train workers to make their own work decisions, and then set before their newly "empowered" employees moral as well as financial incentives. At Amerco, the Total

Quality worker is invited to feel recognized for job accomplishments. Amerco regularly strengthens the familylike ties of co-workers by holding "recognition ceremonies" honoring particular workers or self-managed production teams. Amerco employees speak of "belonging to the Amerco family" and proudly wear their "Total Quality" pins or "High Performance Team" T-shirts, symbols of their loyalty to the company and of its loyalty to them.

The company occasionally decorates a section of the factory and serves refreshments. The production teams, too, have regular get-togethers. In a New Age recasting of an old business slogan—"The Customer Is Always Right"—Amerco proposes that its workers "Value the Internal Customer." This means: Be as polite and considerate to co-workers inside the company as you would be to customers outside it. How many recognition ceremonies for competent performance are being offered at home? Who is valuing the internal customer there?

Amerco also tries to take on the role of a helpful relative with regard to employee problems at work and at home. The education-and-training division offers employees free courses (on company time) in "Dealing With Anger," "How to Give and Accept Criticism," "How to Cope With Difficult People."

At home, of course, people seldom receive anything like this much help on issues basic to family life. There, no courses are being offered on "Dealing With Your Child's Disappointment in You" or "How to Treat Your Spouse Like an Internal Customer."

If Total Quality calls for "re-skilling" the worker in an "enriched" job environment, technological developments have long been de-skilling parents at home. Over the centuries, store-bought goods have replaced homespun cloth, homemade soup and home-baked foods. Day care for children, retirement homes for the elderly, even psychotherapy are, in a way, commercial substitutes for jobs that a mother once did at home. Even family-generated entertainment has, to some extent, been replaced by television, video games and the VCR. I sometimes watched Amerco families sitting together after their dinners, mute but cozy, watching sitcoms in which television mothers, fathers and children related in an animated way to one another while the viewing family engaged in relational loafing.

The one "skill" still required of family members is the hardest one of all—the emotional work of forging, deepening or repairing family relationships. It takes time to develop this skill, and even then things can go awry. Family ties are complicated. People get hurt. Yet as broken homes become more common—and as the sense of belonging to a geographical community grows less and less secure in an age of mobility—the corporate world has created a sense of "neighborhood," of "feminine culture," of family at work. Life at work can be insecure; the company can fire workers. But workers aren't so secure at home, either. Many employees have been working for Amerco for 20 years but are on their second or third marriages or relationships. The shifting balance between these two "divorce rates" may be the most powerful reason why tired parents flee a world of unresolved quarrels and unwashed laundry for the orderliness, harmony and managed cheer of work. People are getting their "pink slips" at home.

Amerco workers have not only turned their offices into "home" and their homes into workplaces; many have also begun to "Taylorize" time at home, where families are succumbing to a cult of efficiency previously associated mainly with the office and factory. Meanwhile, work time, with its ever longer hours, has become more hospitable to sociability—periods of talking with friends on e-mail, patching up quarrels, gossiping. Within the long workday of many Amerco employees are great hidden pockets of inefficiency while, in the far smaller number of waking weekday hours at home, they are, despite themselves, forced to act increasingly time-conscious and efficient.

The Averys respond to their time bind at home by trying to value and protect "quality time." A concept unknown to their parents and grandparents, "quality time" has become a powerful symbol of the struggle against the growing pressures at home. It reflects the extent to which modern parents feel the flow of time to be running against them. The premise behind "quality time" is that the time we devote to relationships can somehow be separated from ordinary time. Relationships go on during quantity time, of course, but then we are only passively, not actively, wholeheartedly, specializing in our emotional ties. We aren't "on." Quality time at home becomes like an office appointment. You don't want to be caught "goofing off around the water cooler" when you are "at work."

Quality time holds out the hope that scheduling intense periods of togetherness can compensate for an overall loss of time in such a way that a relationship will suffer no loss of quality. But this is just another way of transferring the cult of efficiency from office to home. We must now get our relationships in good repair in less time. Instead of nine hours a day with a child, we declare ourselves capable of getting "the same result" with one intensely focused hour.

Parents now more commonly speak of time as if it is a threatened form of personal capital they have no choice but to manage and invest. What's new here is the spread into the home of a financial manager's attitude toward time. Working parents at Amerco owe what they think of as time debts at home. This is because they are, in a sense, inadvertently "Taylorizing" the house—speeding up the pace of home life as Taylor once tried to "scientifically" speed up the pace of factory life.

Advertisers of products aimed at women have recognized that this new reality provides an opportunity to sell products, and have turned the very pressure that threatens to explode the home into a positive attribute. Take, for example, an ad promoting Instant Quaker Oatmeal: it shows a smiling mother ready for the office in her square-shouldered suit, hugging her happy son. A caption reads: "Nicky is a very picky eater. With Instant Quaker Oatmeal, I can give him a terrific hot breakfast in just 90 seconds. And I don't have to spend any time coaxing him to eat it!" Here, the modern mother seems to have absorbed the lessons of Frederick Taylor as she presses for efficiency at home because she is in a hurry to get to work.

Part of modern parenthood seems to include coping with the resistance of real children who are not so eager to get their cereal so fast. Some parents try desperately not to appease their children with special gifts or smooth-talking promises about the future. But when time is scarce, even the best parents find themselves passing a system-wide familial speed-up along to the most vulnerable workers on the line. Parents are then obliged to try to control the damage done by a reversal of worlds. They monitor mealtime, homework time, bedtime, trying to cut out "wasted" time.

In response, children often protest the pace, the deadlines, the grand irrationality of "efficient" family life. Children dawdle. They refuse to leave places when it's time to leave. They insist on leaving places when it's not time to leave. Surely, this is part of the usual stop-and-go of childhood itself, but perhaps, too, it is the plea of children for more family time and more control over what time there is. This only adds to the feeling that life at home has become hard work.

Instead of trying to arrange shorter or more flexible work schedules, Amerco parents often avoid confronting the reality of the time bind. Some minimize their ideas about how much care a child, a partner or they themselves "really need." They make do with less time, less attention, less understanding and less support at home than they once imagined possible. They *emotionally downsize* life. In essence, they deny the needs of family members, and they themselves become emotional ascetics. If they once "needed" time with each other, they are now increasingly "fine" without it.

Another way that working parents try to evade the time bind is to buy themselves out of it—an approach that puts women in particular at the heart of a contradiction. Like men, women absorb the work-family speed-up far more than they resist it; but unlike men, they still shoulder most of the workload at home. And women still represent in people's minds the heart and soul of family life. They're the ones—especially women of the urban middle and upper-middle classes—who feel most acutely the need to save time, who are the most tempted by the new "time saving" goods and services—and who wind up feeling the most guilty about it. For example, Playgroup Connections, a Washington-area business started by a former executive recruiter, matches playmates to one another. One mother hired the service to find her child a French-speaking playmate.

In several cities, children home alone can call a number for "Grandma, Please!" and reach an adult who has the time to talk with them, sing to them or help them with their homework. An ad for Kindercare Learning Centers, a for-profit child-care chain, pitches its appeal this way: "You want your child to be active, tolerant, smart, loved, emotionally stable, self-aware, artistic and get a two-hour nap. Anything else?" It goes on to note that Kindercare accepts children 6 weeks to 12 years old and provides a number to call for the Kindercare nearest you. Another typical service organizes children's birthday parties, making out invitations ("sure hope you can come") and providing party favors, entertainment, a decorated cake and balloons. Creative Memories is a service that puts ancestral photos into family albums for you.

An overwhelming majority of the working mothers I spoke with recoiled from the idea of buying themselves out of parental duties. A bought birthday party was "too impersonal," a 90-second breakfast "too fast." Yet a surprising amount of lunchtime conversation between female friends at Amerco was devoted to expressing complex, conflicting feelings about the lure of trading time for one service or another. The temptation to order flash-frozen dinners or to call a local number for a homework helper did not come up because such services had not yet appeared at Spotted Deer Child-Care Center. But many women dwelled on the question of how to decide where a mother's job began and ended, especially with regard to babysitters and television. One mother said to another in the breakroom of an Amerco plant: "Damon doesn't settle down until 10 at night, so he hates me to wake him up in the morning and I hate to do it. He's cranky. He pulls the covers up. I put on cartoons. That way I can dress him and he doesn't object. I don't like to use TV that way. It's like a drug. But I do it."

The other mother countered: "Well, Todd is up before we are, so that's not a problem. It's after dinner, when I feel like watching a little television, that I feel guilty, because he gets too much TV at the sitter's."

As task after task falls into the realm of time-saving goods and services, questions rise about the moral meanings attached to doing or not doing such tasks. Is it being a good mother to bake a child's birthday cake (alone or together with one's partner)? Or can we gratefully save time by ordering it, and be good mothers by planning the party? Can we save more time by hiring a planning service, and be good mothers simply by watching our children have a good time? "Wouldn't that be nice!" one Amerco mother exclaimed. As the idea of the "good mother" retreats before the pressures of work and the expansion of motherly services, mothers are in fact continually reinventing themselves.

The final way working parents tried to evade the time bind was to develop what I call "potential selves." The potential selves that I discovered in my Amerco interviews were fantasy creations of time-poor parents who dreamed of living as time millionaires.

One man, a gifted 55-year-old engineer in research and development at Amerco, told how he had dreamed of taking his daughters on a camping trip in the Sierra Mountains: "I bought all the gear three years ago when they were 5 and 7, the tent, the sleeping bags, the air mattresses, the backpacks, the ponchos. I got a map of the area. I even got the freeze-dried food. Since then the kids and I have talked about it a lot, and gone over what we're going to do. They've been on me to do it for a long time. I feel bad about it. I keep putting it off, but we'll do it, I just don't know when."

Banished to garages and attics of many Amerco workers were expensive electric saws, cameras, skis and musical instruments, all bought with wages it took time to earn. These items were to their owners what Cassie's fudge bar was to her—a substitute for time, a talisman, a reminder of the potential self.

Obviously, not everyone, not even a majority of Americans, is making a home out of work and a workplace out of home. But in the working world, it is a growing reality, and one we need to face. Increasing numbers of women are discovering a great male secret—that work can be an escape from the pressures of home, pressures that the changing nature of work itself are only intensifying. Neither men nor women are going to take up "family-friendly" policies, whether corporate or governmental, as long as the current realities of work and home remain as they are. For a substantial number of time-bound parents, the stripped-down home and the neighborhood devoid of community are simply losing out to the pull of the workplace.

There are several broader, historical causes of this reversal of realms. The last 30 years have witnessed the rapid rise of women in the workplace. At the same time, job mobility has taken families farther from relatives who might lend a hand, and made it harder to make close friends of neighbors who could help out. Moreover, as women have acquired more education and have joined men at work, they have absorbed the views of an older, male-oriented work world, its views of a "real career," far more than men have taken up their share of the work at home. One reason women have changed more than men is the world of "male" work seems more honorable and valuable than the "female" world of home and children.

So where do we go from here? There is surely no going back to the mythical 1950s family that confined women to the home. Most women don't wish to return to a full-time role at home—and couldn't afford it even if they did. But equally troubling is a workaholic culture that strands both men and women outside the home.

For a while now, scholars on work-family issues have pointed to Sweden, Norway and Denmark as better models of work-family balance. Today, for example, almost all Swedish fathers take two paid weeks off from work at the birth of their children, and about half of fathers and most mothers take additional "parental leave" during the child's first or second year. Research shows that men who take family leave when their children are very young are more likely to be involved with their children as they grow older. When I mentioned this Swedish record of paternity leave to a focus group of American male managers, one of them replied, "Right, we've already heard about Sweden." To this executive, paternity leave was a good idea not for the U.S. today, but for some "potential society" in another place and time.

Meanwhile, children are paying the price. In her book *When the Bough Breaks: The Cost of Neglecting Our Children*, the economist Sylvia Hewlett claims that "compared with the previous generation, young people today are more likely to underperform at school; commit suicide; need psychiatric help; suffer a severe eating disorder; bear a child out of wedlock; take drugs; be the victim of a violent crime." But we needn't dwell on sledgehammer problems like heroin and suicide to realize that children like those at Spotted Deer need more of our time. If other advanced nations with two-job families can give children the time they need, why can't we?

College Athletes
and Role Conflict

Peter Adler and Patricia A. Adler

introduction ■ ■ ■ ■ ■

In earlier societies, there was no separate social institution called education. There were no special buildings called schools, and no people who earned their living as teachers. Instead, as an integral part of growing up, children learned what was necessary to get along in life. If hunting and cooking were the essential skills required for survival and taking on adult roles in their group, then people who already possessed those skills taught them to children. Socialization into adult roles by family and friends was education.

No longer is an informal system of passing on knowledge and skills adequate, and today a formal social institution known as education has become highly significant in social life. With each generation, the amount of education that young people are expected to attain has increased. A hundred years ago, graduating from the eighth grade was considered sufficient education for almost everyone—except for the few who went on to *higher* education in a place called *high* school. Today, in contrast, most young people are asked, "Where are you going to college?" This question is also asked of every top high school athlete, who everyone presumes will be awarded a scholarship to college. Of the athletes who do get scholarships, many fail to graduate from college. Peter and Patricia Adler, a husband and wife team of sociologists, explore reasons for this.

Thinking Critically

As you read this selection, ask yourself:

1. Why is it common for athletes who receive college scholarships to fail to graduate from college? What part does the athlete subculture play in this?

2. What role conflict do college athletes experience? Why?

3. If you were the president of a Top 10 college and you wanted to dramatically increase the college graduation rate of your athletes, based on the findings in this selection, what would you do?

Athletes attend colleges and universities for the ostensible purpose of getting an education while they exercise and refine their athletic skills, but recent studies note that this ideal has become increasingly corrupted. Reports by journalists, former athletes, and social scientists note the commercialization of big-time college athletics, where the money and prestige available to universities have turned their athletic programs into business enterprises that emphasize winning at all costs, often neglecting the education goals of their institutions. The equality of the exchange between college athletes and their educational institutions has therefore been sharply questioned, with many critics leveling charges that universities have exploited their athletes by making excessive demands of them and failing to fulfill their educational promises to them. Several studies have suggested that these factors...result in [athletes] having lower grades and less chance of graduating than other students.... Drawing on four years of intensive participant observation with a major college basketball team, this article examines college athletes' academic experiences....

▪ ▪ ▪ ▪ METHODS AND SETTING

For four years the authors studied a major college basketball program via participant-observation.... The research was conducted at a medium-size private university with a predominantly white, suburban, and middle-class student body. The university's academic standards were demanding as it was striving to enhance its academic reputation. The athletic department, as a whole, had a recent history of success. Players were generally recruited from the region, were 70% black, and ranged from the lower to the middle classes. The basketball program fit what Coakley and Frey termed *big-time college athletics*. Although it could not compare to the really large universities, its recent success had compensated for its size and lack of historical tradition. The national ranking and past success of the basketball team and other teams in sending graduating members into the professional leagues imbued the entire athletic milieu with a sense of seriousness and purpose.

The basketball players' circle of significant others was largely predetermined by athletic environment. The role-set members fell into three main categories: athletic, academic, and social. Within the athletic realm, in addition to their teammates, athletes related primarily to the coaching staff, trainers, team managers, secretaries, and athletic administrators. Secondary role-set members included boosters, fans, and the news media. Within the academic realm, athletes' role-set members consisted of professors, tutors, classmates, and, to a lesser extent, academic counselors and administrators. Within the social realm, athletes related to girlfriends, local friends, and students (non-athletes), but most especially to their college athlete peers: the teammates and dormmates who were members of their subculture.

■ ■ ■ **ROLE EXPECTATIONS**

Most incoming college athletes observed approached their academic role with initial feelings of idealism. They were surrounded by family and cultural messages that college would enhance their upward mobility and benefit their lives in many ways. They never doubted this assertion. Because of their academic experiences in high school, few athletes questioned their ability to succeed in college ("I graduated high school, didn't I?"). Athletes' idealism about their impending academic experience was further strengthened by the positive tone coaches had taken toward academics during the recruiting process. Entering freshmen commonly held the following set of prior expectations about their academic role: (1) they would go to classes and do the work (phrased as "putting the time in"); (2) they would graduate and get a degree, and (3) there would be no problems.

Approximately 47% ($N = 8$) of the entering athletes observed showed their initially high academic aspirations and expectations by requesting to be placed in a preprofessional major in the colleges of business, engineering, or arts and sciences. Despite warnings from coaches and older teammates about how difficult it would be to complete this coursework and play ball, they felt they could easily handle the demands. These individuals planned to use college athletics as a stepping-stone to career opportunities. As one freshman stated:

> I goin' to use basketball to get an education. Sure I'd like to make the NBA someday, but right now I've got to have something to fall back on if I don't.

Another group of freshmen, who had already accorded academics a less salient role (45%, $N = 17$), were enrolled by coaches in more "manageable" majors, such as physical education or recreation. Most of these individuals, though, believed that they too would get a degree. They had few prior expectations about academics, but assumed that they would make it through satisfactorily. Someone had taken care of these matters in high school, and they felt that college would be no different. Only a few individuals from the sample (8%, $N = 3$) entered college expecting to turn professional shortly thereafter. From the beginning these individuals disdained the academic role.

Much of this initial idealism was based on an inaccurate picture of college. Athletes did not anticipate the focus on analytical thinking and writing they would encounter, expecting that college courses would be an extension of their high school experiences. One sophomore reflected back on his expectations:

> I didn't think about it much, but when I did, I thought it'd be more or less the same here as it be back in high school, no big change. I be passin' all my courses there, but I still be goin' out every night.

In their first weeks on campus during their summer program, this early idealism was once again bolstered. Repeatedly the head coach stressed the importance of earning a degree. He cared about his players as people and wanted them to build a future out of their college experience. In fact, one of the main reasons athletes' parents encouraged their sons to attend this university was because of the head coach's integrity and good values. Once the school year began, athletes attended required nightly study halls, were told that tutors were available, and were constantly reminded by the coach to go to class. One freshman, interviewed during the preseason period, showed his idealism through his expectations and impressions:

> I'm here for two reasons: to get my degree and play basketball. I don't think it's goin' to be no problem to get my degree. I want to graduate in four years and I think I will. I think that's really important to Coach, too, because in practice he always mentions how important the degree is and everything.

Contrary to popular sentiment, most of the athletes observed began their college careers with a positive attitude toward academics. While their athletic role was unquestionably the most salient and their social role secondary, the academic role was still a critical dimension of their self-identity. Their behavior in the academic realm reflected this; they missed few classes, and turned in assignments regularly. For most this period lasted anywhere from one semester to two years.

■ ■ ■ ROLE CONFLICT

After two semesters in school and a full basketball season, athletes began to realize that their academic expectations had not been entirely accurate. Their early naive idealism gave way to disappointment and cynicism.... A major change athletes encountered in shifting from high school to college basketball lay in their athletic role. In large part this was due to the professionalization process they underwent. As one junior remarked:

> In high school, basketball was fun and games, but now it's a job. We get to the gym, we gotta work. You gotta put your all into it no matter how you feelin' that day. 'Cause this is big business. There's a lotta money ridin' on us.

Compounding the professionalization was a dramatic increase in pressure. The basketball players were all public figures in the local area who received intense news coverage. They clearly knew how important winning was to the coaches, boosters, and fans.

The players' athletic role often encroached on their academic role. They soon discovered that handling both roles was not always possible. A primary reason was the time conflict: some courses they wanted or needed for their majors were only offered in the afternoons during practice time; road trips caused them to miss key lectures, examinations, or review sessions, and banquets and other booster functions (which occurred at least once a week) cut into their studying time. At some point during this freshman year, most athletes realized that they did not have the time to perform as well as they had originally hoped in the academic role....

Athletes' perceptions of their athletic–academic role conflict was also influenced by the role model of their coaches. While the coaches sincerely cared about their players' academic responsibilities and achievements, they had their own priorities. Once the season began, they were too busy with their athletic work to pay much attention to academics. The pressures of recruiting, funding, and winning absorbed their energy. Despite their best preseason intentions, once practice officially began in October, the coaches became predominantly concerned with their players as athletes and ended up passing on the pressures of their organizational demands and constraints. Like their players, they were faced with a complex situation to which they often reacted, rather than acted. While they verbally stressed the importance of academics, they accorded athletic and team functions higher salience than school obligations: players' athletic time was strictly regulated, but their academic time was not. Players' behavior in practice, at games, at booster events, and on road trips was carefully monitored, yet their performance in class was not. Despite the coaches' concern about academics, the predominant message that athletes received was that, in contrast to academics, athletics had to be strictly adhered to because a powerful role-set member was always present.

ACADEMIC ROLE

During the school year, players began to notice other characteristics of their academic role that undercut their coaches' verbal emphasis on scholarship. One of the first was their lack of autonomy over their course (and sometimes major) selection. An assistant coach picked out classes and registered the athletes without consulting them. Assistant coaches bought their books, added and dropped courses for them, and contacted their professors if they had to be absent or were doing poorly in their work. By taking care of these academic matters for them, the coaches served as intermediaries between players and the academic realm. Consequently, most athletes failed to develop the knowledge, initiative, or the interest to handle these academic matters themselves, or to develop significant relationships with their professors or other academic role-set members. Thus, when the coaches were too busy to attend to these details, the players were unable to manage for themselves. As one senior remarked:

> Most of those guys don't even know how to fill out an add-drop card, so when they want to switch classes they just do it, and they tell the coaches to switch them. They figure it's not their job. But a lot of guys get Fs because the coaches never got around to it. The only reason I got through is that my girlfriend did it for me. I don't even know how to read a schedule of classes or where to get one.

Despite their occasional lapses, the fact that coaches managed these administrative matters gave athletes a false sense of security, a feeling that someone was always looking out for them academically and would make sure that they were given another chance. The athletes believed that they could fail to perform academically and not have to pay the consequences. They developed the perception that...they would be taken care of academically, and that they need not overly involve themselves in this arena....

Concomitant with this lack of autonomy came a new freedom. Unlike high school, their attendance at classes was not compulsory. Being able to skip classes placed a greater responsibility for self-motivation on them. When their motivation waned, athletes developed a pattern of slipping behind in their attendance and classwork until their problems compounded. When athletes did attend class, they often encountered another set of difficulties or disillusionments. In the classroom athletes thought that many professors labeled them as jocks. This image was fostered by the fact that they were surrounded in their classes by other athletes (also placed there by assistant coaches), and that they were identified early in the semester to their professor as athletes (because assistant coaches called or sent out reports to monitor their academic progress). They therefore encountered different expectations and treatment than the general student body. Whether they were given greater tolerance (extra tutoring sessions, relaxed deadlines, relaxed academic standards) or less tolerance ("Those guys think they're entitled to special treatment because they're athletes, and I'm going to show them they're wrong"), they were treated as less than full adults. This special treatment reinforced the differentiation between these two roles and their perceptions of themselves as athletes more than students. When they returned to the dormitory rooms at night, exhausted and sore from practicing, it became easier for them to rationalize, procrastinate, and fritter away their time instead of studying.

Athletes also became disinterested in their academic role because of the content of their classes. The level of disinterest varied between the athletes enrolled in arts and sciences, business, or engineering courses, and those taking physical education or recreation courses. Many of those in the latter category had wanted and expected to take courses in college that were either entertaining, vocational, or in some way relevant to their everyday lives. This was not what they found. Instead, they were enrolled in courses that they considered comical and demeaning. One sophomore articulated the commonly held view:

> How could I get into this stuff? They got me taking nutrition, mental retardation, square dancing, and camp counseling. I thought I was goin' to learn something here. It's a bunch o' BS.

Players enrolled in more rigorous academic courses were often unequipped for the demanding calibre of the work. Many did not have the knowledge, interests, skills, or study habits to compete with other students. With their inadequate training, tight schedules, and waning motivation, athletes became frustrated, bored, and disinterested. Players often stopped going to classes they did not like, yet never officially withdrew from them. When they did poorly on the first test, they gave up on the course, figuring "to hell with it, I'm not gonna try." The positive feedback from their academic role that the athletes anticipated often was replaced by a series of disappointments. As a result they often spent their days lying around the dormitory rooms, watching television, and convincing each other not to go to class. Athletes' academic failures then brought them feelings of inadequacy and uncertainty, as one player described:

> When I first came here I thought I'd be goin' to class all the time and I'd study and that'd be it. But I sure didn't think it meant studyin' all the time. Back in high school you just be memorizin' things, but that's not what they want here. Back in high school I thought I be a pretty good student, but now I don't know.

Players' experiences in the classroom were very different from their preconceptions. The work was harder and they were not taken care of to the extent they had imagined. The intense competition of the athletic arena led them to be obsessed with success. Their frequent academic failures (or at best mediocre grades) led athletes to distance themselves from self-involvement in the academic role. It was better not to try than to try and fail. And they derived plenty of support for this tack within the peer subculture.

■ ■ ■ SOCIAL ROLE

Athletes' social experiences at the university were predominantly with other athletes. Initially they had expected to derive both friendship and status recognition from other students as they had in high school. Instead they found themselves socially isolated. Geographically they were isolated by being housed in an athletic dormitory on a remote side of the campus. Temporally they were cut off by the demands of their practices, games, study halls, and booster functions. Culturally they were racially, socially, and economically different from the rest of the student body. Physically, they were different from other students in size and build, and many students, especially women, found them imposing or occasionally intimidating.

These factors left other athletes as their primary outlets for social relations. Housed together in a dormitory reserved almost exclusively for male athletes (primarily football and basketball players), they bonded together into a reference group and peer subculture. Relations within this group were made especially cohesive by the intensity of their living, playing, and traveling together. A junior described this living situation:

> Living in the jock dorm the privacy is limited. Everybody knows everythin' 'bout what you doin' and who you seein'. You got to live with these same faces twelve months out of the year, they like your brothers, and we all one big family, like it or not. You just got to fit in.

Within the dormitory, athletes briefed each other about what to expect from and think about various individuals, and how to handle certain situations. They formed generalized attitudes and beliefs about what things were important and what things were not. The peer subculture provided them with a set of norms that guided their interpretations of and actions within their various roles.

One of the peer subculture's strongest influences lay in its anti-intellectual and anti-academic character. Typically, dormitory conversation centered on athletic and social dimensions of their lives with little reference to academic, cultural, or intellectual pursuits. In fact, individuals who displayed too much interest, effort, or success in academics were often ridiculed, as one player described:

> When most of the other guys are making Ds or Fs, if I work hard and I get a B on a test, if I go back to the dorm and they all see I got a B, then they goin' "snap on" [make fun of] me. So most of the guys, they don't try. They all act like it's a big joke.

The athletes' peer subculture conflicted with their academic role in five ways: (1) by discouraging them from exerting effort in academics; (2) by providing them with distractions that made it harder for them to study; (3) by providing them with role models who appeared to be getting through college while according their academic role negligible identity salience; (4) by discouraging them from seeking out and associating with other students who could have provided greater academic role modeling; and (5) by providing excuses and justifications that legitimated their academic failures.

The conflict between their athletic, academic, and social roles pulled the athletes in too many directions. One junior expressed his continuing distress over this role conflict:

> When I think about it I get tense and frustrated, you just can't be everything they expect you to be and what you want to be. Something's gotta give. It's either cut off my social life, or flunk out of school, or not do the things I have to do to be able to make pro.

■ ■ ■ ROLE CONFLICT RESOLUTIONS

Athletes' expectations for their academic role were gradually replaced by feelings of anomie as they came to perceive the disparity between the recruiting and cultural rhetoric they had encountered and the reality of college life. In order to successfully negotiate their college experience they had to find some way to resolve this role conflict, which they did by realigning the expectations, priorities, and identity salience [the significance of a role, or how much one identifies with it] of their roles.

The biggest change in their core identity salience lay in the growth of their athletic role. While athletics had always been the first priority for most, it now engulfed them. This shift was brought about by the demands and expectations of their athletic role set and by their own desire to cling to their dreams of making it in the NBA. First, the head coach overwhelmed athletes by the intensity of his power and role demands. He expected them to place basketball before everything else. He influenced their view of their present and future life chances by framing these for them based on athletic priorities. He heard about everything they did and reprimanded them for violations of his behavior code. Yet it was the intensity of the athletic experience itself that ensured their self-immersion in this role. The glamour and excitement of playing for a big-time athletic program offered even the most marginal players their most fulfilling gratification and rewards. One player described the impossibility of maintaining any balance between his athletic and other roles:

> When I go to sleep at night what do you think I be thinking? History? Sociology? No way. I hear coach yelling in my ear, "Run, run, get on the ball, play defense, Robinson. Damn, Robinson, can you move your feet, son?" During the season I sleep, eat, and breathe basketball.

In addition, the athletic role pervaded and dominated the identity of their other roles in social and academic situations. On campus they were recognized as athletes first and students second. Off campus and even out of uniform, they were constantly responsible for "representing the program." Their appearance and demeanor reflected on their teammates, their coaches, their basketball program, and the entire university. They therefore had to relinquish a great deal of privacy and freedom.

The growth of the athletic role's identity salience was further endorsed by their peer subculture. Most of the athletes in their dormitory had reprioritized their roles and become engulfed by athletics. These significant others offered them a model of role conflict resolution that adopted the coach's perspective on the predominance of athletics, maintained the secondary importance of having a social life, and reshuffled academics to an even lower identity salience. All of the athletes realigned the identity salience of these roles in this manner, progressively detaching themselves from academics.

These changes in athletes' identities led to a series of pragmatic adjustments in their academic goals. Of the individuals who began with preprofessional majors, only one-fourth of them stayed with these all the way through college and graduated. They did so primarily without the academic care and concern they had originally anticipated. They ceased attending classes regularly, diminished their efforts to get to know professors, did not bother to get class notes or reading assignments until just before tests, and exerted the minimum amount of effort necessary to get by. More commonly, these individuals reassessed their academic goals and found that some adjustment was necessary. A second group (the remaining three-fourths of this original group) adjusted by both shifting their behavior and by changing from their preprofessional program to a more manageable major. While this shift meant that they had abandoned both their academic idealism and their earlier career goals, they still held to the goal of graduating. The predominant attitude changed to getting a diploma regardless of the major. As one player commented, "When you apply for a job all that matters is if you have that piece of paper. They don't care what you majored in." Many of the athletes in this group managed to graduate or keep on a steady course toward graduation. Much like Merton's innovators, they retained the socially approved goal but replaced their earlier means with a creative alternative.

Athletes who began their college careers with lower initial academic aspirations and who majored in physical education or recreation from the start made corresponding adjustments. Approximately one-fifth of these in this group originally held on to their initial goal and managed to graduate in one of these fields. Like the preprofessional majors, they did so with less concern than they had displayed on entering. The other four-fifths came to the realization, usually relatively late, that their chances for graduating from college were unrealistic. They therefore shifted their orientation toward maintaining their athletic eligibility. A junior's remarks illustrated how this shift to maintaining eligibility affected his attitude toward his academic role:

> I used to done thought I was goin' to school, but now I know it's not for real.... I don't have no academic goals. A player a coach is counting on, that's all he think about is ball. That's what he signed to do. So what you gotta do is show up, show your smilin' face. Try as hard as you can. Don't just lay over in the room. That's all the coach can ask. Or else you may not find yourself playing the next year. Or even that year.

By their senior year, when they had met their final eligibility requirements, many members of this last group abandoned the academic role entirely. They either anticipated going to one of the professional leagues, or they knew that their scholarships would soon expire and they would have to look for a job. In either case, wasting their time in class no longer seemed necessary.

■ ■ ■ DISCUSSION

...In their academic role, many college athletes received poor or marginal grades and had to relinquish or readjust the academic goals they held on entering college. This perception awakened them to the conflict between their expectations that college would be much like high school and their realizations that the academic demands at the university were greater than they could achieve. Their emphasis on competition and winning, derived from their athletic role, made the failure especially difficult to accept.

When faced with extreme role conflict, individuals doing very poorly in their classes engaged in role distance, diminishing the importance of this role to their self-identity. Individuals from stronger academic backgrounds fared slightly better, however, and did not as greatly diminish their [identity with the] academic role.... As individuals assessed their relative strengths and weaknesses within given roles, they accorded higher salience to those in which they were evaluated positively and lower salience to those in which they were negatively evaluated....

Most athletes' initial commitment to the academic role was induced by cultural expectations and by the encouragement of others, but that commitment was not firmly embedded in their self-conceptions. Once they got to college, their commitment to work hard academically was easily dislodged by their first few adverse experiences and by the peer culture's devaluation of academics. In contrast, their commitment to the athletic role was entrenched, because this was their dream since childhood. No matter how little playing time they received or how much the coach criticized them, they clung to the primary self-identification as athletes....

As college athletes learned the nature of their new status they learned that they were seen as basketball players by nearly everyone they encountered. Their athletic identity pervaded and dominated the identity of their other roles in almost all other situations. This designation was true in their academic and social lives both on campus and off, and it grew more pervasive as they progressed through their playing careers and advanced to more visible team positions.... When people are constantly identified by one role to the near total exclusion of their others, they become increasingly committed to that role and it is likely to take precedence in influencing their self-conceptions....

Athletes' position at the university was characterized by "institutional powerlessness," as their coaches had the ability to control all aspects of their lives. By influencing their personal time, academic schedules, and playing role on the team, coaches could dominate not only their athletic role, but their social and academic roles as well. Regardless of the players' own goals, expectations, or desires, they had to take into consideration the wishes and demands of the coach. Players also believed...that the coach could...keep them eligible to play if he wanted, even if they got into academic difficulty. The omnipotence of their athletic over their academic role influenced them to shift greater identity salience to the role where the apparent power lay....

PART

V Social Change

■■■ ■

Like it or not, we are destined to live in the midst of rapid social change. Social change is one of the chief characteristics of our society. It is so extensive that little remains the same from one generation to the next. Social change is so swift that it can be difficult to keep up with it. We have to learn new skills—and relearn old ones. Although U.S. physicians receive a top notch education and are familiar with the latest developments in their profession, if they fail to continue reading journals and taking courses in their specialties, in a short time they fall woefully behind.

Some changes are small and of little consequence for our lives. A fast food outlet opens where a gas station used to be. The new models of cars sprout new lines—ever so slightly. Computers appear in new colors and shapes. Our college adds a course and drops another. A band, singer, author, or actor becomes an overnight sensation, then quickly drops from sight.

Other changes are large and have greater impact on us. Cities grow so greatly that they merge into one another, and no longer can you tell where one ends and the other leaves off. Increasingly, these megacities affect U.S. culture, changing the way we view life. Latinos immigrate to the United States in such vast numbers that they become the largest U.S. minority group. Upset about some social condition, people band together in social movements, their protests echoing through the culture.

In their effects, some changes are huge. As the globalization of capitalism sweeps jobs away from us, transplanting them into other parts of the world, our own economic future changes. The mass media become more powerful, increasingly shaping public opinion, and with it, the affairs of the nation. Computers change the way we work, how we become educated, and even how we fight wars. They even change the way we think, although this fundamental impact is so recent—and so subtle—that we currently have little understanding of it.

To conclude this book, then, we shall consider social change. Joan Moore and Raquel Pinderhughes open this final part by giving us a background for understanding the major changes that Latino immigration is bringing. Marlise Simons reports on a tribe of South American Indians who are facing a major onslaught as industrial life collides with their small group. The final selection that closes this part, written by a team of researchers, examines changes in the sex life of Americans.

14 ....

In the Barrios

Joan Moore and Raquel Pinderhughes

introduction ■ ■ ■ ■

Although they seem remote, urbanization and population changes are two of the most significant social events that affect our society and our own lives. As our society has urbanized—as increasing numbers of people have moved from village and farm to the city—cities have taken on a more significant role in determining U.S. culture and with it a greater significance in our own lives. To say *U.S. culture* today is to say *urban* culture. Similarly significant are changes in population, which sociologists call *demographic shifts*. On a global level, population growth and population shrinkage affect the welfare of nations. They set up conditions for vast migrations, bringing ethnic and cultural changes that transform nations.

A major demographic shift that is having its impact on the United States is the extensive migration of Latinos from Mexico and South America. This migration has been so huge during the past decade that Latinos have replaced African Americans as the largest ethnic group in the country. It is too early to tell what changes this demographic shift will bring to U.S. social institutions and to popular culture, but we can be certain that they will be extensive. In this selection, Joan Moore and Raquel Pinderhughes provide a background for understanding this fundamental change.

Thinking Critically

As you read this selection, ask yourself:

1. What changes to our social institutions and culture is this demographic shift likely to bring?

2. Why do the authors use the term *underclass* in this reading?

3. In referring to Latinos, how are these terms interrelated: economic restructuring, underclass, informal economy, immigration, and urban space?

In the publication *The Truly Disadvantaged,* William Julius Wilson's seminal work on persistent, concentrated poverty in Chicago's black neighborhoods, Wilson used the term "underclass" to refer to the new face of poverty, and traced its origins to economic restructuring. He emphasized the impact of persistent, concentrated poverty not only on individuals but on communities.

...The term "Hispanic" is used particularly by state bureaucracies to refer to individuals who reside in the United States who were born in, or trace their ancestry back to, one of twenty-three Spanish-speaking nations. Many of these individuals prefer to use the term "Latino."...

No matter what the details, when one examines the history of the term underclass among sociologists, it is clear that Wilson's 1987 work seriously jolted the somewhat chaotic and unfocused study of poverty in the United States. He described sharply increasing rates of what he called "pathology" in Chicago's black ghettos. By this, Wilson referred specifically to female headship, declining marriage rates, illegitimate births, welfare dependency, school dropouts, and youth crime. The changes in the communities he examined were so dramatic that he considered them something quite new.

Two of the causes of this new poverty were particularly important, and his work shifted the terms of the debate in two respects. First, Wilson argued effectively that dramatic increases in joblessness and long-term poverty in the inner city were a result of major economic shifts—economic restructuring. "Restructuring" referred to changes in the global economy that led to deindustrialization, loss and relocation of jobs, and a decline in the number of middle-level jobs—a polarization of the labor market. Second, he further fueled the debate about the causes and consequences of persistent poverty by introducing two neighborhood-level factors into the discussion. He argued that the outmigration of middle- and working-class people from the urban ghetto contributed to the concentration of poverty. These "concentration effects" meant that ghetto neighborhoods showed sharply increased proportions of very poor people. This, in turn, meant that residents in neighborhoods of concentrated poverty were isolated from "mainstream" institutions and role models. As a result, Wilson postulates, the likelihood of their engaging in "underclass behavior" was increased. Thus the social life of poor communities deteriorated because poverty intensified....

■ ■ ■ ▪ THE LATINO POPULATION—SOME BACKGROUND

American minorities have been incorporated into the general social fabric in a variety of ways. Just as Chicago's black ghettos reflect a history of slavery, Jim Crow legislation, and struggles for civil and economic rights, so the nation's Latino barrios reflect a history of conquest, immigration, and a struggle to maintain cultural identity....

This is an old population: as early as the sixteenth century, Spanish explorers settled what is now the American Southwest. In 1848, Spanish and Mexican settlers who lived in that region became United States citizens as a result of the Mexican-American War. Although the aftermath of conquest left a small elite population, the precarious position of the masses combined with the peculiarities of southwestern economic development to lay the foundation for poverty in the current period.

In addition to those Mexicans who were incorporated into the United States after the Treaty of Guadalupe Hidalgo, Mexicans have continually crossed the border into the United States, where they have been used as a source of cheap labor by U.S. employers. The volume of immigration from Mexico has been highly dependent on fluctuations in certain segments of the U.S. economy. This dependence became glaringly obvious [in the 1900s]. During the Great Depression of the 1930s state and local governments "repatriated" hundreds of thousands of unemployed Mexicans, and just a few years later World War II labor shortages reversed the process as Mexican contract-laborers (*braceros*) were eagerly sought. A little later, in the 1950s, massive deportations recurred when "operation Wetback" repatriated hundreds of thousands of Mexicans. Once again, in the 1980s, hundreds of thousands crossed the border to work in the United States, despite increasingly restrictive legislation.

High levels of immigration and high fertility mean that the Mexican-origin population is quite young—on the average, 9.5 years younger than the non-Latino population—and the typical household is large, with 3.8 persons, as compared with 2.6 persons in non-Latino households. Heavy immigration, problems in schooling, and industrial changes in the Southwest combine to constrain advancement. The occupational structure remains relatively steady, and though there is a growing middle class, there is also a growing number of very poor people....

[In 2000, 23] percent of all Puerto Rican families were below the poverty line. A growing proportion of these families were concentrated in poor urban neighborhoods located in declining industrial centers in the Northeast and Midwest, which experienced massive economic restructuring and diminished employment opportunities for those with less education and weaker skills. The rising poverty rate has also been linked to a dramatic increase in female-headed households. Recent studies show that the majority of recent migrants were not previously employed on the island. Many were single women who migrated with their young children (Falcon and Gurak 1991). Currently, Puerto Ricans are the most economically disadvantaged group of all Latinos. As a group they are poorer than African Americans.

Unlike other Latino migrants, who entered the United States as subordinate workers and were viewed as sources of cheap labor, the first large waves of Cuban refugees were educated middle- and upper-class professionals. Arriving in large numbers after Castro's 1959 revolution, Cubans were welcomed by the federal government as bona fide political refugees fleeing communism and were assisted in ways that significantly contributed to their economic well-being. Cubans had access to job-training programs and placement services, housing subsidies, English-language programs, and small-business loans. Federal and state assistance contributed to the growth of a vigorous enclave economy (with Cubans owning many of the businesses and hiring fellow Cubans) and also to the emergence of Miami as a center for Latin

American trade. Cubans have the highest family income of all Latino groups. Nevertheless in [2000, 17.3] percent of the Cuban population lived below the poverty line.

In recent years large numbers of Salvadorans and Guatemalans have come to the United States in search of refuge from political repression. But unlike Cubans, few have been recognized by the U.S. government as bona fide refugees. Their settlement and position in the labor market have been influenced by their undocumented (illegal) status. Dominicans have also come in large numbers to East Coast cities, many also arriving as undocumented workers. Working for the lowest wages and minimum job security, undocumented workers are among the poorest in the nation.

Despite their long history and large numbers, Latinos have been an "invisible minority" in the United States. Until recently, few social scientists and policy analysts concerned with understanding stratification and social problems in the United States have noticed them. Because they were almost exclusively concerned with relations between blacks and whites, social scientists were primarily concerned with generating demographic information on the nation's black and white populations, providing almost no information on other groups. Consequently, it has been difficult, sometimes impossible, to obtain accurate data about Latinos.

Latinos began to be considered an important minority group when census figures showed a huge increase in the population. By 1980 there were significant Latino communities in almost every metropolitan area in the nation. As a group, Latinos have low education, low family incomes, and are more clustered in low-paid, less-skilled occupations. Most Latinos live in cities, and poverty has become an increasing problem. On the whole, Latinos are more likely to live in poverty than the general U.S. population: poverty is widespread for all Latino subgroups except Cubans....

■ ■ ■ THE IMPORTANCE OF ECONOMIC RESTRUCTURING

The meaning of economic restructuring has shaped the debate about the urban underclass....

First, there is the "Rustbelt in the Sunbelt" phenomenon. Some researchers have argued that deindustrialization has been limited to the Rustbelt, and that the causal chain adduced by Wilson therefore does not apply outside that region. But the fact is that many Sunbelt cities developed manufacturing industries, particularly during and after World War II. Thus Rustbelt-style economic restructuring—deindustrialization, in particular—has also affected them deeply....

Second, there has been significant reindustrialization and many new jobs in many of these cities, a trend that is easily overlooked. Most of the expanding low-wage service and manufacturing industries, like electronics and garment manufacturing, employ Latinos and some depend almost completely on immigrant labor working at minimum wage. In short, neither the Rustbelt nor the Sunbelt has seen uniform economic restructuring.

Third, Latinos are affected by the "global cities" phenomenon, particularly evident in New York and Chicago. This term refers to a particular mix of new jobs and populations and an expansion of both high- and low-paid service jobs. When

large multinational corporations centralize their service functions, upper-level service jobs expand. The growing corporate elite want more restaurants, more entertainment, more clothing, and more care for their homes and children, but these new
consumer services usually pay low wages and offer only temporary and part-time
work. The new service workers in turn generate their own demand for low-cost
goods and services. Many of them are Latino immigrants and they create what Sassen calls a "Third World city...located in dense groupings spread all over the city":
this new "city" also provides new jobs (1989, p. 70)....

Fourth, even though the deindustrialization framework remains of overarching importance in understanding variations in the urban context of Latino poverty,
we must also understand that economic restructuring shows many different faces. It
is different in economically specialized cities. Houston, for example, has been called
"the oil capital of the world," and most of the devastating economic shifts in that
city were due to "crisis and reorganization in the world oil-gas industry." Miami is
another special case. The economic changes that have swept Miami have little to do
with deindustrialization, or with Europe or the Pacific Rim, and much to do with
the overpowering influence of its Cuban population, its important "enclave economy," and its "Latino Rim" functions.

Finally, economic change has a different effect in peripheral areas. Both Albuquerque and Tucson are regional centers in an economically peripheral area. Histor-
ically, these two cities served the ranches, farms, and mines of their desert
hinterlands. Since World War II, both became military centers, with substantial
high-tech defense industrialization. Both cities are accustomed to having a large,
poor Latino population, whose poverty is rarely viewed as a crisis. In Tucson, for
example, unemployment for Mexican Americans has been low, and there is stable
year-round income. But both cities remain marginal to the national economy, and
this means that the fate of their poor depends more on local factors.

Laredo has many features in common with other cities along the Texas border,
with its substantial military installations, and agricultural and tourist functions. All
of these cities have been affected by general swings in the American and Texan economy. These border communities have long been the poorest in the nation, and their
largely Mexican American populations have suffered even more from recent economic downturns. They are peripheral to the U.S. economy, but the important point
is that their economic well-being is intimately tied to the Mexican economy. They
were devastated by the collapse of the peso in the 1980s. They are also more involved than most American cities in international trade in illicit goods, and poverty
in Laredo has been deeply affected by smuggling. Though Texas has a long history
of discrimination against Mexican Americans, race is not an issue within Laredo itself, where most of the population—elite as well as poor—is of Mexican descent....

■ ■ ■ ■ THE INFORMAL AND ILLICIT ECONOMIES

The growth of an informal economy is part and parcel of late twentieth-century economic restructuring. Particularly in global cities, a variety of "informal" economic

activities proliferates—activities that are small-scale, informally organized, and largely outside government regulations. Some low-wage reindustrialization, for example, makes use of new arrangements in well-established industries (like home work in the garment industry, as seamstresses take their work home with them). Small-scale individual activities such as street vending and "handyman" house repairs and alterations affect communities in peripheral as well as global cities.... These money-generating activities are easily ignored by researchers who rely exclusively on aggregate data sources: they never make their way into the statistics on labor-market participation, because they are "off the books." But they play a significant role in the everyday life of many African American neighborhoods as well as in the barrios.

And, finally, there are illicit activities—most notoriously, a burgeoning drug market. There is not much doubt that the new poverty in the United States has often been accompanied by a resurgence of illicit economic activities. It is important to note that most of the Latino communities...have been able to contain or encapsulate such activities so that they do not dominate neighborhood life. But in most of them there is also little doubt that illicit economic activities form an "expanded industry." They rarely provide more than a pittance for the average worker: but for a very small fraction of barrio households they are part of the battery of survival strategies.

Researchers often neglect this aspect of the underclass debate because it is regarded as stigmatizing. However,...the neglect of significant income-generating activities curtails our understanding of the full range of survival strategies in poor communities. At the worst (as in Laredo) it means that we ignore a significant aspect of community life, including its ramifications in producing yet more overpolicing of the barrios. Even more important, many of these communities have been able to encapsulate illicit economic activities so that they are less disruptive. This capacity warrants further analysis.

■ ■ ■ ■ IMMIGRATION

Immigration—both international and from Puerto Rico—is of major significance for poor Latino communities in almost every city in every region of the country. Further, there is every reason to believe that immigration will continue to be important.

First, it has important economic consequences. Immigration is a central feature of the economic life of global cities: for example, Los Angeles has been called the "capital of the Third World" because of its huge Latino and Asian immigration.... The restructured economy provides marginal jobs for immigrant workers, and wage scales seem to drop for native-born Latinos in areas where immigration is high.... Immigrants are ineligible for most government benefits, are usually highly motivated, and are driven to take even the poorest-paying jobs. They are also more vulnerable to labor-market swings....

Though immigrants have been less important in the peripheral cities of Albuquerque, Laredo, and Tucson, each of these cities is special in some way. Albuquerque has attracted few Mexican immigrants, but it draws on a historical Latino labor pool—English-speaking rural *Manitos*—who are as economically exploitable as are Spanish-speaking immigrants from Mexico. Until recently Tucson was also largely bypassed by most Mexican immigrants. Instead, there is an old, relatively self-contained set of cross-border networks, with well-established pathways of family movement and mutual aid. Similar networks also exist in Laredo. Laredo's location on the border means that many of its workers are commuters—people who work in Laredo but live in Mexico....

The concentration of poverty comes about not only because of market forces or the departure of the middle classes for better housing; in Houston, Rodriguez shows that restructuring in real estate had the effect of concentrating poverty. Concentrated poverty can also result from government planning. Chicago's decision decades ago to build a concentration of high-rise housing projects right next to one another is a clear case in point. Another is in New York's largely Latino South Bronx, where the city's ten-year-plan created neighborhoods in which the least enterprising of the poor are concentrated, and in which a set of undesirable "Not-In-My-Back-Yard" institutions, such as drug-treatment clinics and permanent shelters for the homeless, were located. These neighborhoods are likely to remain as pockets of unrelieved poverty for many generations to come. It was not industrial decline and the exodus of stable working people that created these pockets: the cities of Chicago and New York chose to segregate their problem populations in permanent buildings in those neighborhoods....

■ ■ ■ OTHER ASPECTS OF URBAN SPACE...

Where a poor neighborhood is located makes a difference.

First, some are targets for "gentrification." This is traditionally viewed as a market process by which old neighborhoods are revitalized and unfortunate poor people displaced. But there is a different perspective. Sassen (1989) argues that gentrification is best understood in the context of restructuring, globalization, and politics. It doesn't happen everywhere...gentrification, along with downtown revitalization and expansion, affects Latino neighborhoods in Chicago, Albuquerque, New York, and west side Los Angeles. In Houston, a variant of "gentrification" is documented. Apartment owners who were eager to rent to Latino immigrants when a recession raised their vacancy rates were equally eager to "upgrade" their tenants when the economy recovered and the demand for housing rose once again. Latinos were "gentrified" out of the buildings.

Second, Latinos are an expanding population in many cities, and they rub up against other populations. Most of the allusions to living space center on ethnic frictions accompanying the expansion of Latino areas of residence. Ethnic succession is explicit in Albuquerque and in Chicago.... It is implicit in...Houston, with the immigration of Central Americans to Mexican American neighborhoods and the manipulated succession of Anglos and Latinos. In Albuquerque and East Los Angeles, Latinos are "filling-in" areas of the city, in a late phase of ethnic succession. Ethnic succession is *not* an issue in Laredo because the city's population is primarily of Mexican origin.

It is crucial in Miami, where new groups of immigrants are establishing themselves within the Latino community: newer immigrants tend to move into areas vacated by earlier Cuban arrivals, who leave for the suburbs. In Brooklyn, a different kind of urban ecological function is filled by the Puerto Rican barrio—that of an ethnic buffer between African American and Anglo communities. Los Angeles' Westlake area is most strongly affected by its location near downtown: it is intensely involved in both gentrification and problems of ethnic succession. Here the Central Americans displaced a prior population, and, in turn, their nascent communities are pressured by an expanding Koreatown to the west and by gentrification from the north and from downtown.

These details are important in themselves, but they also have implications for existing theories of how cities grow and how ethnic groups become segregated (and segregation is closely allied to poverty). Most such theories take the late nineteenth-century industrial city as a point of departure—a city with a strong central business district and clearly demarcated suburbs. In these models, immigrants initially settle in deteriorating neighborhoods near downtown. Meanwhile, earlier generations of immigrants, their predecessors in those neighborhoods, leapfrog out to "areas of second settlement," often on the edge of the city....

[In contrast with] the "traditional" Rustbelt pattern of ethnic location and ethnic succession,...new Latino immigrants are as likely to settle initially in communities on the edge of town (near the new jobs) as they are to move near downtown; or their initial settlement may be steered by housing entrepreneurs, as in Houston. The new ecology of jobs, housing, and shopping malls has made even the old Rustbelt cities like Chicago less clearly focused on a central downtown business district.

Housing for the Latino poor is equally distinctive. Poor communities in which one-third to one-half of the homes are owner-occupied would seem on the face of it to provide a different ambience from public housing—like the infamous phalanx of projects on Chicago's South Side that form part of Wilson's focus....

Finally, space is especially important when we consider Mexican American communities on the border. Mexican Americans in most border communities have important relationships with kin living across the border in Mexico, and this is certainly the case in Tucson and Laredo. But space is also important in economic matters. Shopping, working, and recreation are conditioned by the proximity of alternative opportunities on both sides of the border. And in Laredo the opportunities for illicit economic transactions also depend on location. The Laredo barrios in which illicit activities are most concentrated are located right on the Rio Grande River, where cross-border transactions are easier.

In sum, when we consider poor minority neighborhoods, we are drawn into a variety of issues that go well beyond the question of how poverty gets concentrated because middle-class families move out. We must look at the role of urban policy in addition to the role of the market. We must look at the factors that promote and sustain segregation. We must look at how housing is allocated, and where neighborhoods are located within cities. And, finally, we must look at how the location of a neighborhood facilitates its residents' activity in licit and illicit market activities.

REFERENCES

Falcon, Luis, and Douglas Gurak, 1991. "Features of the Hispanic Underclass: Puerto Ricans and Dominicans in New York." Unpublished manuscript.

Sassen, Saskia, 1989. "New Trends in the Sociospatial Organization of the New York City Economy." In Robert Beauregard, ed. *Economic Restructuring and Political Response.* Newberry Park, CA.

Wilson, William Julius, 1987. *The Truly Disadvantaged: The Inner City, the Underclass, and Public Policy.* Chicago: The University of Chicago Press.

Social Change
and Amazon Indians

Marlise Simons

introduction ■ ■ ■ ■

As Chapter 15 of *Essentials* explains, William F. Ogburn identified three processes of social change: *invention* (think of the changes ushered in by the automobile and computer), *discovery* (such as the discovery of gold in California), and *diffusion* (the spread of an invention or discovery from one group to another). Inventions that change our technology are an especially powerful source of social change. Because *technology* (tools—items used to accomplish tasks—and the techniques for using those tools) is integrated into a group's way of life, when a group changes its technology, its culture also changes. If the technological change is extensive, the culture can be transformed.

In contrast with the rapid pace of change in industrial and postindustrial societies, the way of life of tribal groups usually changes so slowly that even in hundred-year intervals little is noticeably different. If a group's environment stays fairly constant, the adjustments that a people have worked out remain viable and stable. Contact with groups that have sharply contrasting ways of life, however—as is happening with the Kaiapo Indians of Brazil featured in this selection by Marlise Simons—can rapidly undermine traditional ways of life. Note how the diffusion of technology from industrial society to the Kaiapo is not simply a matter of changes in housing, diet, and tools. This diffusion alters their traditional relationships and ultimately transforms their values. It even leads to a different way of viewing life itself.

Thinking Critically:

As you read this selection, ask yourself:

1. How is the diffusion of technology affecting the Kaiapo?

2. What difference does it make if settlers take over the Amazon jungle, displacing the tribes that live there? Isn't this simply an inevitable cost of the advancement of civilization?

3. If you were the head of the Indigenous Peoples Department of the government of Brazil and you wanted to help Indian tribes preserve their cultures, what would you do?

It is getting dark when Chief Kanhonk sits down in the yard outside his home, ready for a long evening of conversation. Night birds are calling from the bush that sparkles with fireflies. Whooping frogs make a racket by the river. No one seems worried by the squadron of bats sweeping low overhead.

It is that important moment of the day when Indians of the Amazon, who use no written language, meet to talk, pass on information, and tell stories. The night is when they recall ancestral customs, interpret dreams, and comment on changes in nature and other events of the day. But from a nearby home come the sounds of a powerful rival: a television set is screeching cartoons at a group of children. I under-stand now why, that morning, by way of saying hello, these naked children of the rain forest had shouted things like "He-Man" and "Flintstones."

Three years ago, when money from the sale of gold nuggets and mahogany trees was pouring into Gorotire, Chief Kanhonk agreed to bring in television, or the "big ghost," as it is called here. A shiny satellite dish now stands on the earthen plaza like an alien sculpture, signaling that Gorotire—a small settlement of some 800 people on the Fresco River, a tributary of the Amazon—has become one of the wealthiest Indian villages in Brazil.

Yet Chief Kanhonk appears to regret his decision. "I have been saying that people must buy useful things like knives or fishing hooks," he says darkly. "Televi-sion does not fill the stomach. It only shows our children and grandchildren white people's things."

The "big ghost" is just one of the changes that have been sweeping over Gor-otire, but it seems to be worrying the elders the most. Some believe it is powerful enough to rob them of their culture. Bebtopup, the oldest medicine man in the vil-lage, explains his misgivings: "The night is the time the old people teach the young people. Television has stolen the night."

When I discuss this with Eduardo Viveiros, a Brazilian anthropologist who works with a more isolated Amazonian tribe, he seems less worried. "At least they quickly understood the consequences of watching television," he says. "Many peo-ple never discover. Now Gorotire can make a choice."

It was the issue of choice that first drew me to the Kaiapo Indians of the lower Amazon Basin. They seemed to be challenging the widely held notion that forest In-dians are defenseless in face of the pressures of the competitive and predatory West-ern world around them. Unlike most of Brazil's 230,000 Indians, they go out into the white world to defend their interests, and it is no longer unusual to see Kaiapo men—in their stunning body paint and feathered headdresses—showing up in Congress in Brasilia, the nation's capital, or lobbying by doing a war dance outside a Government office. They have even bought Western gadgets to record and film their festivals.

Once the masters of immense stretches of forest and savannas, the Kaiapo were for hundreds of years among the most skillful farmers and hunters and fiercest war-riors of central Brazil. They terrified other tribes with their raids. From the 17th to the 19th centuries, they not only resisted the slaving raids of the Portuguese invaders but they also attacked white traders and gold prospectors with such a vengeance that

From "The Amazon's Savvy Indians," by Marlise Simons, *The New York Times Magazine*, February 26, 1989. Copyright © 1989 by Marlise Simons. Reprinted by permission of The New York Times Syndicate.

royal orders came from Portugal to destroy the Kaiapo. The white man's wrath and his diseases killed many, yet there are still close to 3,600 Kaiapo in more than a dozen different villages near the Xingu River. They have quarreled and regrouped, but their lands, several vast reservations, are more secure than those of many other tribes.

After many years of isolation to the forest, the Kaiapo now have to deal with the growing encroachments of white society. "They are going through a great transition," says Darrell Posey, an American anthropologist who has worked in Gorotire for more than a decade. "Their survival is a miracle in itself. But I worry whether they can go on making the changes on their own terms."

Colombia, Ecuador, Peru, and Venezuela—four of nine nations in the Amazon Basin, which harbors some 800,000 Indians—each have large numbers of tropical-forest Indians. But nowhere are pressures on Indian land as great as they are in Brazil. As the Amazon is opened up, developers bring in highways, settlers, cattle ranchers, mines and hydroelectric dams. In Brazil alone, more than 90 tribes...disappeared [during the 1900s].

The clearing of large areas of the rain forest and the fate of the Indians are also rapidly becoming an issue of international concern. Interest in the region has risen as ecological concerns, such as ozone depletion, the greenhouse effect, and other changes in the global environment become political issues. More attention is paid to scientists who are alarmed at the destruction of the rain forest—a vital flywheel in the world's climate and the nursery of at least half of the world's plant and animal species.

This has also prompted an increasing interest in the highly structured world of the forest Indians and their ancient and intricate knowledge of nature that permits them to survive in the tropical jungle without destroying it....

As Indians find greater support among environmentalists, they also get more organized in their fight to protect their habitat. The Kaiapo held their first international congress...in Altamira, in central Brazil, protesting Government plans to build several massive dams that would flood Indian land.

In Brazil, Indian tribes occupy 10 percent of the nation's territory, although much of their land has not been demarcated. Brazil's past military regimes elevated Indian affairs to a national-security issue, because many tribes live in large areas of border land. It is official policy to integrate Indians into the larger society, and the National Indian Foundation, with its 4,900 employees, is in charge of implementing this.

In my 18 years in Latin America, I have heard many politicians and anthropologists discuss what is usually called "the Indian problem," what to "do" about cultures that have changed little in thousands of years. One school of thought holds that the remote tribes should be kept isolated and protected until they can slowly make their own choices. Another school accepts that the Indian world is on the wane, and talks about "guiding" the Indians toward inevitable change—a process that should take several generations.

But some anthropologists and politicians, including the Brazilian Government, believe in still more rapid integration. When Romeo Jucá was head of the Indian Foundation, he said that it was only right for Indians to exploit their wealth, even if it meant acculturation. "We have to be careful how fast we go," he said, "but being Indian does not mean you have to be poor."

Gerardo Reichel-Dolmatoff is one of Latin America's most respected anthropologists. He insists that the Indians are their own best guides into Western society. An Austrian-born Colombian, Reichel-Dolmatoff has worked in Colombia's forests, at the Amazon's headwaters, for almost fifty years. "We cannot choose for them," he insists. "And we cannot put them into reserves, ghettos, ashokas. They are not museum exhibits.... If Indians choose the negative aspects of our civilization, we cannot control that. If there is one basic truth in anthropology, it is that cultures change. Static cultures do not exist."

The Indians themselves are pleading for more protection and respect for their cultures. Conrad Gorinsky, son of a Guyana Indian mother and himself a chemist in London, recently said: "We don't want the Indians to change because we have them comfortably in the back of our mind like a kind of ShangriLa, something we can turn to even if we work ourselves to death in New York. But we are hounding and maligning them instead of recognizing them as the guardians of the forests, of the world's genetic banks, of our germ plasm and lifelines."

The aboriginal peoples we call Indians are as different from one another as, say, Europeans are. Even the most isolated groups remain separate fiefdoms with widely varying experiences, beliefs, and histories. The degree of contact they have with the outside world is just as varied.

I first met Kaiapo tribesmen three years ago in Belém, a large city at the mouth of the Amazon. I saw them again in Brasilia, the capital. In both places, they demonstrated their political skills and capacity to mobilize, showing up in large numbers to protest measures by the Government. They seemed particularly adept at commanding the attention of the press. Their body paint, feathers, and other paraphernalia made them appear warlike, exotic, and photogenic.

Back in Gorotire, as it turns out, they are more "ordinary." Wearing feathers and beads, explains Kubei, a chief's son, is for special occasions. "It's our suit and tie." Besides the satellite dish, the Kaiapo also have their own small airplane. Their new wealth has also given them the luxury of hiring non-Indians to help plant new fields. But they remain ready to attack white intruders; some of the adult men have markings on their chests that record the number of outsiders they have killed.

Two roads fan out from the center of Gorotire. A new sand track leads east on a five-hour drive to the town of Redenção. The other road goes south and, in a sense, it leads into the past. Dipping into the forest, it becomes a path that meanders through open patches where the Kaiapo women grow corn, sweet potatoes, bananas, manioc. On the plain ahead, it joins an ancient trail system that once reached for hundreds of miles into northern and western Brazil.

One morning, Bebtopup (medicine man, shaman, connoisseur of nature), the anthropologist Darrell Posey (who speaks the Kaiapo language), and I wander into the bush. Bebtopup walks past the plants the way you go down a street where you know everyone. Stopping, nodding, his face lighting up with happy recognition, he sometimes goes into a song—a soft, high-pitch chant for a particular plant.

He picks leaves, each one familiar, each one useful. One serves to remove body hair. Another, he says, can prevent pregnancy. The underside of one leaf is so rough it is used to sandpaper wood and file fingernails. Bebtopup collects his plants in the morning, he says, because "that is when they have the most strength."

Stopping at a shrub, we look at the large circle around its stem, where nothing grows. "This and other plants have been sent to a laboratory for analysis," says Posey. 'We think this one has a natural weedkiller."

Bebtopup holds up a branch of what he calls the "eye of the jaguar." "This was our flashlight," he says, showing how to set it afire and swing it gently so its strong glow will light one's path.

One afternoon, when the heat has crept into everything, the women and children come back from the fields to their village. They stop and sit in a creek to escape the swirling gnats and buzzing bees. Others sit outside their homes, going about their age-old business. One woman plucks the radiant feathers of a dead macaw. Another removes her eyebrows and eyelashes, because the Kaiapo women think they are ugly. (A nurse once told me that this custom might have a hygienic origin—to ward off parasites, for instance.) Kaiapo women also deepen their foreheads by shaving the top of their head in a triangle that reaches the crown—a fearsome sight to the unaccustomed eye.

I envy a mother who is clearly enjoying herself fingerpainting her three children. She draws black designs with genipap juice. On the face and the feet she puts red dye from the "urucu," or annatto, plant; Indians say it keeps away chiggers and ticks.

Change has come to Gorotire along the other road, the one leading east to Redenção. Recent Kaiapo history is full of "firsts," but a notable turning point came when prospectors struck gold on Gorotire land in 1980. The Kaiapo raided the camp, 20 miles from the village, but failed to drive away the trespassers. Then they made a deal.

Last fall, when I was visiting Gorotire, about 2,000 gold diggers were stripping the land to the bone farther upstream, and the River Fresco passed the village the color of mud, its water contaminated with oil and mercury. I heard no one complain about that. Gorotire gets 7 percent of the mine's profit—several pounds of gold a week.

In 1984, a lumber company completed the first road. It signed a contract with the Indian Foundation for Gorotire's mahogany (the Indians are wards of the Brazilian Government). Most of the mahogany is gone now, and the Government agency split the profits with the Kaiapo. Gorotire chose to spend its gold and timber profits on new water and electricity lines and rows of brick houses. Only about half of the inhabitants now live in traditional palm-frond huts.

The young Kaiapo who earn a salary as supervisors at the gold camp have bought their own gas stoves, radios, sofas, and mattresses. For the community, the four tribal chiefs ordered several boats, trucks, and a small plane that ferries people and goods among nearby Kaiapo villages.

One evening, a truck arriving from Redenção—bringing rice, sugar, bottled gas, oil for the generator—is another reminder of how fast Gorotire is adapting to a Western economy. From being a largely self-sufficient community of hunters and farmers, it is now increasingly dependent on outside goods. In Gorotire, it is clearly money, no longer disease or violence, that has become the greatest catalyst for change. Money has given the Kaiapo the means and the confidence to travel and lobby for their rights. At the same time, it is making them more vulnerable.

I have seen other villages where Indians have received large sums of money—for the passage of a railroad or a powerline, or from a mining company. Such money is usually released in installments, through banks, but its arrival has put new strains on the role of the chiefs. Money and goods have introduced a new, materialistic expression of power in societies that have been egalitarian. Among most Indians, a man's prestige has always depended not on what he acquires but on what he gives away.

In Gorotire, some of the young men complain that the chiefs are not distributing community money and goods equally, that the chiefs' relatives and favorites are getting a bigger share and more privileges.

Darrell Posey, the anthropologist, believes the greatest political change came with the road. With it, he says, "the Kaiapo chiefs lost control of which people and what goods would come in." Previously, the chiefs had been the sole distributors. They had also played the vital roles of keeping the peace and leading the ceremonies. Now, the chiefs hardly know the liturgy of the ceremonies; their main task seems to be to deal with the outside world.

The transition is also changing the role of the medicine man. Bebtopup, for example, has an arsenal of remedies for the common ailments—fevers, diarrheas, snake bites, wounds. But he and his colleagues have lost prestige because they do not know how to deal with the diseases brought to Gorotire by white men, such as the pneumonia that strikes the children and the malaria spreading from the gold miners' camp.

Anthropologists sometimes say that when outsiders visit the Indian world, they often focus on themes central not to Indians but to themselves. This might explain why I was so bothered by the garbage, the flotsam of Western civilization.

Gorotire's setting is Arcadian. It lies on a bluff overlooking the River Fresco, with views of the forests across and the mountains behind. Spring rains bring waterfalls and blossoms. But these days the village is awash with rusting cans, plastic wrappers, tapes sprung from their cassettes, discarded mattresses, and clothes. New domestic animals such as dogs, pigs, and ducks have left a carpet of droppings. And giant rats, which suddenly appeared some years ago, seem to be everywhere; some have bitten small children.

"Indians have never had garbage that was not biodegradable," says Sandra Machado, a Brazilian researching Kaiapo farming techniques here. "No one wants to take care of it."

It is a mild moonlit evening, and in the men's house many Kaiapo are watching soccer on television. The bank of the river is a quieter place to talk.

"If you look beyond the garbage and the stone houses, this is still a strong and coherent indigenous culture," says Darrell Posey, speaking of the mixed feelings he has about a decade of developments in Gorotire. "Despite everything, the language is alive; the festivals and initiation rights are observed."

Posey says that the Kaiapo in Gorotire and in other villages continue with their age-old natural farming techniques, using plants to fix nitrogen in the soil, chunks of termite nests instead of chemical fertilizers, plant infusions to kill pests, the nests of ferocious ants to protect fruit trees from other ant predators.

Biologists often complain that there have been many studies of exotic rituals, paraphernalia, and kinships of Indians, but that Western science has paid scant attention to the Indians' use of animals and plants.

Like others working in the Amazon region, Posey worries about the gap between the old and the young. "The old chiefs are turning over decisions to the young because they can drive a truck or operate a video machine or go to the bank," he says, "But the young people don't see the relevance of learning the tribal knowledge, and it's being lost."

"You can afford to lose one generation," he adds, "because grandparents do the teaching of their grandchildren. But you cannot afford to lose two generations."

Gorotire has a small Government school, designed to help Indians integrate into the national society. The teacher, who speaks only Portuguese, has started organizing annual Independence Day parades. On the blackboard is a list of patriotic holidays, including Independence Day and the Day of the Soldier. I ask the children later what a soldier is, "Something of white people," one of them says.

Chief Poropot agrees that everyone must learn Portuguese. "The language of the Kaiapo is very ancient, and it will never end," he says. "But the women and the children need to learn Portuguese to defend themselves."

Defend themselves?

"If they go to shop in Redenção, they have to talk," he says. "If they get sick, they cannot tell the doctor what they have."

Thirty miles from Gorotire, in the village of Aukre, another Kaiapo tribe is choosing a different strategy for change. Its best-known member is Paiakan, 37 years old, the son of Chief Tikiri.

Calm and articulate, Paiakan has been named to "keep an eye on the whites" in the state capital of Belém. He acts as a kind of roving ambassador for the Kaiapo, even though each village is autonomous. When Kaiapo interests are threatened, he sends out warnings to the communities.

Paiakan's contacts with the outside world and the many pitfalls it holds for Indians have made him more conservative, he says, more so than in the early days, in the 1970's, when he first left home to work on the Trans-Amazonian Highway. As his father's main adviser, he has insisted that Aukre remain a traditional village.

It is built in the age-old circle of mud-and-thatch huts. There is no television, running water, pigs, or piles of garbage. Paiakan and his father have also banned logging and gold digging. This appears to have saved Aukre from the consumerism—and widespread influenza and malaria—of Gorotire.

"The lumber men have come to us with their bags of money," he says. "And we know we have a lot of gold. But we do not want to bring a lot of money in. The Indian still does not know the value of white man's objects or how to treat them." Paiakan cites clothing as an example. "The Indian wears something until it is stiff with dirt; then he throws it out."

But people now want things from the "world of the whites," he continues. "Pressure from the white society is so strong; there is no wall that can stop it." It is the task of the chief to measure the change, provide explanations, he says. "If someone wants to get a radio or a tape recorder, the chiefs cannot stop it."

In Aukre where two aging chiefs are still in charge of buying goods for the community, they say that they will not buy gadgets. "We explain we cannot buy this thing for you because we do not have the batteries you need, and we cannot repair it," Paiakan says.

Of late, Paiakan has been invited abroad to campaign for the protection of the rain forest. He knows the problem only too well. Ranchers have moved almost to the reservation's doorstep, felled trees, and set massive forest fires. Because of deforestation, there have been unusual changes in the water level of the Fresco River.

"Our people are getting very disoriented," says Paiakan. "It would be as if people from another planet came to your cities and started to tear down your houses. The forest is our home." With all the destruction going on, he continues, "the breath of life is drifting up and away from us."

At the age of 78 and retired from teaching at the University of California at Los Angeles, the anthropologist Gerardo Reichel-Dolmatoff lives in Bogotá, Colombia, and is still writing. After studying changes in the Amazon for five decades, he is not optimistic about the prospects for the Indians.

"In Colombia, I don't know of a single case where an aboriginal culture has found a strong adaptive mechanism," he says. "Physical survival is possible. But I have not seen the ancient values replaced by a workable value system. I wish I could be more positive. But in 50 years I have seen too many traditions being lost, too many tribes disappear.

"For 500 years we have witnessed the destruction of the Indians. Now we are witnessing the destruction of the habitat. I suggest more field work, and immediate field work, because soon it will be too late."

At a conference on ethnobiology..., Reichel-Dolmatoff urged scientists to insist on spreading the message that Western science has much to learn from Indians, from their well-adapted lives and deeply-felt beliefs, their view that whatever man subtracts he must restore by other means.

What suggestions has he made to Indians?

"Indians have to stay in touch with their language—that is absolutely essential," he says. "It embodies their thought patterns, their values, their philosophy." Moreover, he says, talented young Indians should be given a modern academic education, but also the chance to keep in touch with their people. "They come from cultures based on extraordinary realism and imagery. They should not be forced to enter at the lowest level of our society."

One night, I ask the chiefs in Gorotire: What happens if the gold runs out? After all, most of the mahogany is already gone. Young tribesmen have wanted to invest some of the income, and the chiefs have accepted the idea. Gorotire has bought a home in Belém for Kaiapo who travel there, as well as three houses in Redençáo. There is talk of buying a farm, a curious thought, perhaps for a community that lives on eight million acres of land. But the Kaiapo, so they say, want it so that white farmers can grow rice for them.

And there is talk of planting new mahogany trees. Soon the conversation turns to a bird that a tribesman explains is very important. It is the bird, he says, that spreads the mahogany seeds.

READING 16 ■

How Many Sexual Partners Do Americans Have?

Robert T. Michael, John H. Gagnon, Edward O. Laumann, and Gina Kolata

introduction ■ ■ ■ ■ ■

Human sexual behavior is one of the many fascinating aspects of social life that sociologists study. This aspect of social life is significant because it involves not only social relationships but also a central part of our personal identity—our feelings of self, of who we are. Yet when sociologists investigate this vital area of human behavior, they meet resistance and suspicion. Resistance comes from people who feel that human sexuality is solely a private matter and no prying sociologist should examine it. Suspicion is generalized, coming from a great number of people who feel that the sociologist's motives are somehow impure and improper. If sociologists do research on teenage sexuality, they are thought to harbor secret fantasies. If they do research on prostitutes, they are thought to visit prostitutes under cover of night. If they gather data on homosexual behavior, they are thought to be closet homosexuals. No matter what area of sexual behavior they investigate, they are suspected of fantasies, secret longings, or some sort of sexual deviance.

This risk to reputation and relationships (which often comes with side remarks and smirking) is not faced by sociologists who investigate voting behavior or changes in food preference. These researchers do not come under suspicion or derision as people who may covertly want to undermine democracy or who harbor secret food longings. As a consequence, few sociologists investigate human sexual behavior, despite its high significance for understanding social life. Some do, however, and this selection by Robert Michael, John Gagnon, Edward Laumann, and Gina Kolata provides an update on changing human sexual behavior.

Thinking Critically

As you read this selection, ask yourself:

1. In the introduction to this selection, the editor says that unlike those who do research on political behavior, sociologists who study human sexual behavior risk reputation and relationships. Why do you think this is so?

2. This selection underscores the significance and influence of marriage. What evidence do you find for this statement?

3. Based on this reading, how has the sexual behavior of Americans changed? Why?

Sometimes, the myths about sex contain a grain of truth. The common perception is that Americans today have more sexual partners than they did just a decade or two ago. That, it turns out, is correct. A third of Americans who are over age fifty have had five or more sexual partners in their lifetime. But half of all Americans aged thirty to fifty have had five or more partners even though being younger, they had fewer years to accumulate them.

Still, when we ask older or younger people how many partners they had in the past year, the usual reply is zero or one. Something must have changed to make younger people accumulate more partners over a lifetime, yet sustain a pattern of having no partners or only one in any one year. The explanation is linked to one of our most potent social institutions and how it has changed.

That institution is marriage, a social arrangement so powerful that nearly everyone participates. About 90 percent of Americans have married by the time they are thirty, and a large majority spends much of their adulthood as part of a wedded couple. And marriage, we find, regulates sexual behavior with remarkable precision. No matter what they did before they wed, no matter how many partners they had, the sexual lives of married people are similar. Despite the popular myth that there is a great deal of adultery in marriage, our data and other reliable studies do not find it. Instead, a vast majority are faithful while the marriage is intact....

So, yes, many young people probably are having sexual intercourse with a fair number of partners. But that stops with marriage. The reason that people now have more sexual partners over their lifetimes is that they are spending a longer period sexually active, but unmarried. The period has lengthened from both ends and in the middle. The average age at which people have their first sexual intercourse has crept down and the average age at which people marry for the first time has edged up. And people are more likely to divorce now, which means they have time between marriages when they search for new partners once again.

To draw these conclusions, we looked at our respondents' replies to a variety of questions. First, we asked people when they first had heterosexual intercourse. Then, we asked what happens between the time when people first have intercourse and when they finally marry. How many partners do they have? Do they have more than one partner at any one time or do they have their partners in succession, practicing serial monogamy? We asked how many people divorced and how long they remained unmarried. Finally, we asked how many partners people had in their lifetimes.

In our analyses of the numbers of sex partners, we could not separately analyze patterns for gay men and lesbians. That is because homosexuals are such a small percentage of our sample that we do not have enough people in our survey to draw valid conclusions about this aspect of sexual behavior.

If we are going to look at heterosexual partners from the beginning, from the time that people first lose their virginity, we plunge headfirst into the maelstrom of teenage sex, always a turbulent subject, but especially so now, in the age of AIDS.

While society disputes whether to counsel abstinence from sexual intercourse or to pass out condoms in high schools, it also must grapple with a basic question: Has sexual behavior among teenagers changed? Are more having sexual intercourse and at younger ages, or is the overheated rhetoric a reaction to fears, without facts? The answer is both troubling and reassuring to the majority of adults who prefer teenagers to delay their sexual activity—troubling because most teenagers are having intercourse, but reassuring because sexual intercourse tends to be sporadic during the teen years.

We saw a steadily declining age at which teenagers first had sexual intercourse. Men and women born in the decade 1933–1942 had sex [for the first time] at an average age of about eighteen. Those born twenty to thirty years later have an average age at first intercourse that is about six months younger, as seen in Figure 1. The figure also indicates that the men report having sex at younger ages than the women. It also shows that blacks report a younger age at first intercourse than whites.

Another way to look at the age at first intercourse is illustrated in Figure 2. The figure shows the proportions of teenagers and young adults who experienced sexual intercourse at each age from twelve to twenty-five. To see at what age half the people

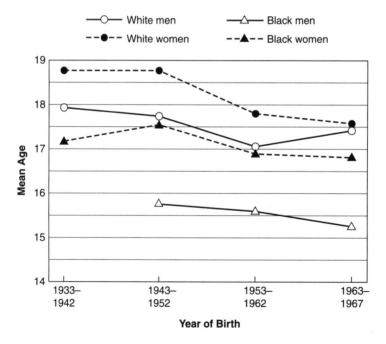

FIGURE 1   Mean Age at First Intercourse

Note: This includes respondents who had vaginal intercourse no later than age twenty-five and who have reached their twenty-fifth birthday by the date of the interview. [There were an] insufficient number of cases [to show Hispanics]. Whites computed from cross-section sample; blacks computed from cross-section and the over-sample.

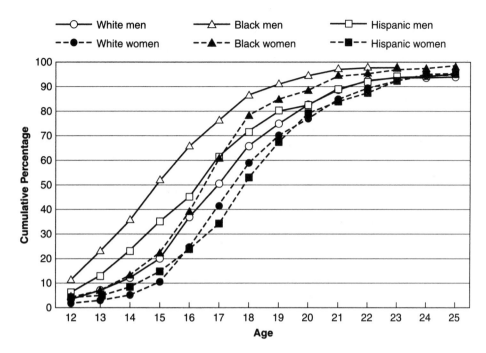

FIGURE 2   Cumulative Percentage Who Have Had Intercourse [by Age 25]

Note: Cumulative percentage indicates the proportion of respondents of a given group at a given age. This figure only includes respondents who have reached their twenty-fifth birthday by the date of the interview.

had intercourse, for example, follow the…horizontal line that corresponds to a cumulative frequency of 50 percent. It shows that half of all black men had intercourse by the time they were fifteen, half of all Hispanic men had intercourse by the time they were about sixteen and a half, half of all black women had intercourse by the time they were nearly seventeen, and half the white women and half the Hispanic women had intercourse by the time they were nearly eighteen. By age twenty-two, about 90 percent of each group had intercourse.

The patterns are crystal clear. About half the teenagers of various racial and ethnic groups in the nation have begun having intercourse with a partner in the age range of fifteen to eighteen, and at least four out of five have had intercourse by the time their teenage years are over. Since the average age of marriage is now in the mid-twenties, few Americans wait until they marry to have sex….

It's a change that built up for years, making it sometimes hard to appreciate just how profound it is. Stories of what sex among the unmarried was like decades ago can be startling. Even people who were no longer teenagers, and who were engaged, felt overwhelming social pressure to refrain from intercourse before marriage….

In addition to having intercourse at younger ages, many people also are marrying later—a change that is the real legacy of the late 1960s and early 1970s. This period was not, we find, a sexual revolution, a time of frequent sex with many partners for all. Instead, it was the beginning of a profound change in the sexual life course, providing the second reason why Americans have accumulated more partners now than in decades past.

Since the 1960s, the route to the altar is no longer so predictable as it used to be. In the first half of the twentieth century, almost everyone who married followed the same course: dating, love, a little sexual experimentation with one partner, sometimes including intercourse, then marriage and children. It also was a time when there was a clear and accepted double standard—men were much more likely to have had intercourse with several women before marrying than women were to have had intercourse with several men.

At the dawn of the millennium, we are left with a nation that still has this idealized heterosexual life course but whose actual course has fragmented in the crucial years before marriage. Some people still marry at eighteen, others at thirty, leading to very different numbers of sexual partners before marriage. Social class plays a role, with less-educated people marrying earlier than better-educated people. Blacks tend to marry much later than whites, and a large number of blacks do not marry at all.

But a new and increasingly common pattern has emerged: affection or love and sex with a number of partners, followed by affection, love, and cohabitation. This cycles back to the sexual marketplace, if the cohabitation breaks up, or to marriage. Pregnancy can occur at any of these points, but often occurs before either cohabitation or marriage. The result is that the path toward marriage, once so straight and narrow, has begun to meander and to have many side paths, one of which is being trodden into a well-traveled lane.

That path is the pattern of living together before marriage. Like other recent studies, ours shows a marked shift toward living together rather than marriage as the first union of couples. With an increase in cohabitation, the distinctions among having a steady sexual partner, a live-in sexual partner, and a marriage have gotten more fuzzy. This shift began at the same time as talk of a sexual revolution. Our study shows that people who came of age before 1970 almost invariably got married without first living together, while the younger people seldom did. But, we find, the average age at which people first move in with a partner—either by marrying, or living together—has remained nearly constant, around age twenty-two for men and twenty for women. The difference is that now that first union is increasingly likely to be a cohabitation....

With the increase in cohabitation, people are marrying later, on average. The longer they wait, however, the more likely they are to live with a sexual partner in the meantime. Since many couples who live together break up within a short time and seek a new partner, the result has been an increase in the average number of partners that people have before they marry....

Finally, we can look at divorce rates, another key social change that began in the 1960s and that has led to increasing numbers of partners over a lifetime.... For example, we can look at how likely it is that a couple will be divorced by the tenth anniversary of their marriage. For people born between 1933 and 1942, the chance was about one in five. For those born between 1943 and 1952, the chance was one in three. For those born between 1953 and 1962, the chance was closer to 38 percent. Divorced people as a group have more sexual partners than people who remain married and they are more likely, as a group, to have intercourse with a partner and live with a partner before they marry again.

These three social trends—earlier first intercourse, later marriage, and more frequent divorce—help explain why people now have more sexual partners over their lifetimes.

To discern the patterns of sexual partnering, we asked respondents how many sexual partners they had. We could imagine several scenarios. People could find one partner and marry. Or they could have sex with several before marrying. Or they could live with their partners first and then marry. Or they could simply have lots of casual sex, never marrying at all or marrying but also having extramarital sex.

Since our respondents varied in age from eighteen to fifty-nine, the older people in the study, who married by their early twenties, would have been married by the time the turbulent 1960s and 1970s came around. Their premarital behavior would be a relic from the past, telling us how much intercourse people had in the days before sex became so public an issue. The younger people in our study can show us whether there is a contrast between the earlier days and the decades after a sexual revolution was proclaimed. We can ask if they have more partners, if they have more than one sexual partner at a time, and if their sexual behavior is markedly different from that of the older generations that preceded them.

Most young people today show no signs of having very large numbers of partners. More than half the men and women in America who were eighteen to twenty-four in 1992 had just one sex partner in the past year and another 11 percent had none in the last year. In addition, studies in Europe show that people in the United Kingdom, France, and Finland have sexual life courses that are virtually the same as the American life course. The picture that emerges is strikingly different from the popular image of sexuality running out of control in our time.

In fact, we find, nearly all Americans have a very modest number of partners, whether we ask them to enumerate their partners over their adult lifetime or in the past year. The number of partners varies little with education, race, or religion. Instead, it is determined by marital status or by whether a couple is living together. Once married, people tend to have one and only one partner, and those who are unmarried and living together are almost as likely to be faithful.

Our data for the United States are displayed in Table 1.

The right-hand portion of Table 1 tells how many sexual partners people had since they turned eighteen. Very few, just 3 percent, had no partners, and few, just 9 percent, had a total of more than twenty partners.

The oldest people in our study, those aged fifty-five to fifty-nine, were most likely to have had just one sexual partner in their lifetimes—40 percent said they had had only one. This reflects the earlier age of marriage in previous generations and the low rate of divorce among these older couples. Many of the men were married by age twenty-two and the women by age twenty.

TABLE 1   Number of Sex Partners in Past Twelve Months and since Age Eighteen

	SEX PARTNERS PAST TWELVE MONTHS				SEX PARTNERS SINCE AGE EIGHTEEN					
	0	*1*	*2 to 4*	*5+*	*0*	*1*	*2 to 4*	*5 to 10*	*10 to 20*	*21+*
Total	12%	71%	14%	3%	3%	26%	30%	22%	11%	9%
Gender										
Men	10	67	18	5	3	20	21	23	16	17
Women	14	75	10	2	3	31	36	20	6	3
Age										
18–24	11	57	24	9	8	32	34	15	8	3
25–29	6	72	17	6	2	25	31	22	10	9
30–34	9	73	16	2	3	21	29	25	11	10
35–39	10	77	11	2	2	19	30	25	14	11
40–44	11	75	13	1	1	22	28	24	14	12
45–49	15	75	9	1	2	26	24	25	10	14
50–54	15	79	5	0	2	34	28	18	9	9
55–59	32	65	4	0	1	40	28	15	8	7
Marital status										
Never married, noncohabiting	25	38	28	9	12	15	29	21	12	12
Never married, cohabiting	1	75	20	5	0	25	37	16	10	13
Married	2	94	4	1	0	37	28	19	9	7
Divorced, separated, widowed, noncohabiting	31	41	26	3	0	11	33	29	15	12
Divorced, separated, widowed, cohabiting	1	80	15	3	0	0	32	44	12	12
Education										
Less than high school	16	67	15	3	4	27	36	19	9	6
High school graduate or equivalent	11	74	13	3	3	30	29	20	10	7
Some college, vocational	11	71	14	4	2	24	29	23	12	9
Finished college	12	69	15	4	2	24	26	24	11	13
Master's/advanced degree	13	74	10	3	4	25	26	23	10	13
Current Religion										
None	11	68	13	7	3	16	29	20	16	16
Mainline Protestant	11	73	13	2	2	23	31	23	12	8
Conservative Protestant	13	70	14	3	3	30	30	20	10	7
Catholic	12	71	13	3	4	27	29	23	8	9
Jewish	3	75	18	3	0	24	13	30	17	17
Other religion	15	70	12	3	3	42	20	16	8	13
Race/Ethnicity										
White	12	73	12	3	3	26	29	22	11	9
Black	13	60	21	6	2	18	34	24	11	11
Hispanic	11	69	17	2	4	35	27	17	8	9
Asian	15	77	8	0	6	46	25	14	6	3
Native American	12	76	10	2	5	28	35	23	5	5

Note: Row percentages total 100 percent.

The left-hand portion of Table 1 shows the number of sexual partners that people had in the past twelve months. These are the data that show how likely people are to remain faithful to their sexual partner, whether or not they are married. Among married people, 94 percent had one partner in the past year. Couples who were living together were almost as faithful. Seventy-five percent of people who had never married but were living together had one partner in the past year. Eighty percent of people who were previously married and were cohabiting when we questioned them had one partner in the past year. Two-thirds of the single people who were not living with a partner had no partners or only one in the past year. Only a few percent of the population had as many as five partners for sexual intercourse in the past year, and many of these were people who were never married and were not living with anyone. They were mostly young and mostly male.

One way to imagine the patterns of sexual partners is to think of a graph, with the vertical axis showing numbers of partners and the horizontal axis showing a person's age. The graph will be a series of blips, as the person finds partners, interspersed with flat regions where the person has no partners or when the person has just one steady partner. When the person marries, the line flattens out at a height of one, indicating that the individual has only one partner. If the marriage breaks up, the graph shows a few more blips until the person remarries, and then it flattens out again.

For an individual, the graph is mostly flat, punctuated by a few areas of blips. But if we superimposed everyone's graph on top of each other, we would have a sort of supergraph that looked like it was all blips. That, in essence, is what has led to the widespread impression that everyone is having lots of partners. We see the total picture—lots of sex in the population—without realizing that each individual spends most of his or her life with only one partner.

These findings give no support to the idea of a promiscuous society or of a dramatic sexual revolution reflected in huge numbers of people with multiple casual sex partners. The finding on which our data give strong and quite amazing evidence is not that most people do, in fact, form a partnership, or that most people do, in fact, ultimately get married. That fact also was well documented in many previous studies. Nor is it news that more recent marriages are much less stable than marriages that began thirty years ago. That fact, too, was reported by others before us. But we add a new fact, one that is not only important but that is striking.

Our study clearly shows that no matter how sexually active people are before and between marriages, no matter whether they lived with their sexual partners before marriage or whether they were virgins on their wedding day, marriage is such a powerful social institution that, essentially, married people are nearly all alike—they are faithful to their partners as long as the marriage is intact. It does not matter if the couple were high-school sweethearts who married after graduation day or whether they are in their thirties, marrying after each had lived with several others. Once married, the vast majority have no other sexual partner; their past is essentially erased. Marriage remains the great leveler.

We see this, for example, when we ask about fidelity in marriage. More than 80 percent of women and 65 to 85 percent of men of every age report that they had no partners other than their spouse while they were married....

The marriage effect is so dramatic that it swamps all other aspects of our data. When we report that more than 80 percent of adult Americans age eighteen to fifty-nine had zero or one sexual partner in the past year, the figure might sound ludicrous to some young people who know that they and their friends have more than one partner in a year. But the figure really reflects the fact that most Americans in that broad age range are married and are faithful. And many of the others are cohabiting, and they too are faithful. Or they are without partners altogether, a situation that is especially likely for older women.... We find only 3 percent of adults had five or more partners in the past year. Half of all adult Americans had three or fewer partners over their lifetimes.

Name Index

Subject Index